The Ethical Demand

The Ethical Demand

by

KNUD E. LØGSTRUP

translated by

THEODOR I. JENSEN

foreword by

JAMES M. GUSTAFSON

FORTRESS PRESS

Philadelphia

This book is a translation of pages 1–243 of the eighth
edition of *Den etiske Fordring* published in 1969 by Gyl-
dendals Forlagstrykkeri in Copenhagen, Denmark (first
edition 1956). Omitted in this English edition are pages
244–295 of the original, the "Polemisk epilog."

Library of Congress Catalog Card Number 75–141253

2651J70   Printed in U.S.A.   1-54

Contents

Foreword

Knud Løgstrup's classic book on ethics, now in its eighth Danish edition, has evoked extensive discussion in Europe as a result of its early translation into German. With this English translation it can now achieve also the place it deserves in the American discussion. I regard it as a privilege to introduce to the American reader a book which for more than a decade has functioned, along with another Danish book by Niels Hansen Søe, as a "conversation partner" in my own work. *The Ethical Demand* will be of interest here in the American scene for several reasons, not least of all because of a particular thrust which is immediately suggested in one of the chapter titles. Whereas Søe entitles his book as such *Christian Ethics,* Løgstrup asserts in Chapter 5 "The Impossibility of 'Christian' Ethics."

Løgstrup provides a philosophical and theological foundation for ethical programs which take into serious account the uniqueness and concreteness of the particular situations or circumstances of moral action. His "phenomenology" of moral experience, which is akin to that which informs some of the most creative contemporary Catholic thought, portrays human existence in terms of the root relationship of trust between persons. Indeed, Løgstrup begins his ethical reflection with this description. Readers of Marcel, Buber, Royce, and others who have introduced personalistic categories into American ethical thought will find that he evokes familiar tones. Within this relationship of trust, according to Løgstrup, there is an element of mutual obligation, an "unspoken demand" as he calls it. This view of the occasion of moral response offers little comfort to those who wish to develop more generalized and

abstract notions of the human situation, such as the defenders
of traditional Thomistic natural law, or of the concept of orders
of creation.

There is an implicit, but undeveloped assumption in Løgstrup's argument which is akin to the "perceptual intuitionism"
that the American philosopher, Maurice Mandelbaum, has developed in *The Phenomenology of Moral Experience.* Løgstrup's
position thus runs counter to the preoccupation with the development of generalized moral rules that American readers recognize to be the thrust of much of Paul Ramsey's recent work, as
well as with rational casuistry that has characterized much of
Catholic moral theology. Epistemologically, then, with reference
to how one knows what he ought to do, Løgstrup is more akin to
his mentors Bultmann and Gogarten, and to existentialist moral
philosophers, than he is to Christian ethicians who are deeply
informed by recent British and American moral philosophy.

Løgstrup's use of creative literature as a source for understanding the nuances of human existence will appeal to American
readers who for a long time have not confined their sources of
ethical ideas to technical theology and philosophy. In this book,
D. H. Lawrence is extensively used and E. M. Forster is also
referred to. In a subsequent book, *Kunst og Etik (Art and
Ethics),* the author has brought together further reflections on
the relations of the affective aspect of moral experience to the
work of creative artists. He reveals himself to be a scholar who
is open to the winds of modernity.

Americans who have been interested in the ethics of "secu-
larity" will find that Løgstrup's book provides additional
theological and philosophical backing for this approach. Surely
Gogarten, the principal discernible influence on Løgstrup's
book, offered a basis for this range of impulses long before they
gained currency in the Anglo-Saxon world; Løgstrup provides
a refinement and extension of the same thrust.

Although I have some rather radical disagreements with
Løgstrup's thesis and argument, it is with enthusiasm that I
commend the book to American readers. His thesis is compelling enough to warrant serious consideration, and distinctive

enough to evoke sharp counterarguments. There is also a humaneness, a moral sensibility, to the book that makes it yield insight and understanding not only to the professional theologian and student, but also to others who grapple with the meaning of the human.

JAMES M. GUSTAFSON
Professor of Christian Ethics
Yale University

Introduction

The Task

If a proclamation is to have any relevance for us it must answer to something in our own existence: a perplexity in which we find ourselves, an inescapable contradiction, a fate we refuse to accept, experiences we anticipate, or difficulties that loom up before us. This is not to say that the proclamation, in order to be taken seriously, must explain our perplexity and contradiction in the same way we ourselves do, or call our expectations and difficulties by the same names that we use, much less solve our problems, answer our questions, save us from our fate, or fulfill our desires in the ways we have imagined. Indeed, the proclamation may express itself in a manner which is strange to us, it may even be at odds with everything we have imagined, without our necessarily turning a deaf ear to it—provided that it does speak to something in our existence.

Furthermore, the proclamation may answer to something in our existence of which we are totally unaware until we are made aware of it by the proclamation's speaking of it. It is quite conceivable that a particular proclamation will bring to our attention, for example, some contradiction in our existence of which we could hardly be aware before the proclamation in question had actually taken place. Once the proclamation has shown us this feature of our existence, however, we are then able to recognize it by ourselves without recourse to the proclamation. It is also conceivable that we may accept this particular feature of our existence, once the proclamation has disclosed it to us, while otherwise rejecting the proclamation itself and all that it entails and intends.

If the proclamation in question is of a religious nature, then the task becomes one of defining in strictly human terms those

1

features of our existence to which the proclamation speaks and which—possibly for the first time—it helps us to see. Why is this necessary? For two reasons.

First, it is necessary in order that we may understand the proclamation. If a religious proclamation is not understandable in the sense that it answers to decisive features of our existence, then to accept it is tantamount to letting ourselves be coerced —whether by others or by ourselves—for faith without understanding is not faith but coercion. Only if we understand the proclamation can we accept it for the sake of its content. To accept it without understanding it is to accept it for other reasons, out of illegitimate motives; that is to say, we force it upon ourselves. In fact, if a proclamation is not characterized by understandability, then it is an exercise in obscurantism. This is true even in the case of a religious proclamation which —to use a theological expression—claims to be revelation.

However, as we have already said, the understandability of a proclamation does not mean that it must concur with our own formulations or accommodate itself to the solutions we have ourselves imagined; it does not mean that we cannot take offense at it. On the contrary, understandability means only that the proclamation answers to decisive features of our existence. It is one thing for a proclamation to be understandable in the banal sense that it reinforces our own wishful thinking. It is quite another thing for it to be understandable in the personal and objective sense that it discloses to us our existence. A proclamation may conceivably arouse us to an opposition so intense that we constantly seek to evade it, but this does not negate the fact of its understandability in this personal and objective sense.

The second reason for trying to express in strictly human terms what it is in our existence that is disclosed to us by a religious proclamation, such as the proclamation of Jesus of Nazareth, is that precisely as religious proclamation it is not limited to what it discloses. On the contrary! If it were entirely or even mainly limited to the disclosure of existence, it would be more a philosophy than a proclamation. The fact is, though, that it is a religious proclamation, and therefore the decisive thing about it is what it says over and above this disclosure, namely, its message to the individual existence thus disclosed. But in order to make clear that which is unique about the proclamation, namely the thing proclaimed, we must differentiate it from that which is merely disclosed.

The one thing in our existence which the proclamation of Jesus touches upon more than any other is the individual's relation to the neighbor. The question therefore arises with respect to this proclamation: What attitude to the neighbor is implicit in it? What does it conceive to be the essential thing in our life together and how can that be stated in strictly human terms? The question thus introduces a distinction between the content of Jesus' proclamation—which in a very general and vague sense is religious—and the attitude to the neighbor which, although it is included in the religious content of the proclamation, should be susceptible of formulation in strictly human terms. This distinction, by the way, is one that people often make in their attitude to Christianity as such: they tend to reject Christianity out of hand because it is a religion, while at the same time they approve—or think they approve—the attitude to the neighbor which is set forth in and through the religious proclamation![1]

1. From a theological point of view some object that the question here raised and the distinction implied in it are illegitimate. It is illegitimate, they say, to differentiate between the content of Jesus' proclamation and the attitude to the neighbor implicit in it, and to attempt to formulate the latter in strictly human terms. The proclaimed attitude to the neighbor, they assert, cannot be isolated and distinguished from the rest of the religious content of the proclamation.

Why not? What is the point of this objection? For the present we can disregard the purely formal considerations, such as the fact that the unity and inner coherence of the proclamation would be violated and a foreign aspect introduced, for all this is beside the point. More closely considered, the objection must rather mean one of two things. It may mean that any attempt to define in strictly human terms the attitude to the neighbor implied in the religious proclamation of Jesus inevitably distorts, that is, reduces this attitude. Or it may mean that construed as a purely human attitude the attitude becomes absurd, since it has no meaning apart from its locus within a religious proclamation. Indeed, these two objections are combined in the argument that through the desire to make the attitude human we actually reduce its meaning. The people who advance these objections can cite plenty of literary examples to show that those who reject the religious content of the Christian message while approving the attitude

4　　　　　　　　　　　　　　　　　　THE ETHICAL DEMAND

The Relation to God and the Relation to the Neighbor

Friedrich Gogarten characterizes the proclamation of Jesus concisely but with precision when he says that according to this proclamation the individual's relation to God is determined wholly at the point of his relation to the neighbor. This characterization sets the proclamation of Jesus into sharp contrast with all other religions. In contrast to the general and vague conception of religion—and of Christianity as a religion—the proclamation of Jesus sets Christianity apart from all other religions.[2] Without pursuing this matter further, I would simply make use of Gogarten's characterization for posing the question at issue in our present context: What must my relation to the neighbor be if that relation is the one and only place at which my relation to God is determined? What must the man-to-man relationship involve if it is so closely tied in with the relation to God?

The answer to this question—an answer by no means exhaustive but nonetheless of decisive importance in this context—is that when according to the proclamation of Jesus it is at the point of my relation to the neighbor that God determines his own relation to me, then God, through this relationship to me, must also be doing something decisive with respect to the neighbor. All the while that God is determining his relation to me he is also caring for that other person, the neighbor. If this were not true, my relation to God would be an exclusively religious relationship, and my relation to the neighbor would

to the neighbor contained in the proclamation are in reality espousing a depreciated attitude.

To me, none of these objections seems convincing. A strictly human definition of the attitude to the neighbor set forth in Jesus' proclamation often has meant and probably always will tend to mean a modification of that attitude, but this does not mean that such modification is *inevitable*. And as far as the other objection is concerned, one cannot with finality assert that the attitude set forth in the proclamation of Jesus is undefinable in strictly human terms until he has actually made the attempt so to define it. Hence, despite all objections, I shall proceed to tackle the question before us and attempt the indicated distinction and definition.

2. "Through his radical repudiation of all forms of religion Jesus made the most elementary and fundamental phenomenon of human existence and history, namely, men's relation to one another, the one and only point at which the relation to God is determined." Friedrich Gogarten, *Die Verkündigung Jesu Christi* (Heidelberg: Schneider, 1948), p. 115.

be reduced to the status of a mere means to the end of a right relationship with God.

This implies, further, that the other person must to such a degree be dependent upon me that what I do and say in the relationship between us—I alone and nobody else, here and now and not at some other time or in some other manner—is of decisive importance. If my relation to the other person is the place where my relation to God is determined, then it must at the same time be the place where that person's existence is so totally at stake that to fail him is to do him irreparable damage. In other words, what I withhold from him in one situation he will not be able to recoup in another situation, either from me or from anyone else. If human beings were so independent of one another that the words and deeds of one were only a dispensable luxury in the life of another and my failure in relation to the life of the neighbor could easily be made up later, then God's relation to me would not be as intimately tied up with my relation to the neighbor as the proclamation of Jesus declares it to be.[3] In short, the close connection in which Jesus places our relation to God and our relation to the neighbor presupposes that we are, as Luther expressed it, "daily bread" in the life of one another. And this presupposition for the close connection Jesus makes between the two great commandments in the law can indeed be described in strictly human terms.

Methodology

Before proceeding with the investigation a few comments on methodology are in order. Methodologically, our task will be one of making distinctions. We will have to make those distinctions which are necessary in order to understand the silent, radical, one-sided, and impossible character of the demand contained in the proclamation of Jesus.

As we do so it will be important not to allow ourselves to be carried away by some particular distinction and the perspective

---

3. That which takes place in my relation to the neighbor would in that event be only a *result* of God's relation to me; the two relationships would not be internally connected in any decisive way.

it affords, as all too frequently happens in philosophy and theology. By means of some particular distinction the theologian perhaps succeeds in solving a problem and in illuminating certain essential interconnections, whereupon he enthusiastically supposes that the same distinction can help him solve a whole series of attendant problems and throw light upon many related topics. Hence there arises the extended analysis which fixes on one particular perspective and presses it home with mindlessly rigorous consistency. Now such an analysis is not necessarily without worth. By no means! Often it involves the application of a truly illuminating distinction. The mistake is in employing the distinction beyond its legitimate limits, using it as a means to explain everything under the sun. When that happens the result is usually nothing more than a process of thinking in abstractions. Abstract concepts, after all, are both easy to come by and easy to understand, and they do manifest an apparent clarity.[4]

We must never be content to stop with any particular key distinction. Our task is rather to regard each new ambiguity and each new problem as an occasion for advancing yet another distinction, and so proceeding until all the elements in the proclamation under consideration have been characterized as precisely as possible. To a large extent systematic theology consists precisely in this business of disentangling problems which have been inadmissably lumped together.

There are, among others, three ways in which to clarify experiences, situations, and outlooks on life. We can deal with them by way of poetic metaphors and images, or by way of philosophical and theological analogies and distinctions, or—if we may put it thus—by way of a perverted philosophy, theology, or culture analysis which monomaniacally explains every-

---

4. We often find the same error among the innumerable analyses of culture in our day. To be sure, the cultural analysts often come up with valuable insights, but they go astray when they try to lump together under the same formula as many problems as possible. When that happens, the explanations for most of the phenomena get too farfetched and people lose sight of the problems themselves.

thing in terms of a single distinction, a distinction which may be perfectly all right in itself but is simply incapable of explaining everything.[5]

If we are to understand the demand contained in the proclamation of Jesus we must proceed from the standpoint of our own existence, to which that proclamation after all is addressed. Certain perspectives are required if we are to make the distinctions which will enable us to understand and express the silent, radical, one-sided, and impossible character of that demand. These perspectives must be found in the contexts, contradictions, and conflicts of our own existence—whether our understanding and formulations precede or are the result of the revealing encounter with the proclamation and its demand.

This is by no means to say that the individual, if he is to know them at all, must always experience personally at first-hand these situations, contradictions, and conflicts of our existence. He may also come to know them through what he has read or personally observed of the experiences of others.

5. If a theologian is the least bit systematically disposed, it is not long before he sets his conceptualizing apparatus in motion. But this is something more difficult to stop than to start. Indeed, if he has a tendency to verbosity, he may never get it stopped!

The interconnections between his various presentations then come to occupy his attention more than the substance of the thoughts themselves. Every time he undertakes a further development of his thought he gets up a head of steam by starting from the very beginning and repeating at least in summary form everything he has already said before.

Even systematic thinking has its rules, of course, but they involve more than merely the matter of consistency. There is also the requirement that everything must depend upon the illuminating thought which comes in the form of a new idea or insight, and that one must refrain from filling the time—and the books —between such ideas and insights with merely spewing out concepts.

This is not to say that the systematic theologian can altogether escape this practice of harping on a single theme. However, he ought at least to be clear that such repetition is not a virtue but a sign of his own incapacity.

1.

The Source of
the Silent Demand

Trust as a Fundamental Part of Human Existence

It is a characteristic of human life that we naturally trust one another. This is true not only in the case of persons who are well acquainted with one another but also in the case of utter strangers. Only because of some special circumstance do we ever distrust a stranger in advance. Perhaps some informer has destroyed the natural trust which people spontaneously have toward one another, so that their relationship becomes oppressive and strained. Perhaps because of strife in the land, where the land is ruled by men who have no respect for law and justice, people lose confidence in one another. Under normal circumstances, however, we accept the stranger's word and do not mistrust him until we have some particular reason to do so. We never suspect a person of falsehood until after we have caught him in a lie. If we enter into conversation on the train with a person whom we have never met before and about whom we know absolutely nothing, we assume that what he says is true and do not become suspicious of him unless he begins to indulge in wild exaggerations. Nor do we normally assume a person to be a thief; not until he conducts himself in a suspicious manner do we begin to suspect him. Initially we believe one another's word; initially we trust one another. This may indeed seem strange, but it is a part of what it means to be human. Human life could hardly exist it it were otherwise. We would simply not be able to live; our life would be impaired

8

and wither away if we were in advance to distrust one another, if we were to suspect the other of thievery and falsehood from the very outset.

To trust, however, is to deliver oneself over into the hands of another.[1] This is why we react vehemently when our trust is "violated," as we say, even though it may have been only in some inconsequential matter. Violated trust is trust that is turned against the person who does the trusting. The embarrassment and danger to which we are subjected by the violation is bad enough. But even worse is the fact that our trust was scorned by the other person. For the other person to have been able to violate it, our trust must simply have left him cold. However much he may seem to have accepted it outwardly, he did not actually accept it but merely exploited it. And it is a question whether it is not the indifference thus manifested toward us in his violation of our trust, even more than the unpleasant consequences of the violation itself, which evokes our bitter reaction.

That trust and the self-surrender that goes with it are a fundamental part of human life is seen not only when trust is violated. We see it fully as much in those conflicts which are caused by a collision between two persons' respective spirits and worlds.

The peculiar point here is that while the collision is due to the fact that a purely personal expectation is not fulfilled by the other person, it takes the form of moral accusations—even though moral evaluations of the other person's behavior are quite beside the point and the accusations themselves are therefore obviously unreasonable. Why is this? We need to know the answer. We need to explain why conflicts which in themselves have nothing to do with morality or immorality, with right or wrong, but which are entirely due to a difference between our

---

1. Gogarten makes this point in some of his helpful remarks concerning the basis of law. Friedrich Gogarten, *Die Verkündigung Jesu Christi* (Heidelberg: Schneider, 1948), p. 108.

respective spirits and worlds—why these conflicts nevertheless turn into questions of sheer morality and self-justification and cause reproaches and accusations which are plainly unreasonable.

First, an expectation which requires that the other person personally fulfill it usually makes itself apparent in one way or another, perhaps through general attitude or conduct, or perhaps directly through some particular word or action. Whatever its form, whether articulated or silent, the expectation manifests itself on the presupposition that the other person is to fulfill the expectation. This is to say that by manifesting the expectation one has already surrendered himself to the other person—even before it is certain that there will be any fulfillment. In other words, the manifestation is necessary for bringing about the fulfillment—perhaps simply in order to make the other person aware of what we expect from him.

Now, if the fulfillment does not take place, the manifestation is in vain and perhaps meaningless. But what is worse is the fact that in the manifestation one has exposed himself. One's expectation, exposed through its manifestation, has not been covered by the other person's fulfillment of it. And it is this exposure which causes the encounter to erupt in moral reproaches and accusations.

Second, when one dares to extend himself in the hope of being accepted, and then is not accepted, this gives the conflict such an emotional character that even though no one has done anything-wrong, one must turn it into the kind of conflict that results from the other person's having committed a wrong. One finds it necessary to invent a suffered wrong by which to motivate his strong and deep emotional reaction. In short, it is the emotional element in the situation which causes one to grasp at the moral reproaches and accusations which, precisely because of their moral character, are emotionally loaded.

The simple conflict within a conflict, namely, that one has dared to extend himself in the hope of being accepted but was not accepted, makes everything either black or white and makes one's accusation correspondingly irrevocable. For it is precisely to the degree that things are black or white in our moral evaluations, that our moral accusations become irrevocable.[2]

But there is a third reason why the conflict vents itself in moral accusations. It must at all costs never become apparent to the other person, and preferably not even to ourselves, that it is a matter of disappointed expectation, because though we have been exposed we are at pains not to admit it. We would much rather admit blemishes and weaknesses, mistakes and stupidities than admit to our having been exposed. The collision in the encounter must therefore be covered up. It must be externalized even though we may have to go far afield for the reproaches and may have to invent the most unreasonable accusations in an effort to cover up the real conflict. The accusations, having nothing to do with morality, betray the fact that it is a matter of a conflict which at all costs must be covered up, even at the cost of our having to invent the most absurd accusations.[3]

If communication between persons in conflict with each other is cut off, sparks of moral reproach and accusation begin to fly, because there is self-surrender in all forms of communication. Rejected self-surrender expresses itself in moral accusations because the situation is emotional and plain, and because the exposure must at all costs be kept covered up.

In E. M. Forster's novel, *Howards End,* we have the account of a rift between Leonard Bast and the Schlegel sisters. Their

2. Regardless of how vehemently our opponent may refute our moral accusation and inveigle us into replying and getting involved in discussion, and though the discussion may have a moderating effect upon us and even cause us to revoke our moral accusation—that accusation is nonetheless final and irrevocable in its original intention.

3. We have reference here to resentment. The person who has been offended advances unreasonable reproaches and accusations. He will not admit that they are unreasonable, though he knows very well that they are. By nourishing his resentment he is unable to reason clearly. He allows himself to be dominated by the purely emotional inertia of his resentment. It is characteristic of resentment that it wants to hide its own emotional origin in the exposure, and to divert our own and others' attention from it by unreasonable accusations. It is an opaqueness which knows that it is opaque without wanting to become transparent. Consequently it must in self-pity, one might say, cling to its own unreasonable accusations and reproaches. Resentment is the cheapest form of taking pleasure in pain, because the pain is imagined, and one knows that it is imagined.

respective milieus were as different from one another as they could possibly be. Leonard was a penniless office clerk whose married life was very drab and whose entire existence would be bleak indeed were it not for his consuming interest in culture. However, he was not equal to this interest; his hunger for books and music was and remained artificial. The Schlegel sisters, on the other hand, had never known anything but economic security. They were fairly wealthy. Since they had grown up in an atmosphere of cultural appreciation and had become the center of a large social group where these things were discussed, their life was rich in terms of experience and delightful variety.

On an altogether casual occasion Leonard Bast came into contact with the Schlegel sisters. He received an invitation to an afternoon tea with them. It turned out to be a fiasco. Leonard was disappointed in his expectations for the afternoon. He had hoped to discuss books and to keep his visit with them in a romantic vein and at all costs to keep it from getting mixed up with his routine, uninteresting life at the office.

The Schlegel sisters had an entirely different purpose in inviting him, however, a very practical purpose, namely, to get him out of the firm in which he was employed inasmuch as they had secret information that the firm was about to go bankrupt. And they had another, an indirect, purpose too: to help him in his interest in culture, because though his love of books was artificial they detected that underneath there lay a desire for authenticity.

The ensuing conflict was inevitable. It could not be warded off. For the Schlegel sisters' idea in issuing the invitation was entirely different from Leonard's idea in accepting it. The two parties were blind to one another's world. Leonard's anticipation of an afternoon spent in undisturbed enjoyment of books blinded him to the Schlegel sisters' desire to help him. Disappointed and embittered, he was carried away with outrageous and stupid accusations that they had low motives in inviting him, namely, that they wanted to use him for spying upon his firm. As for the Schlegel sisters themselves, not until afterwards did they have any inkling of the two worlds in Leonard's life and of how important it was for him to keep them isolated from each other.

Leonard Bast and the Schlegel sisters disagreed about many things, but it was not an objective disagreement which caused the collision between them. Nor was the collision caused by one of them committing wrong and the other being wronged. Rather it was because Leonard was disappointed in his expectation that the Schlegel sisters would satisfy his cultural craving by engaging him in conversation about books. Their failure to do this immediately turned into a moral issue.

Those who are implicated in it never, or at least very seldom, are aware that the conflict has nothing to do with right or wrong. Only observers on the outside who have an incisive insight into the worlds of both parties—dramatists and novelists, theatergoers and readers—are able to see this.

The fundamental character of trust is revealed in yet another way. In love and sympathy there is no impulse to investigate the other person's character. We do not deliberately try to picture to ourselves who he or she is. In the event that we already have such a picture, it shows only those features which immediately stand out. We are aware only of those peculiarities which force themselves upon our attention. Of ourselves we make no conscious effort to picture the other person for the simple reason that there has been nothing about him to arouse our suspicion.

If, on the other hand, we are not in sympathy with the other person, or if there is a certain tension between us and him because of something about him regarding which we are uncertain or against which we react with irritation, dissatisfaction, or antipathy, then we begin to form a picture of his character. We then begin to see in him a variety of dispositions because we are on our guard in relation to him.

However, when we are in direct association with him this picture usually breaks down; his personal presence erases it. It is not erased because of any particular words, deeds, or conduct; this would of course only mean that the facts contradict the picture we have had of him, forcing us either to correct it or to set it aside entirely. No, it means something altogether different. It means that the actual presence of the other person leaves no room for a mere picture. His presence and my picture of him are irreconcilable. They exclude each other, and it is the picture that must give way. Only where the proof of his unreliability has in the most positive sense become an ingrown distrust, or where the irritation and antipathy have shut me off from him completely, does the picture continue to stand.

Why does the picture break down? This is a difficult question to answer, because what happens in this connection is something fundamental, something anterior to morality and convention. An adequate explanation is impossible. Only through paraphrase and metaphor, only by approaching the phenomenon from different angles are we able to suggest the answer.

To associate with or encounter personally another person always means to be "in the power of" his words and conduct. Psychology refers to this as the power of suggestion. There are many degrees of suggestion. It may be very weak, only strong enough to understand what the other person says and does, or it may be so strong that we are, as we say, grasped, or taken captive by it.

But there is also something more fundamental than this. Not to let the other person come into his own through words, deeds, and conduct, but to hinder him instead by our suspicion and by the picture we have formed of him as a result of our antipathy toward him is a denial of life, his life and our own. It is in the very nature of human existence that it does not want to be reduced to reactions—even wise reactions—which are determined solely by what has already transpired. It is in the very nature of human existence that it wants to be just as new as the other person's new words, new deeds, and new conduct. We assume, as it were, that because they are contemporary they are new, and so we also insist upon taking a similarly new attitude to them. We might call this a trust in life itself, in the ongoing renewal of life. Later we discover that the words, deeds, and conduct were after all not new, and we vow that we will never again let ourselves be tricked or fooled or be naive or in any other way let our trust get the better of us.[4]

In its fundamental sense trust is essential to every conversation. In conversation as such we deliver ourselves over into the hand of another. This is evident in the fact that in the very act of addressing a person we make a certain demand of him. This demand is not merely for a response to what we say. And the self-surrender is not essentially a matter of what is said: its content or importance or intimate character. What happens is that simply in addressing him, irrespective of the importance of the content of what we say, a certain note is struck through which we, as it were, step out of ourselves in order to exist in the speech relationship with him. For this reason the point of the demand—though unarticulated—is that as the note struck by the speaker's address is accepted, the speaker is himself accepted. For a person inadvertently or even intentionally not to hear the note in what we say, therefore, means that it is we ourselves who are being ignored, provided it is we ourselves who made the overture. That all speech takes place in such fundamental trust is evident in the fact that the most casual comment takes on a false note if one believes that it is not accepted in the sense that it is intended.

A particular point of the analysis we have made thus far—one might call it an analysis of a phenomenological character—is in fact supported by such sciences as psychology and psychiatry. Their investigations have clearly shown how a child's life may be permanently determined by the manner in which adults

4. This is not to say that it is in the nature of human existence for a person to try to prevent his being in any way determined by what has already happened. To be determined by the past can mean two things. It can mean that out of what one has heard, said, done, experienced, and thought there arises an outlook on life which gives perspective to one's judgment. It can also mean that these give rise only to security measures and, especially, countermeasures whose purpose is to prevent one from undertaking anything regarding the outcome of which we are uncertain. This makes the word old even before it is spoken, the action old even before it is taken.

behave toward him. For example, one might mention parents'
ambitious pride in relation to their children. In the ambiguity
of everyday living this is regarded as very commendable, but
humanly speaking it is a detriment to the children because it
can result in an upbringing which deprives them, perhaps forever, of something of paramount importance, namely, joy in
living, the courage to be. This is due not least of all to the fact
that the child, in contradistinction to the adult, is never content
to trust only partially. To trust with reservation is possible only
for one who has learned to hold back something of himself. But
this the child has not learned consciously and deliberately to do.
For him reservation takes place as a matter of psychic automa-
tism. This is why the disappointed trust, restlessness, and insecurity which go with it create in the child far-reaching and
fateful consequences.

Although it is in the child's relation to the adult that the one
is surrendered to the other in the most far-reaching and fateful
sense—which is why science has here been able to establish it
—it is nonetheless in one degree or another true also of all the
relationships in which we deal with one another. A person
never has something to do with another person without also
having some degree of control over him. It may be a very small
matter, involving only a passing mood, a dampening or quick-
ening of spirit, a deepening or removal of some dislike. But it
may also be a matter of tremendous scope, such as can determine the very course of his life.

Unconsciously, we nonetheless have the strange notion that
one person has nothing to do with another person's world. We
have the curious idea that a person constitutes his own world,
and that the rest of us have no part in it but only touch upon
it now and then. If the encounter between persons therefore
means, as it normally does, nothing more than that their respective worlds touch upon each other and then continue unaffected on their separate courses, the encounter can hardly be
very important. According to this reasoning, it is only when a
person accidentally breaks into another person's world with

good or bad intentions that anything important is at stake.

This is really a curious idea, an idea no less curious because we take it for granted. The fact is, however, that it is completely wrong because we do indeed constitute one another's world and destiny. That we usually ignore this fact can easily be explained.

It is a common observation that the most elementary phenomena of our existence are the ones we are least aware of. It should be added that the phenomenon we are discussing here is highly disquieting. For the sake of our own peace of mind it is perhaps fortunate that we are not more aware of the extent to which, by what we were or said or did in our relationship with them, we have actually determined other people's joy or pain in living, their sincerity or duplicity.

In describing the nature of trust, we have in the foregoing used several different expressions. We have spoken of a person surrendering himself, of his going out of himself, of his placing something of his own life into the hands of the other person. These expressions are metaphorical and subject to misunderstanding. In order to avoid one serious misunderstanding, one that is easily suggested by the metaphors themselves, it should be said that trust does not mean to turn oneself inside out. Trust has nothing to do with the abandonment of all spiritual modesty. To surrender oneself by turning oneself inside out in the presence of another does not require trust. In fact this sort of thing is rarely even related to trust; it usually demands nothing of the other person except that he play the role of an observer.

It is quite another thing, however, to surrender oneself in that trust of the other person whereby a requirement is always imposed upon him insofar as one comes to him with an expectation. In expecting something of the other person we undertake an action which amounts to a delivering of ourselves over into his hand. This self-surrender, whatever form it may take, need not necessarily mean that we confide in the other person. It can of course mean that too, but it can also mean all kinds of other things; for example, it may mean that we rely upon him to speak the truth, or that in speaking to him we adopt a particular tone of voice. Correspondingly it means that the self-exposure, through the trust which was not accepted, consists in one's having risked the chance of being rejected. It has nothing to do, however, with exposure in an exhibitionist sense.

The Demand That Grows out of Trust

Through the trust which a person either shows or asks of another person he surrenders something of his life to that person. Therefore, our existence demands of us that we protect the life of the person who has placed his trust in us. How much or how little is at stake for a person who has thus placed his trust in another person obviously varies greatly. It depends upon many different factors: upon his psychic constitution and momentary condition, and upon the situation, which is determined not least of all by who and what the other person is. But in any event this trust means that in every encounter between human beings there is an unarticulated demand, irrespective of the circumstances in which the encounter takes place and irrespective of the nature of the encounter.

Regardless of how varied the communication between persons may be, it always involves the risk of one person approaching the other in the hope of a response. This is the essence of communication and the fundamental basis of ethical life. Therefore, a consciousness of the resultant demand is not dependent upon a revelation, in the theological sense of the word, nor is the demand based on a more or less conscious agreement between the persons with respect to what would be mutually beneficial.

If trust and the self-surrender that goes with it were determined by our own arbitrary decision, so that without any loss to ourselves we could ignore the trust and the surrender, then life together with other people would present no demands other than those which one person might arbitrarily decide to place upon another person, whether they be conventional, sentimental, or paranoiac demands. Such is not the case, however.

Trust is not of our own making; it is given. Life is so constituted that it cannot be lived except as one person surrenders something of himself to the other person either by trusting him or by asking him for his trust.[5]

By our very attitude to one another we help to shape one another's world. By our attitude to the other person we help to determine the scope and hue of his world; we make it large or small, bright or drab, rich or dull, threatening or secure. We help to shape his world not by theories and views but by our very attitude toward him. Herein lies the unarticulated and one might say anonymous demand that we take care of the life which trust has placed in our hands.[6]

The Twofold Function of Conventional Forms

Usually we trust one another with great reservation. We hold ourselves in reserve and do not allow ourselves completely to trust one another. Not even in an emergency situation when we desperately need help do we trust without some reservation. Hence what is normally expected of us in everyday living is not concern for a person's life but for the things which belong to conventional courtesy. Social convention has the effect of reducing both the trust that we show and the demand that we take care of the other person's life.

The conventional forms have a twofold function. For one thing, regardless of how these forms originated, they facilitate

5. Trust and distrust are not two parallel ways of life. Trust is basic; distrust is the absence of trust. This is why we do not normally advance arguments and justifications for trust as we do for distrust. To use a modern philosophical expression, distrust is the "deficient form" of trust.

6. Someone will probably argue that the fact that a person gives himself to another person by trusting him is one thing whereas the demand that we take care of the life thus committed to us through trust is quite another thing; in other words, that there must be a difference between a fact and a demand, between an opinion about what is and an opinion about what ought to be. This argument raises a number of questions too extensive for treatment in this book; they must be dealt with elsewhere.

Our concern here is only to point out the intimate connection between the fact and the demand, to point out that to a great extent the demand grows out of the fact. In other words, the fact forces upon us the alternative: either we take care of the other person's life or we ruin it. Given man's creatureliness, there is no third alternative. To accept the fact without listening to the demand is to be indifferent to the question whether life is to be promoted or ruined.

our relationship with one another, making it smooth and effortless, not least because they protect us against psychic exposure. Without the protection of the conventional norms, association with other people would be intolerable.

When we thus refer to "spiritual modesty" does this mean that there are certain things which simply are not to be mentioned? Must we, by keeping silent about them, act as if they did not exist? Are there feelings which can exist only as long as we refrain from expressing them but which die the moment we allow them to come to the surface in speech? Does that which is most vital in life wither in the light of day?

No, what we mean is rather that there are certain things which cannot exist in a formless state. That which is most vital in a person's life cannot tolerate banality. Formless expression destroys it. Spiritual immodesty is not a harmless affair.

Spiritual modesty keeps the most vital human relationships from being spoiled by banality. It gives form to a person's life. That which is most vital demands a controlled, structured, indirect expression.

The will to form is not limited to the elect, to creative artists. It is something fundamentally human, something native to any person even though he may have very little to do with what we usually call art. And because we cannot ourselves create the necessary forms we adopt the conventional forms.

Life has been given to us. We have not ourselves created it. This is why we cannot give it a direct expression. If we attempt to do so all the same, we falsify it in pathetically or sentimentally unstructured effusion.

In the second place, however, we employ the very same conventional forms for reducing trust and its demand. Instead of allowing convention to give needed form to our life, we use it as a means for keeping aloof from one another and for insulating ourselves. The one who trusts has in advance, by way of convention, guarded himself; he has rendered his trust conventionally reserved, and the one who is trusted is thus relieved of hearing the demand contained in that trust, the demand that he take care of the trusting person's life.

The important thing is that if a person's trust is not accepted, it turns into distrust. This distrust is not necessarily the result of animosity; it is just as likely the result of indifference, reservation, and rejection. Not wanting to run the risk of being distrusted, one neutralizes his own trust in advance. The alternative given in and with human existence, namely, that whatever is not in the nature of care for the trusting person's life ruins it, is thus broken by a third possibility, which is the neutral possibility of social convention. Unable to bear the given alternative of care or ruin, we tacitly agree to avail ourselves of convention as a form of existence whereby we avoid the alternative.

The child, however, will not go along with this. He is able to trust only without reservation. When he shows trust he gives himself completely. The child, being yet outside of convention, still stands in the power of the given alternative. If he fails to encounter love, his future possibilities are destroyed —as psychology and psychiatry have amply shown.

The Unspoken Demand

The demand which is present in any human relationship is, however, unspoken and is not to be equated with a person's expressed wish or request. It is not expressed in his spoken or implied expectations. Any correspondence between the spoken and the unspoken demand is purely accidental; usually they are not at all alike. The other person's interpretation of the implications of the trust offered or desired is one thing, and the demand which is implicit in that trust as, one might say, a "fact of creation" which I must interpret is quite another thing. And these two interpretations may well conflict with each other. The situation may be such that I am challenged to oppose the very thing which the other person expects and wishes me to do for him, because this alone will serve his best interest. In other words, the challenge rests on the assumption that I know better than he does what is best for him.

If this were not true, communication between two persons would in fact be impossible. If it were merely a matter of fulfilling the other person's expectations and granting his wishes, our association would mean nothing less than—irresponsibly— making oneself the tool of the other person. Our mutual relations would no longer present any challenge but would consist merely in reciprocal flattery. However, what we are speaking of is a demand for love, not for indulgence. The risk of conflict is therefore an ever present possibility.

This is not mere theory. What is regarded in ordinary parlance as a "very good" or "very kind" thing to say is usually only a case of accommodating oneself to the other person, abstaining from any contradiction which we know would irritate him, refraining from any criticism which would offend him, avoiding the confrontation which would not be well received. It is a matter of shying away from contradiction in an effort to lead the conversation on to something regarding which one knows that the other person can agree with him. It is refraining from criticism and instead looking for something for which one can praise him. It is an avoidance at all costs of confrontation in order to be able to settle down cozily in mutual agreement about something irrelevant. What men commonly commend as good or kind usually represents in reality the kind of accommodation that results in an insecure relationship. What men commonly call love is usually an affectation which shuns like the plague truth between people. And this situation is not altered by the fact that sacrifice is sometimes both demanded and given. Where there is no will to truth, even sacrifice turns to flattery. In short, if there were no difference between the challenge implicit in every relationship and the other person's expressed request, our life together would consist in abandoning ourselves to the crowd. And the crowd can very well consist of only one person. Indeed, this is the case if it is a person I am willing merely to follow—however much that following may involve me in great sacrifice and may even be interpreted as goodness or kindness.

In other words, the demand implicit in every encounter between persons is not vocal but remains silent. The individual to whom the demand is directed must himself in each concrete relationship decide what the content of the demand is. This is not to say that a person can arbitrarily and capriciously determine the content of the demand. In that event there would be no demand. But the fact is that there is a demand. And since the demand is implied by the very fact that a person belongs to the world in which the other person has his life, and therefore holds something of that person's life in his hands, it is therefore a demand to take care of that person's life. But nothing is thereby said about how this caring is to be done. The other person himself cannot say anything about this, even though he is the one directly concerned, since, as we said before, it might very well involve something diametrically opposed to his own expectations and wishes. It is of the essence of the demand that with such insight, imagination, and understanding as he possesses a person must figure out for himself what the demand requires.

The Sovereignty of the Individual

In the light of what has been said one might ask: Does not the demand then encourage arrogant encroachment upon the other person? How can one know what is best for him, especially if that which presumably is best for him is clearly disappointing to him or even resisted by him? The answer is that this is something which one learns from one's own outlook on life. But of what concern is my outlook to the other person, who perhaps does not even share it? Why must he have an outlook imputed to him or even forced upon him which is entirely strange to him and which he can neither use nor appreciate?

A prominent idea in the idealistic ethics of the nineteenth century, largely through the influence of Kant, was respect for the other person's independence. Idealistic ethics is severely criticized today both by philosophers and theologians, and not without some justification, because this matter of mutual respect for one another's independence threatened to become the major consideration. Morality came to consist in self-realization, and respect for the other person in his self-realization. Respect for the other person's independence was used to legitimate one's own self-realization, and this inevitably resulted in a kind of adulation of personhood. At the base of this idea was the notion that every person is a world unto himself and that others are not a part of that world. Consequently there was no awareness of the conflict in which the idea of respect for the other person's independence arises and belongs. This conflict may be expressed in the form of a question: What does my outlook have to do with the other person if it leads me to think I know better than he what is best for him?

Outlook on life is a very abstract concept. It can mean many different things. It can even be a matter of something very fundamental. To disappoint a person's desire for flattery could hardly, except by the disappointed person himself, be regarded as an attempt to impose a foreign outlook upon him. We may even assume that there is a certain basic conception of human existence which is inevitable and common to all.

However, the outlook on life can take on more and more definite features; it can take on a firm structure and thereby become more and more narrow. It can become hardened into an ideology which a person comes to regard as something absolute. The more this happens, the more the relation of the individual to other people becomes an occasion for arrogance and possibly for encroachment upon them. In other words, the ideologically hardened outlook becomes, so far as the individual is concerned, his life's meaning, but in the sense that the order of values is inverted so that his life exists for the sake of his outlook on life instead of the reverse. It is not so much a case of his own life giving content to his outlook as of his outlook determining the content of his life, a life which without the outlook is empty. The outlook simply becomes a cause for which he exists. Whatever concerns his own life must logically concern the life of all others as well. The ultimate truth which he possesses must be the ultimate truth also for them—obviously, because otherwise it would of course not be ultimate truth! In the name of this ultimate truth he therefore also knows—with incontrovertible certainty—what is best for the other person. Consequently he need not concern himself with the idea of respect for other people's independence. It follows that the farther this process advances, the easier it becomes with a good conscience to violate the other person. You see, it is the ultimate truth, the perfect outlook for which one is responsible!

It is possible to lose all sense of the problem here under discussion through a pandering to the lower instincts, through a mutual admiration of one another, or through indifference toward one another—always under the guise of respect for the other person in his own world. But it may also be lost when the outlook on life becomes so hardened and so religiously ultimate that we come to believe that we know what is best for the other person, when we come to believe that it is only through our outlook that not only our own life but also the lives of other people have meaning and content.

We are, in other words, dealing with two different perversions of communication between people. The one is the kind of association which, due to laziness, fear of people, or a propensity for cozy relationships, consists in simply trying to please one another while always dodging the issue. With the possible exception of a common cause against a third person, there is nothing which promotes a comfortable relationship quite so much as mutual praise. At any rate mutual admiration can hardly fail to create such a relationship. The understanding here revealed is not the kind which in the interest of honesty is willing to be uncharitably received. It is rather the kind regarding which one knows in advance that he will be warmly welcomed; the other comes to covet such understanding, almost as a tribute which is his due.

That which makes this kind of association so attractive is that it calls for no appreciable inconvenience. It demands very little of us. So long as the other person is accorded all the understanding he desires, and even a little more, he causes no further inconvenience. When each one receives his due in the form of the desired praise and understanding, we can enjoy the peace of indifference toward one another. In reality, however, no communication takes place, despite the fact that to all appearances the persons involved are very much taken up with their association.

We commonly think that it is only among persons who are comparative strangers to one another that men say always what the other person wants to hear; we tend to think that honesty increases only as the degree of acquaintance increases. However, the opposite may equally well be true, namely, that the closer persons are united in friendship, the more dishonest they become in their relation to one another; they find it easier to be honest toward persons they do not know quite so well.

An opposite form of perverted communication consists in our wanting to change other people. We have definite opinions about how they ought to be. These opinions are lacking in understanding, because the more definitive the opinions are, the more necessary it becomes that we not be distracted by too much understanding of those who are to be changed. Understanding must be temporarily suspended. The mania for perfection turns everything which is said and done into something provisional and preparatory. Understanding must be postponed until perfection has been attained.

Taking these two perversions of communication into consideration we are, in other words, caught in the conflict between a regard for others which is in fact indulgence, compliance, and flattery on the one hand, and a disregard for others which in the interest of our own outlook turns into arrogance and violation on the other hand. Although this conflict can be resolved only in specific instances by the exercise of one's own individual judgment, we can nonetheless advance some fundamental considerations to guide us in such judgment.

In our discussion up to this point we have spoken metaphorically of having something of the other person's life "in our hands" or "delivered over to us." Precisely what in the other person's life is in our hands, what of the other person has been delivered over to us, may vary greatly. It may vary all the way from his most passing mood to his entire destiny.

However, there is one thing which a person does not directly surrender, and that is his individuality which determines his reactions to what we say and do. The fact that we are one another's world does not mean that we hold another person's will in our hands. We cannot intrude upon his individuality and will, upon his personhood, in the same way that we can affect his emotions and in some instances even his destiny.

We often have the other person's more or less passing mood in our hands in the most direct way. However, we are not able in the same direct way to determine how he either conquers or succumbs to the despondency, for example, which we have caused in him. Correspondingly, an individual often in a most direct way holds another person's destiny in his power. For example, he may determine the success or failure of his spouse's marriage. Inconsiderateness of one kind or another on his part may turn the marriage into lifelong suffering for his spouse. However, this does not mean that the inconsiderate partner has power in the same direct way to determine how his spouse reacts to his inconsiderateness, how he defends or does not defend himself against it. The partner who by his inconsiderateness determines his spouse's fate does not in the same way hold his spouse's individuality and will in his power. In other words, he cannot control whether the spouse resigns or does not resign himself to his fate.

Nevertheless, the boundary between one's ability to determine another person's fate and one's inability to determine how that other person will react to his fate is fluid. The individuality and the will of both adults and children—particularly children —may be affected through assaults upon their emotions and their fate.

This much can therefore be said: whatever a person may say or do out of concern for what he believes will best serve the other person's welfare, it is not his prerogative to control the other person's reactions to what he says or does. One is not to try to determine what use the other person makes of what is said or done. To this we have no right, be our intentions ever so good. The will to determine what is best for the other person —and to speak or remain silent, or to act in harmony with our insight into what we believe to be best for him—must be coupled with a willingness to let him remain sovereign in his own world. The demand to guard that part of the other person's life which has been delivered over to us, irrespective of the words and actions which the demand may indicate, is always at the same time a demand that the other person be given ample time and opportunity to make his own world as expansive as possible. The demand is always also a demand that we use the surrender out of which the demand has come in such a way as to free the other person from his confinement and to give his vision the widest possible horizon.

On the other hand, the person who out of a fierce perfectionism tries to refashion people will stop at nothing, not even at the violation of their personalities and wills. In his effort to dominate their reactions, even to the point of crowding out their individualities, he capitalizes upon the fact that the boundary line is fluid. The other person is to be completely changed from the ground up, including his will.

However, no one has the right to make himself the master of another person's individuality or will. Neither good intentions, insight into what is best for him, nor even the possibility of saving him from great calamities which would otherwise strike him can justify intrusion upon his individuality and will.[7]

To "have something in one's hand" is a metaphor. Usually it is used in speaking of the comparatively rare situation in which

7. Lady Bertha in Henrik Pontoppidan's *De Dødes Rige* is not in the least doubt about what would be best for her daughter Jytte—a life together with Torben Diehmer. But Jytte Abildgaard is completely unnerved by an unconquerable distrust of life. She does not dare to face it. One day her love for Torben Diehmer conquers, but she has no sooner said yes to him than the unconquerable distrust asserts itself and causes her the next morning to retract her yes to him. At this point Lady Bertha's wrath is aroused. She is angered by the lighthearted trifling with life and death and she is struck by the wild notion that it might be her duty to bring force to bear upon Jytte. But this notion has no sooner come to her than she dismisses it, because there is nothing which gives a person the right to dominate another's will, not even if to do so would save that person from the greatest catastrophe. Says Pontoppidan: "It was only a momentary flash of anger in Bertha. She knew too well that she would never dare to wrest her child's fate out of the hands of life's hidden powers in order to shape it according to her own will. She found herself here at the boundary of her courage and acknowledged her impotence. Though she was certain about the path Jytte would have to follow to attain peace and fortune, she dared not take the responsibility upon herself" (Vol. 1 [Copenhagen: Gyldendal, 1918], p. 111).

everything hangs in the balance. The situation is one of suspense; the scales may tip in either direction, leading to one outcome or the other. Added to this is the fact that the entire weight of the situation rests upon the individual. He determines the outcome of the situation. Therefore, everything which happens or does not happen is traced back to him; it is the consequence of what he does or fails to do.

To speak as we do here of "holding another person's life in one's hand" endows this metaphor with a certain emotional power. The emotional significance of the metaphor grows out of the contrast in the relationship to which it refers, namely, that we have the power to determine the direction of something in another person's life, perhaps merely his mood or in an extreme case his entire destiny. Now it is altogether reasonable that we should have power to control things and animals. It is reasonable that legal authorities should have definite delegated and legally defined power over people in order to keep them from violating others. But it is altogether unreasonable that one person should possess direct power over another person, because such power has not been delegated to him, has not been defined by existing law, and does not serve to protect other people's rights. Wielding such power over another person is unreasonable because every person is an independent and responsible individual; yet we are to a large extent inescapably dependent upon one another so that, whether the thing at stake is our mood or our destiny, we are mutually and in a most immediate sense in one another's power.

Out of this fundamental dependence and direct power arises the demand that we take care of that in the other person's life which is dependent upon us and which we have in our power. However, this same demand forbids that we ever attempt, even for his own sake, to rob him of his independence. Responsibility for the other person never consists in our assuming the responsibility which is his.

2.

The Problem
of Motivation

The Spontaneity of Relationship in D. H. Lawrence

The problem is far from solved, however, simply by the admission that the demand to care for the other person's life never means to deprive him of his own responsibility. We must therefore return to our starting point and take up the problem once again. We pointed out that the individual, if he is not to become merely a tool of the other person, must from the standpoint of his own outlook on life try to determine what is best for that other person. But for this very reason he is in danger of violating that other person, because the outlook of one person may not be pertinent to another.

If the outlook upon life can thus bring people into conflict with one another, this is because our relations with one another are normally motivated *(formidlede)*. And it is precisely when our relation to the other person is motivated by an ideology which we believe meets the need of everyone that such violation is inevitable. But to seek the solution of the problem in the unmotivated relationship is not possible either. Granted, we may violate someone in the name of an ideology, but we may certainly do so also out of a sheer lack of any outlook. The motivating factor *(mediet)* may lead to violation, but spontaneity—the absence of such a factor—may do so as well. We see this very clearly in the writings of D. H. Lawrence. An analysis of his love concept will throw light upon the question of motivation *(formidlingen)*.

It is characteristic of many of Lawrence's short stories and novels that they do not concern themselves with any form of

30

ethical outlook. This is not to say that the ethical outlook is ignored or repudiated. It simply does not exist. Its absence is therefore a case neither of innocence nor of rebellion; it is rather in the nature of a defect. On the one hand, this means that his universe is insecure. In the passion of love his characters are in a strange and impersonal way abandoned to one another. If there were pity in their love, the love would no longer be pure. On the other hand, it means that all forms of sentimentality, to which an ethical outlook is tempted, are excluded. This is why Lawrence's descriptions of love relations are sometimes characterized by an incomparable delicacy and intensity. One need only recall the meeting between Lydia Lensky and Tom Brangwen at the vicarage in the opening chapter of *The Rainbow,* though the literary effect is also attained through the fact that Tom Brangwen is a person deprived of the power of coordination and expression in order that he may be pure emotion and sensitivity.

The fact that we cannot at all employ ethically weighted words or expressions in connection with Lawrence's description of love relations does not mean, however, that his descriptions make no demands, because they do in fact. But what they demand they demand solely for their own sake.

What is demanded is the integrity of personhood. Mere sexual gratification threatens the vital unity of the person and thereby the possibility of fulfillment through the love relationship. In *The Rainbow* Tom Brangwen is seized by fear of having ruined his relation to women and of having lost the unique possibility of love because of his having involved himself with a promiscuous girl one time when he was drunk. Consequently he does not let it happen again. His expectation is so intense and so absolute that it constitutes a demand and in fact makes his life so desolate in its transitoriness that he must from time to time resort to drink. In the same way the vital unity of the person is threatened by a merely erotic relationship, as in the case of Gudrun and Gerald in *Women in Love.*

In the purely sensual relationships sensuality proves inadequate; it is gratified but not fulfilled. Fulfillment is attained when one loves another person with his whole self. The sensual can be fulfilled only in such a love relationship. Love-less sexual gratification may therefore simply attest a failing sensual vitality.

It must be added that in Lawrence's estimation the love rela-tionship is the acid test of the integrity of the person. At any rate Lawrence is apparently unable to see that the integrity of personhood can be tested anywhere else in a person's life. This accounts for the incredible one-sidedness of his writings. They are dominated entirely by those conflicts in which personal integration and fulfillment of life through the love relationship are at stake. This is also why triangular conflicts are of no interest to him.

As inimitable as Lawrence's descriptions of ecstatic love are his descriptions of hate. But how does one explain the fact that the experiences of sublime love and of blind hate alternate like the tides? And how does one explain the fact that even when there is not this oscillation between love and hate—which is sometimes the case in Lawrence's writings—the characters in his stories are nevertheless presented as always on the brink of being destroyed by hate toward one another? One gets this impression, even in instances where the relationship is happy, as in the case of Ursula and Birkin in *Women in Love.*

The reason is not that for Lawrence happiness is devoid of adversity. It is not a case of love being reduced to the merely sexual or erotic. No, the reason is the consistent spontaneity *(mediumløse)* of love.

Lawrence describes love in such a manner that the one part-ner will not tolerate having the other partner develop himself in all directions and realize his nature as fully as possible. For example, love is not able to manifest itself in joy over the other person's work; it cannot bear such a joy. Love is such that it cannot allow the individual to share with the other person what he himself has experienced. It does not admit any sharing of activities or interests. The one partner simply wants to possess the other, one might say, as an unattached individual who exists and realizes himself solely through his relation to him or her. Lawrence's description of love as seclusion from the world, and as desire to possess the other as an individual with no attachment to or interest in the world, is an extraordinarily precise expression of how spontaneous in his view ecstatic love is and must be. In an absolutely exclusive manner the one partner wants to possess the other for himself.

Lawrence is of course correct in maintaining that spontaneity is the unique characteristic of the love relationship. That is what constitutes its intimacy.

But it is just as characteristic of Lawrence that he sets the intensity of the love experience over against its inclusiveness. To think of love as at one and the same time motivating and being motivated by something outside of itself is to bring in something irrelevant. Lawrence will not allow the notion that love has power to motivate the other person's self-development and in that manner also cause him to love that self-development. According to his thinking it is false, weak, and one might almost say irreligious to regard love as something motivated. This is a falsification of the love experience. The purity and vitality of love consist in its being intensified without becoming inclusive. Its intimacy is not to be understood as having been motivated, as something secondary. No, the intimacy is everything, absolutely everything!

This is due to the fact that while it is indeed the other self who is being loved, Lawrence expresses in incredibly varied manner how love at the same time ecstatically transcends both the emotional and the personal life. In the happiness of love intimacy is absolute, and it is precisely this absoluteness of intimacy which often makes Lawrence resort to religious categories in describing love.

Since motivation is never seen as an effect of the vitality of love but always as a false exploitation of it, that is, since love is consistently unmotivated and spontaneous, it is always in danger of turning into hate, because if any passion is spontaneous it is hate. Indeed, this is the difference between anger and hate. The pathos of anger is moral because it arises out of the conviction that a wrong has been committed either against oneself or others. This wrong is the issue. And it is a real issue, for there is in anger a determination to communicate, that is, to effect a settlement of the issue: the other person must be brought to an acknowledgment of his wrong. Therefore, through the outburst of anger one admits that he has been violated either personally or on behalf of others.

It is different with hate. Admittedly there is an issue here too, namely, that a wrong has presumably been committed. But in this case the objectivity of the issue is in doubt. The particular wrong only appears to be the issue; it serves as an occasion for hating but is not the thing itself.

The fact is that hate is impotent, either because the other person is out of reach or because, for whatever reason, we cannot bring ourselves to let him know we are angry with him.[1]

There are many reasons why we do not want to let him know that we are angry with him, but they are reasons which we never really want to admit. This is why in hate there is always an element of simulation. We will not admit our own impotence, and therefore the other person is to be blamed for it. Not only is he to be blamed for the wrong which he presumably has committed but also for the fact that he is beyond the reach of our wrath, though this is clearly not his fault. While anger is honest, hate involves simulation.[2]

Never is one more dependent upon another person than

1. "One tends to hate that to which one is not equal. In other words, one hates that which, one might say, is beyond his strength if he were to fight it." Hans Lipps, Die menschliche Natur (Frankfurt: Klostermann, 1942), p. 129.
2. Anger is suppressed but is too powerful to be hemmed in and therefore changes into hate. This is the decisive thing (see Knud Hansen, Søren Kierkegaard. Ideens Digter [Copenhagen: Gyldendal, 1954], p. 367). But the question is whether there is not also always an element of simulation involved. When we suppress our anger is it not because of reasons we do not really want to admit? The reasons we give—to ourselves and perhaps also to others—are, for example, that we do not wish to be petty, we do not want to make a big issue out of nothing. But all the while we refuse to admit either to ourselves or to others that the real reasons are entirely different: that we had been offended, that we refused to face up to the painfulness of an accounting, or that we lacked the will to deal with the other person as in the case of anger. But in this way the simulation adds to the hate. The other person is also to bear a part of the blame for our anxiety over having to reveal that we have been violated, possibly in an insignificant manner. He is to share the blame for our cowardly shrinking

when he hates him, for hate is forever going in circles about that other person. But circling is as far as it gets, because the person hated is beyond reach; one never gets to him. This is why hate must content itself with merely going around in circles, always at a distance.

This is also why it is hard to imagine anyone more occupied with himself than the person who is in a state of hate. Since his dependence upon the other person has this peculiar negative character, he is not only thrown back upon himself, but out of sheer impotence the isolation and barrenness of his occupation with himself becomes complete.[3] And therefore there is not the slightest desire to communicate, to come to terms with the other. While anger is an outburst, hate maintains itself by the fact that it is incapable of—in fact does not want—an outburst.

The original root of the conflict becomes less and less significant. It is reduced to a mere fuel for keeping the hate alive, a fuel which can also be procured in many other places. In fact, everything which the other person is and does nourishes the hate. The connection between hate and the substantive problem very soon becomes purely incidental.[4] There is no longer any issue between the parties. The other person is simply to be annihilated. The unmotivated and spontaneous character of hate manifests itself in the will to annihilate. "Hate wants to kill in order to annihilate."

Hate can therefore be overcome only if the issue actually gets

from the painfulness of an accounting and for our own unwillingness to communicate. Thus, hate is a kind of obsession, because in addition to the wrong which the other person has committed, he is also to be blamed for our own failure to come to a settlement, which in the case of anger is the only right course to take.

3. But always in such occupation with self there is simulation. The nurture and enjoyment of one's own righteousness are hidden both from oneself and from others because of one's constant and impotent preoccupation with the wrong and the meanness of the other person.

4. Lipps puts it this way: "It is characteristic of our hate that it develops and establishes itself with the help of reasons. It looks for points to latch onto, points on which it can dwell and thus entrench itself. . . . It does not actually clear up anything but finds what it needs for its own justification. Hate is intemperate."

Then he goes on: "We can as it were persecute a person in our thoughts, unable to dismiss him from our minds. We have a compulsion to think about him. . . . We try to convince ourselves that he deserves our hate. Hate wants to be pure." It is a "brooding and thinking"; it "entrenches itself in its object." *Die menschliche Natur*, pp. 129–130.

a fair hearing, for example, by letting the substance of the conflict express itself in the outburst of anger. Only a preoccupation with the thing itself, the motivating factor in the relation between two people, can break the vicious circle of hate.

Lawrence sets love's intimacy and love's inclusiveness over against one another. He denies that love is able to motivate or be motivated by a person's free development in a free world of his own. He makes love so unmotivated and spontaneous that it can turn into the equally unmotivated and spontaneous hate, just as hate can turn into love only through the emergence of the ecstatic experience.

In hate the other person is constantly one's entire universe —and that in the most narrow sense. Hate is intimacy in thought, a perverted intimacy. This is expressed in the impotent desire of the hate-love relationship always to deny the other person his own existence. Hate lives by this complete impotence, and it consumes a person.[5]

It is Lawrence's thesis that the fulfillment of love is experienced with religious or metapyhsical intensity. Does this mean then that love which manifests itself also through the creation of motivating relations to someone is a treasonable compromise? Is it a betrayal of love when the other person is allowed to live a life of his own, in a world in which the individual is only tangentially included?

To this one might reply that it simply is not possible to live one's life, be it long or short, in ecstasy. And only if we face that fact are we able to replace the alternation between love and hate, which we meet so often in Lawrence's writings, with a realization of love involving a fluctuation between the intensity of experience and the creation of motivations. We might add that the erotic-religious view of existence, as found in some modern nature religions, is too narrow; one cannot in this

5. There is an "ingrown hate out of which one is not able to extricate himself and in which one destroys himself." Lipps, *Die menschliche Natur*, pp. 129–130. Lawrence's descriptions of hate illustrate Hans Lipps's definitions of it. The Lawrence descriptions are as precise as the Lipps definitions.

manner rule out the cultural perspective altogether. Love must therefore also be an inclusive relationship which includes in one's own world the self-development of the other person.

If, however, we are satisfied in this way to suggest that the intimacy and the inclusiveness of love should, so to speak, be allowed to alternate as haphazardly as the weather, instead of letting love and hate follow upon each other as certainly as the tides, then we have thereby made one clear-cut admission: There is no necessary connection between the love experience and love's creation of motivations.

But this is hardly a significant admission. For to the degree that the love experience is found to be compatible with an understanding of life as something given to the individual, to that degree love must necessarily manifest itself in inclusiveness. And this is neither compromise, treason, nor fortuitous alternation. To the degree that in the love experience we are willing to understand the other person and his reciprocal love as something received, to that degree it is natural to let him remain free and not turn the intimacy of love into a form of captivity.

Lawrence is right in giving the exclusiveness of intimacy its due; he is right when he glorifies the experience which fully absorbs a person. But we do not see why this should force him to say that exclusiveness and inclusiveness are in conflict with one another. He does this actually for quite a different reason: to make something religious out of the exclusiveness of intimacy. But in so doing he transforms the experience of love. He turns it back, one might say, so that it is no longer open as it once was. He makes the love experience incompatible with an understanding of life as something received. The happiness is intensified to the point of ecstasy, but is not allowed to work itself out in terms of joyfulness, zest for life, the courage to be.

In the novel *The Rainbow* Lawrence describes the marriage of Will Brangwen and Anna. It seemed to them as if the whole world had collapsed and as if they, the only two survivors, were sitting there in the midst of the ruins unspeakably happy in a new world. It happened very suddenly. One day he was absorbed in the world and its affairs. The next day, together with Anna, he was infinitely removed from it. All knowledge and experience of the world had been left behind. True, the world was still there, but on the periphery of their existence—in the cry of the street peddler, the noise of the traffic, and the laughter of children outdoors at play.

At first Will's conscience troubled him a bit because his happiness in love was so remote from the world. Was there not something out there calling to him, something which he was disregarding? Was it right thus to exclude himself from the world and, so to speak, deny its existence? He could not help but think himself guilty: Here he was with Anna, feeling as secure as if their house were the ark floating upon the waters in which everything else had been drowned; yet if he were to open the door, the world would still be there—as if to accuse him. Nonetheless, his uneasiness gradually subsided. Why should he hesitate while Anna had no scruples in the matter. Besides, the very happiness of love matured him and freed him from such pangs of conscience.

The unfortunate thing was, however, that the less restrained Anna was, the sooner she desired an excursion back into the world. And this made Will miserable and unhappy. He was seized by the fear that he would lose everything that had recently become his. His marriage to Anna was such a transformation of his life, and he had had to liberate himself from such deep-seated conventional inhibitions that the happiness of love, once experienced, had become his entire universe. For this reason he could not allow her to move in another universe, a universe in which he would still be there but nothing more. And when she nevertheless did move out into that other universe, he felt as though she were discarding the living fruit for the sake of the rind, and he began to hate her for it.

Anna for her part would not allow him to lead an independent existence either. That which satisfied him was so foreign to her that when he was living in his own universe he might as well have been a fabled monster as a human being. When he was absorbed in his own concerns he paid no attention to her, and this completely embittered her; she was determined to ruin his life, and she succeeded in doing so. Through her aversion and derision his experiences turned sour for him, and this naturally revived his hate. Then she cried over their marriage being again out of kilter, but at the same time she was happy at having been able to wreck something of his life.

They had gotten themselves into a vicious circle. The more Anna succeeded in wrecking that which was his, the more dependent upon her Will became. But to her this dependence seemed only an attempt to hem her in, an attempt which she had to resist and which she could resist effectively only by hurting him even more. But this in turn caused him to cling to her even more, with the result that she came to feel still more hemmed in and tyrannized. She became obsessed with a desire to get rid of him and was ready to do anything to achieve that end. It seemed to her that he was determined to drag her down to himself. Her freedom was giving way to the subtle pressure of his will. She felt as though he would not allow her to live, that he wanted at every moment to destroy her.

However, she was unaware that it was in fact she herself who caused him thus to dote upon her, because the more she resisted him the more he felt himself abandoned by her. And out of his fear of being abandoned he pressed himself upon her, which in turn further accentuated her aversion.

"He felt, somewhere, that she did not respect him. She only respected him as far as he was related to herself. For what he was, beyond her, she had no care. She did not care for what he represented in himself. It is true, he did not know himself what he represented. But whatever it was she did not really honour it."[6] Neither his work as an artist, the fact that he was the breadwinner, nor what he thought about life, society, and mankind had any significance to her. She was able, entirely independently of him, to judge concerning all of these matters. Yes, even his spirit was the object of her ridicule, because he was

6. D. H. Lawrence, *The Rainbow* (New York: Viking Press, 1961), p. 167.

pure emotionality, incapable of articulating his thoughts. She had contempt for everything to which he passionately clung. He felt himself violated.

He was determined to be respected for something, anything. Hence every time she took something away from him, he asserted himself and tried to find a new place where he might be the master. But nothing was he permitted to keep. And if he accused her of not respecting him, she ridiculed him for that. For her it was sufficient that she loved him.

He felt disgraced because, while she was everything to him, she did not hesitate to ridicule him for that very fact, and the feeling became a consuming fire within him. If she were to be taken away from him he would crumble as a house whose foundation is torn away. Wildly and wretchedly he clung to her. He desired nothing more passionately than to leave her, but this he was unable to do, because where should he turn? He would be like a swimmer in the ocean in the dead of night with nothing to hold on to. And he had the feeling that she was stubbornly and mercilessly pushing him out into the deep.

Finally it seemed as though his hate was complete, and he remained only a determined, dark will. In fact he refused to admit that she existed. His soul became one single passion, centered about his hate and completely in its power. His will was turned in upon himself, animallike: hidden under cover of darkness, motionless yet incessantly active.

It was a vicious circle of a peculiar character. Why were Will and Anna so affected by the fact that each of them lived in his own world? Why did they hate the unknown in one another? Because they loved one another! The absurdity of it was the fact that it was also because of the strange and the unknown that they loved one another. The one was disposed, alive, youthful in relation to the other when he was absorbed by that which was his own, by that which was strange to the other. Will loved her because of that in her which was strange to him, just as she loved him because of the mystery that his spirit and world were so entirely different from hers. However, the strange and the unknown were only incitements to love, never its object. Hence there was a constant fluctuation between love and conflict.

Objective and Personal Motivation

Having referred to D. H. Lawrence in an attempt to show that we do not find the solution to our problem in the spontaneous relationship, we shall consider the matter of motivation a little further.

There are persons regarding whom one might say that it is physiologically impossible for them to establish connection with others except by way of some objective issue. If such a person is invited some evening into the company of other people whom he does not know and who have come together simply for the sake of getting together and visiting with each other, he is the most awkward person imaginable. The moment he enters the room he becomes speechless, not only because he is unacquainted with the people who are present but fully as much because the thought of having to endure an evening in conversation with them completely paralyzes him. He is unable to utter a word from the moment he arrives until he leaves. It may indeed be pleasant to meet him, because while most people in that kind of situation indulge in a few trivial comments and polite questions, it is absolutely impossible for him to say something simply for the sake of saying it. Rather he prefers to remain silent despite the embarrassment of it and the fact that the others will regard him as impossible. This is not something he deliberately decides upon; that would be affectation.

But let him get together some evening with another group of strangers who have come together for the purpose of discussing a particular subject in which they are interested and regarding which they desire information, and he may be as lively, creative, uninhibited, and full of humor as the rest of the party. Why is this? Because the gap between him and the others has been bridged by their common interest in an objective matter. With a bridge to support him he can get along; without it he is left hanging in midair.

This gap between persons may be bridged in many different ways. But one thing is certain: if persons are to encounter one another in a manner which is redeeming and liberating to the individual's spirit and energies, it will be effected through some intermediate agent as the motivating factor. We must be united in some common enterprise, some common interest or distress.

That which often makes conversation so emaciating and fatiguing is the fact that though we have nothing to say to one another, we are not able to remain silent. Convention does not allow us through silence to admit of the spontaneous in our mutual relationship.

However, the objective relationship between individuals is not maintained solely by the object in question, for even the most objective relationship is also personal. The objective and the personal are intertwined in one motivation. The comparative importance of the objective and the personal will obviously vary greatly from person to person. It will also vary according to the different kinds of relationship. The object of common concern to teacher and student calls for a greater degree of personal contact than the object of common concern to merchant and customer.

That the relationship is personal means that we are, as we say, sure of one another. We can count on one another. Each of the parties involved has so committed himself to norms that there is unity and constancy in their makeup, as they also understand and consent to the content of these norms. In other words, to them the norms have the character of an outlook on life.

But this naturally means that persons may disagree with one another. One outlook may be at variance with another outlook, and the disagreement may be violent. But this is the condition for our living together. The unity and constancy which characterize people's makeup mean at one and the same time that they can depend upon one another and that they may come into conflict.

To avoid the possibility of conflict by allowing the personal relationship to develop spontaneously is no solution. On the contrary, the spontaneous relationship carries even greater possibilities of conflict. The personal relationship is spontaneous, for example, whenever we compare ourselves with others. When we compare ourselves with others out of envy or for the purpose of establishing our own superiority or for whatever reason, we touch the other person—even if only in our thoughts—at a very sensitive point. It is the same as in the case of resentment or hate; hence the close connection between the two: hate and resentment on the one hand, and the practice of comparing ourselves with others on the other hand. Comparison gives rise to resentment just as resentment expresses itself in comparison.

In conflict situations the weight of importance is shifted from the issue itself to the personal. The issue comes to be merely, as we say, the "occasion" for the conflict. But this is not all. To the degree that the issue is merely the occasion and the personal becomes the dominant factor, the relationship also threatens to become a spontaneous personal relationship. Indeed we can prevent this by self-righteously arguing about the issue which now in a different sense has "come between us." But if this proves too ineffective, the relationship threatens to become a spontaneous personal relationship of resentment and hate.

This can be avoided only if a norm or outlook can be interpolated as the thing which has "come between us" and attracted attention. But this again raises the question posed in the preceding chapter: Does this not mean that we become guilty of encroaching upon one another in the name of the norm or the outlook? The answer is that this need not happen if a person, not only for himself but also as regards the other person, can at one and the same time remain committed to the norms but also keep his distance from them.

First, a word concerning this matter of keeping one's own distance from the norms. To keep one's distance is to acknowledge that the norm is not his own. It is not he who has set it up or given it its content. Nor is it he who has endowed it with power to stimulate, regulate, educate, protect, and whatever else it has power to do. To understand the norm and consent to it but without regarding it as something we have ourselves set up, to accept it in such a way that we master it only as we bow before it—this is what is meant by simultaneous commitment to and distance from the norm.

What, then, is meant by the "distance" from the norm which one must observe with respect to the other person? This question arises in the situation of conflict where one is of the opinion that the other has acted contrary to the norm. The distance then consists in our not using the norm utterly to write him off, to liquidate him. His action will indeed be censured to the extent that it was contrary to the norm. However, the distance means that we concede that he himself is something other and more than his action. And this in turn means that in our censure or protest there remains a desire to communicate with him about the norm. There is a desire to involve him, as there is also a willingness to allow him latitude in his relation to the norm in order that his compliance may be voluntary. In the confrontation concerning the norms love has a chance, provided that we refrain from laying exclusive claim to the norms and from using them as an ax for bludgeoning him to death.

The demand that I take care of the other person's life makes my relation to the norms uncertain in the sense that it reveals how I arrogate the norm to myself as though I were its author. I insist upon this norm, I exult over it, I use it for lording it over the other person, I take vain pride in defending it. I remove all distance between the norm and myself and thereby also remove the distance between the other person and the norm. I use the norm to write him off once and for all and to make my own situation respectable. Along with this one more thing happens: I cease to exercise judgment, because when both my own and the other person's distance from the norm has been removed, there is no longer any space in which judgment can be exercised.

In order not to be misunderstood we should perhaps add that what has just been said does not mean that we must continually go about wondering whether or not we made the right decision. In many situations the right course of action is perfectly clear. Judgment is not to be equated with uncertainty. Decisions need not be made in uncertainty just because judgment is involved. The alternative of uncertainty or precise directives is a false alternative. Judgment is neither the one nor the other. It may be very clear what we should do, or it may be doubtful. But to exercise judgment does not mean that we make doubtful that which is clear.

These two things must be distinguished. The certainty gained by claiming the norm as our own and using it to write the other person off is one thing; it rules out all judgment and turns the demand to take care of the other person's life into a matter of uncertainty. The certainty we have when a case is clear, however, is another thing; the ethical demand does not turn this certainty into uncertainty.

We have said that the ethical demand makes uncertain the certainty won through our claiming the norm as our own. If we believe that it also makes every clear decision doubtful, then we have embraced a philosophy of uncertainty and have turned uncertainty into a doctrine.

There is indeed a connection between these two things. We imagine that a certainty gotten from our claiming the norm as our own is based upon the clarity of the case in question. But this does not change the fact that we are dealing here with two different things. Indeed the deception is possible only for this very reason.

3.

The Radical Demand
and the Social Norms

The Radicality of the Demand

The demand, precisely because it is unspoken, is radical. This is true even though the thing to be done in any particular situation may be very insignificant. Why is this? Because the person confronted by the unspoken demand must himself determine how he is to take care of the other person's life. If what he does is to result in something of real value to the other person, he must act unselfishly. Regardless of how significant or insignificant that which is to be done may appear on the surface, the demand is radical because in the very nature of the case no one but he alone, through his own unselfishness, is able to discover what will best serve the other person.

It is different in the case of the demands which inhere in prevailing morality and law. They concern themselves with more or less specific actions. Once these specific actions have been carried out, the matter is closed and nothing is said about whether the person who carried them out is then at liberty to turn to his own benefit all the other actions and words occasioned by the mutual relationship. The point of the unspoken demand, however, is that everything which an individual has opportunity to do and say in his relation to the other person is to be done and said not for his own sake but for the sake of him whose life is in his hand.

The radicality of the demand consists, further, in the fact that it asks me to take care of the other person's life not only when to do so is pleasant for me but also when it is very unpleasant, unpleasant because it intrudes disturbingly into my own existence. And this is not all. Even in distrust the other person is still delivered over into my hands. Even my enemy is to a large degree dependent upon me and upon the manner in which I respond to him. How often my thoughts are determined by someone's animosity toward me. How often a person is more dependent upon someone he hates than upon someone he loves. The demand therefore asks us to take care of whatever in the other person's life has been placed in our hands, regardless of whether he is one of our loved ones or a stranger, and regardless of the manner in which he has been placed in our hands, whether it be through a confidence in us which we appreciate or through an enmity which arouses us to self-assertion.

The radicality of the demand manifests itself in various ways. It prevents the encounter in which the demand arises from becoming a fellowship in which we lose ourselves completely. It would become such a fellowship if the demand were to come to us as a spoken or implied demand from the other person himself. In that event the encounter would result in a fellowship which would completely absorb us and in which we would lose our identity as individuals. The radicality of the demand means that it is up to the individual himself to determine what will best serve the other person. And since, as we have said, this could prove to be the very opposite of what the other person asks for and desires, the demand has the effect of making the person to whom the demand is directed an "individual" in the precise sense of the word. Ethically speaking the demand isolates him.

The radicality manifests itself also in the fact that the other person has no right himself to make the demand, even though it has to do with the care of his own life. Such demands as the other person from his own point of view has a perfect right to make are of an entirely different nature. They are conditioned by the social norms, by the moral, legal, and conventional criteria implied in our life together with and over against one another. They are well-founded demands of which the other person is conscious and which he is able to formulate, or of which he might have been conscious and which he might have been able to formulate. At any rate he can lay claim to these demands because he is fully within his right to assume that he and I are in agreement concerning the morality, the law, and the convention in question. If his demands are valid he must therefore also be able to show that they correspond to the social norms.

On the other hand, he has no right to make the radical demand that everything I say and do in our mutual relationship must be said and done for his sake rather than for my own. This is a demand regarding which he and I have *not* mutually agreed. Here there is no prevailing norm to guide us. The fact out of which the demand arises, namely, that his life is more or less in my hands, is a fact which has come into being independently of either him or me. Therefore, he cannot identify himself with this fact and assume that its demand is his own.

Because of its radicality the demand has in philosophical language been called "unconditional," "infinite," and "absolute." We shall return to this later.

Radicality versus Limitlessness

As we have said, radicality means that the demand can be fulfilled only through unselfishness. This does not mean, however, that a person has unlimited responsibility for everything under the sun, including all sorts of things having nothing to do with him.[1]

Concern for everything and everybody, even where it is not indicated by personal relations, social position, or economic factors, has the appearance of selflessness. However, it can equally well be an attempt on the part of a frustrated person

---

1. This is a basic idea in H. Østergaard-Nielsen's study of Luther: *Scriptura sacra et viva vox* (Munich, 1957), and in his earlier articles.

to give content to his own life. His own work, his own life together with his family and the people with whom he is associated in his occupation fail to supply this content. He derives no excitement or inspiration from any of it; these he feels he must seek elsewhere. He looks for some responsibility which can lift him out of his dull existence in the daily treadmill. Without being aware of it he has actually inverted the roles, because to be responsible means that very definite demands are placed upon him. There is some work, some action, a decision, or whatever it may be which he must carry out, not for his own sake but for the sake of the other person for whom he has assumed responsibility. In the search for a responsibility that can inspire, however, it is actually he himself who is making the demand, and he himself who is to be served thereby. He is searching for a hitherto unknown content, some great inspiration for his own life.

If in this search he absorbs himself in political activity, it is a foregone conclusion that this activity will be strongly ideological and utopian. Only in this way will it be able to satisfy him, to give him what he seeks, because in ideology and utopia the responsibility is as great as he could possibly want it to be.

But to carry responsibility to the point of limitlessness leads to encroachment. For example, in the political realm it leads to the conviction that it is not only legitimate but an unselfish act to coerce people, so long as this is done in their own best interest and only as a temporary expedient. The unlimited consists in assuming responsibility for what best serves the welfare of everyone. This very soon results in taking the responsibility away from the people by coercing them against their own will in the interest of what is best for them. In short, if one arrogates to himself a responsibility which goes beyond the bounds of humanity, he inevitably violates those for whom he has assumed responsibility.

We observe the same thing in the area of parent-child relations. That which parents hold in their hands is not least of

all the child's freedom and independence. Therefore, the very
point of child rearing—and this is also the limit of parental
responsibility—is that parents give their children freedom and
independence in relation to themselves. Very often, however,
parental concern does the very opposite. The rules of conduct
will themselves to a very large degree form the child's character. But parents are not content to leave it at that. Instead
they try to do something to make sure that the rules will actually
take effect. They want to make sure that the rules will indeed
shape the child's character, and so with that end in view they
add to their directives various moralizings and admonitions.[2]
But when parents try to form the child's character and direct
his actions they are assuming unlimited responsibility. The
limitlessness of the responsibility expresses itself in the fact
that by their moralizings and admonitions they try to direct
their child's future through remote control. And therein lies
the encroachment upon the child. It is an encroachment upon
him whether or not he suffers under it, whether out of a

---

2. For example, one rule is that the child must suffer the consequences of what
he does. To allow this rule to operate means that the matter is completely closed
when the child has suffered the consequences of what he has done and that
parents (or teachers) will make no further reference to it. There are no more
bad feelings, and the child is certain that he will find his parents in the same
good mood they were in prior to the wrong he committed. To allow the rule to
do its own work means that the parents allow their child the freedom and independence which are rightly his under this rule, namely, the freedom and
independence to learn for himself that one must suffer the consequences of his
acts.

On the other hand, a desire to determine the effects of the rule in order
directly to form the child's character is seen in the common parental admonitions: "You no doubt remember what happened yesterday (or a week ago or
last month). You surely are not about to do that again! Remember what happened." This is to deprive the child of his freedom and independence and to
spoil one's relation to him. Few things are as effective as this kind of admonition in making the relationship between parents and children banal and
uninteresting.

Furthermore, the attempt to assume responsibility for that which is beyond
one's power to control either by action or admonition brings its own retribution.
One wears himself out through insufferable worry. If parents have the time and
the means to give free rein to their worry it can easily run amuck. In their
relation to their children they will always be ready with some admonition. And
when such admonition is not always expressed, it is only because of the additional worry that a repetition of the admonition may create resentment or
indifference and thus have the opposite effect from the one intended. Only
through effort are they able to restrain themselves. The concomitant of unlimited
responsibility is incessant worry.

desire to please his parents he reacts favorably or is instead strong enough to rebel.[3]

In this discussion concerning a confusion of the radical demand and the unlimited responsibility we must, however, add that the problem takes on a particular character in a democratic order of society. At any rate there appears to be something in democratic society which encourages the idea that responsibility is unlimited.

In a democracy the individual citizen shares responsibility in a certain sense for the manner in which the society and the people of which he is a part are governed. Logically each citizen also shares the guilt with respect to the distressing situation into which his fellow citizens are brought by inefficient and poor government. Very pointedly stated, political responsibility means sharing responsibility for the actions of others, specifically, the actions of those who govern.

But what then is the difference between political responsibility and that nonentity commonly referred to as collective responsibility? Through the idea of collective responsibility and its corollary of collective guilt an attempt has been made to revive primitive religious ideas. The result is a great deal of metaphysical nonsense about the fellowship of family, nation, or race according to which each individual shares the responsibility and the guilt of other people's actions.

The difference between this and political responsibility is clear if we pose the question whether there is anything else which makes the individual a participant in the responsibility for and guilt of what others do. The fact is that there is indeed something else, and that something is power. Is an individual

3. Admonitions usually have one of two effects. In the case of the weak person the admonition results in a pharisaic desire to please. Whether or not he has in fact erred, whether or not there is any reason for the admonition, the admonition causes the weak person to be concerned about how he appears in the eyes of those who do the admonishing. The admonition calls forth self-reflection. In the case of the strong person, on the other hand, it calls forth a desire to rebel. It makes the honest person a liar, the industrious person lazy, the dependable person unreliable, because these are the only ways by which the strong person can keep from being forced into a desire to please. Moralizing and admonitions force the strong person into rebellion and the weak person into the pharisaism of wanting to please.

guilty of the oppression of another person by some third party
even though he himself had no overt part in it? We must
answer in the affirmative *if* the individual is in possession of
power, because a person is given power primarily for the
purpose of hindering oppression and for the purpose of making
and enforcing laws.

But does not this power reside with those who govern
rather than with the individual citizen? Yes, in predemocratic
society, but not in democratic society. For the very thing that
makes democratic society democratic is that all of us share in
this power. We say this on the strength of the idea of the
sovereignty of the people which is the basis of democracy and
which determines our contemporary understanding of political
responsibility and its problems. The acts of those who govern
are in a certain sense the acts of the individual citizen, because
in the name of the sovereignty of the people the individual
citizen participates in the power through which those acts are
carried out.

This will be further clarified if we consider the thinking
which prevailed in predemocratic society. As an example we
may refer to Luther's view, which is characteristic of the
thinking of his time. For an individual to take the initiative in
public life outside the area of his own calling or occupation
was regarded by Luther as irresponsible assumption of a
responsibility which God has reserved for himself. But suppose
we see a person outside the area of our own calling or
occupation who is in abject misery and about to perish, and we
believe it should be possible through private initiative outside
the area of our own competence to come to his aid—are we
not then to overstep the boundary of our own calling or
occupation and intervene? Luther says no, not even in such a
case. We must leave the matter in God's hands. Suppose, he
says, that I as a preacher see that sectarians are carrying on
with their false doctrine to the detriment of people's souls,
must I not in such a case intervene? No, "I have no right to do
this even if I hear that false doctrine is being taught and that
souls are being seduced and condemned which I could rescue

from error and condemnation by my sound doctrine. But I should commit the matter to God, who in His own time will find the opportunity to call ministers lawfully and to give the Word."[4]

It is obvious how with reference to such thinking the idea of the sovereignty of the people and of citizens' political responsibility has turned everything upside down. We have come to share responsibility for whatever happens in another city. In Luther's day only the government was responsible; in a democracy we all are responsible, because every individual citizen is in a certain sense the government inasmuch as all participate in the sovereignty.

The decisive change of view expresses itself, for example, in the modern concept of "social consciousness." This is the idea that every citizen shares the responsibility for all undeserved suffering and misery. Social consciousness is not a nobility of spirit ascribed only to a few so-called philanthropists. On the contrary, we expect to find it in everyone, simply because each citizen is a member of the same society and state as those who in one way or another suffer innocently. Therefore, it is not only reprehensible to oppress our fellow citizens, to exploit them, and to serve our own interests at their expense. It is fully as reprehensible, from the standpoint of our political responsibility, to remain unconcerned about the unfortunate and leave them to their own fate—regardless of how perfect we may be personally or how well we may manage our own affairs. Merely to refrain from doing harm is not enough.

But this view has not always prevailed. For centuries all of this was the sole responsibility of the government, primarily because the individual citizen, having no share in the sovereignty, had no power. This in turn meant that no one was responsible for other people's miserable circumstances except those who in one way or another were equipped with governmental power. With the advent of industrialization,

4. Martin Luther, *Luther's Works,* vol. 26, ed. J. Pelikan (Saint Louis: Concordia Publishing House, 1963), p. 18. There is of course a good deal more in Luther's view than a mere reference to state government and the patriarchal social order, but we will not go into that here.

however, came the universal phenomenon whereby individual citizens who have absolutely no state authority oppress fellow citizens purely on the basis of their economic power.

This explains the peculiar history of the idea of the sovereignty of the people. It originated as a concept in support of people's rights in the face of violation at the hands of those who possessed power. The concept was employed in this sense by the revolutionary movements in the Middle Ages and by the Peasants' Revolt in Luther's day. It was a protest against the idea that the people were merely the ruler's property over which he could rule as he pleased. It was an assertion that the people were the real sovereign and that the ruler held his office for the sake of the people, in order to uphold that order without which life is impossible and in order to protect the people and assure them of peace. However, now that we have all come to participate in the sovereignty, we discover that this participation has its price. The sovereignty of the people which formerly was a weapon in the people's hand against the tyrants and the privileged few has now turned into a demand upon the people themselves, a demand which expresses itself, for example, in the "social consciousness" concept.

Immediately, then, the question arises as to whether political responsibility has not thereby become limitless. One thing is certain: if there is nothing more to be said here than what has already been said, then obviously there are indeed no limits to the individual's responsibility, and we are in a situation where ethics no longer has any meaning.

The fact is, however, that there is more to be said on the subject. As we have pointed out, political responsibility is based upon individual participation in political power in the name of the sovereignty of the people. But this very basis also places limits upon responsibility. Though I share in the power, the fact remains that it is not actually I who rule or legislate, but the government. As an individual citizen I have only a certain measure of influence upon legislation and upon the course of government, influence which is partly indirect and partly direct. Within the democratic system of representative government the indirect influence consists in the exercise of my voting right through which I temporarily delegate my share in governmental power to the man or woman I believe best qualified to represent my viewpoints and interests in legislation and government. There is therefore a significant difference between the political responsibility of the voter and that of the political office holder, inasmuch as there is a great difference between the influence they each exercise.

Nevertheless, each individual citizen also has opportunity to influence directly the decisions of the government and legislative assembly through his influence upon public opinion. Influence here, however, varies greatly according to individual differences of ability and position. The word of some carries great weight, while the word of others does not.

Finally, we should add that political responsibility is also limited in the respect that sovereignty belongs to the entire citizenry. I personally only participate in the power of the state. I must share my influence with all other citizens of the land. At the voting booth all individual citizens are equally powerful whereas, as we have seen, the power of individuals in the forming of public opinion actually varies greatly. In one way or another political responsibility is thus limited and of varying degree.

Legal, Moral, and Conventional Regulations

That life together with and over against one another consists in one person being delivered over to another person means that our mutual relationships are always relationships of power, the one person being more or less in the power of another person.

It was said earlier that a person does not arbitrarily deliver himself over to someone else as a matter of trust. Rather, this self-surrender is a part of his life, irrespective of any decision on his part. Also it was said that this implies the demand that we take care of the life which has been placed in our hands. We did not at that time go into any detailed discussion of the relationship between the fact that a person is delivered over to another person and the demand thereby implied. We said only that to accept the fact and refuse to heed the demand is to be indifferent to the question whether one is to take care of the other person's life or ruin it.

In other words, it is impossible to avoid having power over the person with whom we associate. We may very much dislike the idea of having another person's life in our hands, even in the least degree. We possibly find it to be unworthy of both of us. We might wish instead that every contact between persons were a free meeting of free spirits. Nevertheless, this is wishful thinking which has nothing to do with reality. For in reality we do influence other people's moods every day, and eventually we will have someone's entire destiny in our power.

The fundamental phenomenon of ethical life, therefore, is not unstructured and spontaneous charity. This would be possible only if our existence were a life of mutual esteem and respect for one another's independence, only if life were entirely of unproblematic character. The fact remains, however, that this is not the case, and therefore the fundamental phenomenon of ethical life is something else. Because power is involved in every human relationship, we are always forced to decide in advance whether to use our power over the other person for serving him or for serving ourselves. There are many motives for the latter, all the way from the gratification of a lust for power on the part of those who possess power to a use of power as security against one's own fears. But in the moment of decision we are confronted by the demand that our power over the other person be used in such a way as to serve him. That we are inescapably confronted at all times with this given alternative is brought out very nicely by the word "responsibility." To acknowledge that our mutual relationships are relationships of power while ignoring the demand thereby implied is to remain indifferent to the question whether the power we have over the other person is to be used to serve him or to serve ourselves at his expense.

The demand here under discussion, this radical demand, is not being met. It arose out of the fact that something of the other person's life has been delivered into my hands and is in my power. But insofar as the demand is ignored, the other person becomes the object not of my care but of my exploitation. When the demand is despised, the fact on which it rests comes to mean that the other person is subjected to my self-assertion and to my desire to promote myself. The radical demand gives no protection against this sort of thing, since through our disobedience to it we render it impotent.

That a person is more or less in the power of another person is a fact we cannot alter; it is a fact of life. We do not deliberately choose to trust, and thereby deliver ourselves over to another. We constantly live in a state of being already delivered—either through a passing mood or in terms of something which in a fundamental way affects our entire destiny. We are therefore subject to being exploited. It is not possible to profit from our experience of being exploited and avoid the delivery.

Does this mean that the individual is subject in an unlimited way to being exploited by another person? Is there no alternative for him except either to surrender to the other person's favor—or disfavor—on the one hand, or to retaliate by exploiting him in a kind of war of all against all on the other hand? The situation is not that bad, thanks to law, morality, and convention. They protect us against one another, each in its own way. In their respective jurisdictions they impose limits upon the ability of one person to take advantage of another person, and they prevent entirely certain forms of force and violence.[5]

---

5. In that sense they are rational. Their actual rational function does not, however, account for their origin. I shall not discuss this any further here; the problem really belongs to the areas of history, history of religion, and sociology. Research in these fields, however, has shown that not all social norms by any means had their origin in a rational consideration of how we can in one way or another best defend ourselves against each other, of how best to maintain a certain social order, or how to make social life as easy as possible. The actual function of the social norms affords no clue as to their origin. Furthermore, the boundary between them is also fluid. A moral norm in one period becomes a legal norm in another period. Also there are legal, moral, and conventional norms whose origin can be traced back to primitive cultic-religious ideas and regulations.

Why do we seem to have a natural antipathy toward the radical demand while at the same time we accept the legal, moral, and conventional norms? After all, their purpose or function is at least to a certain degree the same. Entirely apart from questions concerning their origin, the social norms actually protect the other person. And for that matter one might say that in their own way they represent an appeal to us to have consideration for him.

The answer lies in the difference between the radical demand and the social norms. The radical demand says that we are to care for the other person in a way that best serves his interest. It says that but nothing more. What this means in a given situation a person must discover for himself in terms of his own unselfishness and in the light of his own understanding of life. This is why in the very nature of things it is impossible to obey the radical demand on the basis of motives which are foreign to the demand. We might say that in order to obey the radical demand one must have the same purpose as it has.

The social norms, on the other hand, give comparatively precise directives about what we shall do and what we shall refrain from doing. We are usually able to conform to these directives without even having to consider the other person, much less take care of his life. We may very well live in harmony with at least many of the social norms even though we may have an entirely different purpose in doing so. We may do so, for example, as a matter of habit, or because we are afraid that the social order might otherwise disintegrate or become unstable, or out of fear of sanctions, or in order to make ourselves meritorious in our own and other people's estimation.

Moreover, the more precise the regulations are, the easier it is to determine whether or not a person is living in harmony with them. And this in turn enables us to react in specific ways to any acts of disobedience. Infractions against legal regulations simply result in sanctions enforced by physical power. Reactions against a breach of the moral and conventional norms run all the way from censuring the act as irresponsible and evil to characterizing it as tactless and unfitting. And if the breach also results in actual sanctions, such sanctions are of a mere private or social character.

But all of this—habit, lack of concern for the other person, sanctions—explains why the demands of the social norms are to such a large extent respected, and why the protection which they afford is, comparatively speaking, so effective.

The Unspoken Demand

The radical demand is thus unspoken. We referred to it earlier as silent in contradistinction to the expectations and requests which the other person expresses or implies. There is no correspondence between these expectations and requests on the one hand, and the radical demand on the other hand; at least any such correspondence would be purely accidental. But the radical demand is silent also in contradistinction to the social norms. The radical demand arises out of the simple fact that one person is delivered over into the hands of another person. The demand gives no directions whatever about how the life of the person thus delivered is to be taken care of. It specifies nothing in this respect but leaves it entirely to the individual. To be sure, the other person is to be served through word and action, but precisely which word and which action we must ourselves decide in each situation. And we must make this decision on the basis of our own unselfishness and our own understanding of life.[6]

The demands arising out of the social norms on the contrary can be formulated, more or less precisely. They determine, each in its own way, the order without which our life together with and over against one another cannot be maintained. They are more or less specific. Their specificity consists in the fact that the situation to which they address themselves is defined as its circumstances are enumerated. Given such and such

6. This is something which has been emphasized not least of all by Rudolf Bultmann. See, e.g., his *Jesus and the Word,* trans. Louise Pettibone Smith and Erminie Huntress Lantero (New York: Charles Scribner's Sons, 1958). pp. 93–101, 117, 123–125; also *Glauben und Verstehen* II (Tübingen: J. C. B. Mohr, 1952), p. 70.

circumstances, the demands of the social norms are supposed to elicit such and such actions.

These social norms may be more or less detailed. In this respect there is a great deal of difference among them. Some of them can be followed through actions of such external character that they can be carried out while we are thinking about something entirely different. Others call for judgment on our part of such a nature that we become deeply involved in what we do.

In this connection we should add, however, that the distinction between the radical demand and the socially conditioned demands is not that the radical demand alone calls for total involvement on our part. It is not as if the socially conditioned demands call only for certain actions which can be carried out equally well whether or not we are ourselves involved in the action; this is not the case. Many of the social demands require insight and cannot be obeyed blindly. For example, to bring up children, to maintain a good marriage, to be an employer calls for insight. It is not sufficient to know the letter of these demands is not that the radical demand alone calls for total actions matching the demands. Furthermore, often there are no final formulations. The demands can be fulfilled only through judgment on our part; they therefore call for insight. And since judgment is necessary, a person must be totally involved in the fulfillment of the law. Carefully to observe the letter of the law without ˙exercising judgment may well result in actions diametrically opposed to the spirit of the law. A person must through the exercise of judgment be involved in his action; he must be guided by the spirit of the law.

The Guidance of the Social Norms

We have in various ways tried to show the difference between the radical demand and the social norms. Though they are fundamentally different, there is also the most intimate connection between them.

A person's life ought to be taken care of through words and actions of a concrete, appropriate, and sensible kind; he is to be served with insight and intelligence. For example, we must use good sense in the upbringing of our children. We might say, therefore, that every ethical decision has both an inward and an outward direction. In its inward direction the decision is on whether we will take care of the other person's life or provide rather for ourselves at his expense. In its outward direction the decision is about what we should or should not do, what we should say or refrain from saying, in order that the inward decision may be realized, and in a concrete, appropriate, and sensible way.

In order to be able to make that kind of decision we must know something about what a person's expectations are and how they may be realized. Also we must know something about the dangers his life holds for him and how he may be shielded against them. The content of his life, his expectations and problems, has been determined by the psychic content of the various particular human relationships and institutions in which he is reared and of which he becomes a part. Just how his life in the given situation is best provided for we will therefore in a great many instances have to learn from the social norms, because it is precisely these norms which protect the various human relations and institutions whose spiritual content has determined the content of the other person's life, his expectations and problems. The social norms thus serve as a guide in helping us to decide what will best serve the other person.

Furthermore—and this is characteristic of our time—the various particular human relationships and institutions are subjected to scientific investigation both as concerns their natural origin and their cultural form. According to the nature of these relationships and institutions and according to whether it is a question of their natural origin or their cultural form, their empirical laws are classified as being, for example, of biological, psychological, political, or economic character. The results of these investigations often concern all of us, not because they directly repudiate some of the social norms or set up new ones, but because the scientific investigation may show that the empirical data assumed by a legal, moral, or conventional regulation either never existed, no longer exists, or no longer has the character which the regulation assumes. Scholarly investigation may thus call in question indirectly the prevailing legal, moral, and conventional norms, suggesting new and better norms. For example, it has for centuries been customary to recommend an authoritarian upbringing of children. Today child psychology and psychiatry maintain that the empirical data on which the authoritarian upbringing is predicated, namely, the patriarchal social order, no longer exists. In an earlier day the authoritarian upbringing of children caused no particular harm and was probably legitimate since it was in harmony with the patriarchal social order of the times. Now that the cultural structure of society has changed, there arises a tension between it and an authoritarian kind of child rearing, with a number of unfortunate results which the authoritarian approach did not have before.

In order to determine what will best serve the other person, however, it is not enough simply to follow the letter of the social norms. As we said earlier, our judgment must also come into play. But if we are to exercise judgment, the same psychic content of the human relationships and institutions which gave content to the other person's life must also have contributed to the shaping of our own understanding of life. This is why—as we have pointed out—the radical demand refers us to our own unselfishness and our own outlook on life to learn what the concrete situation calls for.

Our own outlook on life and our own understanding of what another person expects of life ought therefore to be on a level with the outlook on which the social norms are based. To give an example: A person does not trust himself sufficiently to rely entirely upon his own judgment but always seeks support in the approval and good will of others. He does not dare to ignore the opinions of others, least of all their opinions of himself. An inner uncertainty impels him to look at himself in the light of their opinions as in a mirror. Such an outlook is certain to perpetuate itself in his view of his children's upbringing, the sole purpose and meaning of which is that they turn out to be, as we say, "well-behaved" children. The judgment that they are well-behaved is of course made by other people. The child is not brought up for his own sake but with a view to the opinion which the parents hope others will have of his conduct. According to the best and most sensible prevailing norms this is a demeaning of the purpose and meaning of child upbringing. Bringing children up to become well-behaved is in fact a petty bourgeois caricature of upbringing. One person's understanding of life will simply not serve to take care of another person's life, in this instance the life of the child; it fails to afford adequate protection. The individual's insight is inadequate—inadequate because of his own understanding of life.

The Inadequacy of the Social Norms

Since there is such an intimate connection between the radical demand and the social norms, can we not then rely upon the social norms? Can we not be satisfied with them and the guidance they afford? Is it not a matter of indifference whether a person's motives in obeying these norms are selfish or unselfish? Is not the important thing simply that the norms be obeyed? Does not the other person derive the same benefit from my obedience whether it issues from the most selfish or the most unselfish motives?

Before attempting to answer these questions it should be emphasized that when the social norms guide the individual who stands under the radical demand, there are not two mutually independent decisions, an inward decision which concerns itself only with one's motive, and an outward decision which concerns itself with the question of precisely what is to be done. No, it is one and the same decision, in respect of which we distinguish between an inward and an outward aspect. In actual life motive cannot be isolated from its expression in action, word, and conduct any more than action, word, and conduct can be devoid of motive. Motive and action can be separated only in the abstract, only for the purpose of clarifying certain interconnections and situations.

Nevertheless, the question remains whether the selfish and the unselfish motives do not produce the same form of action, words, and conduct, provided of course that the form is in harmony with the social norms. Is not the guidance provided by the social norms so effective that a difference of motive will not affect the results? Is not motive something internal which does not affect our actions, words, and conduct? After all, do the radical demand and our attitude to it even count in a world that is now governed by social norms which become increasingly exacting as their scientific validity is more and more established?

The answer to these questions is that motive is unimportant only in the case of social norms which can be fulfilled in purely legal, outward acts. There are social norms which can very well be fulfilled even though one's head and heart are not in the act at all. The object of the action derives the same benefit and pleasure regardless of the motive behind the action.

However, in cases where the social norms call for judgment, motive may be all-important. Here motive is often very influential in determining whether or not our obedience to the social norms will really be of help to a person. At any rate we must be deeply concerned with the question.

But this is not always enough. There are also social norms which can be fulfilled to the benefit of the other person only if we are indeed moved by concern for him. This indicates how intimately the radical demand and the social norm are related to one another—and how inadequate the social norms may be.[7]

To mention an example: The more or less coherent norm complex which obtains with respect to the parent-child relationship, both as regards its psychic content and as regards the family as an institution, places upon the parents duties which in terms of their concreteness are as different as can be imagined. These duties range all the way from the most

7. This is why we said before in our discussion of social norms that they can "usually" be followed without concern for the other person.

concrete to the most abstract.[8] Some of these duties can be precisely formulated, for example, the legal duty of parents to see to it that their child learns to read and write and attain to a certain body of knowledge. They also have the task of helping him attain to a state of independence in relation to themselves. But this is a task which requires judgment on their part. It cannot be accomplished simply by following a number of precise directives for carrying it out. What is required is that they love their child.

Since the legal duty to educate their child can be met in an outward and specific way, simply by sending him to school when he reaches the prescribed age, parents may meet this duty with no other motive than to avoid the penalty for non-compliance. The child's benefit from his education is not reduced by the fact that his parents' compliance with the law is not motivated by concern for his welfare. He still learns the necessary subjects and receives sufficient knowledge, though the only motive his parents have in sending him to school is to avoid the fine which would otherwise be imposed upon them.

It is entirely different in the matter of helping the child to become independent of his parents. Though they would hardly be interested in this aspect of child rearing if they did not also have real concern for their child's welfare, let us nevertheless imagine that they address themselves to this task for no other reason, let us say, than that they have heard that this is the way it's done. Obviously they would not then succeed in accomplishing the task. Child psychiatry has shown that a loveless attempt on the part of parents to make their child independent of them may instead have the opposite result. If in the process the child is not loved by his parents, if he does not sense that it is for his own sake that they are helping him to become independent, the result may be that he will become pathologically dependent upon them. In such case their efforts do

8. In view of the dispute concerning child rearing we admittedly cannot speak of "the" prevailing norm complex if we want to speak accurately, since there are divergent views on this matter. I am not taking this into account here since it is not important in this context.

not remain fruitless; they accomplish exactly the opposite effect from the one intended.

This is only an example. But it is generally true that help which is rendered in keeping with the applicable social norms may sometimes be rendered in such a way that he who receives the help would just as soon not have it. It may be because the person rendering the help is eager that it be received as a highly meritorious deed on his part. Or it may be because he has become so scientifically convinced of its soundness that he deals with the recipient in an impersonal way: as a psycho-physical mechanism which he would help to function in the right way.

In short, the social norms are simply not adequate. The guidance they afford does not remove the tension between them and the radical demand.

Moreover, the guidance of the social norms may fail alto-gether. We may be doing great harm if we continue to defend the social norms after the psychic content of the particular human relationships and institutions have changed while the norms themselves remain unchanged. The more our motive in following the social norms is concern for the preservation of the social order, the less alert we will be to the fact that the social norms may no longer be consonant with the psychic content of those institutions which they were supposed to protect, and hence instead of protecting persons they may actually be doing violence to them.

4.

The Changeableness
of the Social Norms

Need, Claim, and Form

There are two things which must be considered further. First, we must consider the desire to endow one's needs with a form which corresponds to the fact that a person is the object of claims. Second, we must consider the changes which over the course of history constantly take place in the forms. Both of these may be illustrated in terms of the relationship between eros and ethos. The changes in the norm systems may also be illustrated by way of examples from the political sphere.

It is in a sense characteristic of human existence that something is constantly being demanded of us. This sounds like a strange and perhaps even unfounded statement, for we are of course not aware of this constant demand. How then do we know of it? We know of it from the circumstance that it is characteristic of human existence that we always give our needs a definite form. Formless striving and formless satisfaction are not human; they characterize the animal. From the form with which we endow our needs we know that even in its broadest and most vague sense it is characteristic of the life of man as man that something is, so to speak, constantly being demanded of us. The form which we give to our life is a consequence of this demand.

Stated differently, our behavior takes the form of conduct and demeanor. In the case of man—in contradistinction to the animal—we speak not only about his behavior but also about his conduct and demeanor. In describing the behavior of an animal, it is the behavior of the *species* to which we refer. One must be an individuality, a self, to be able to *conduct* oneself in a definite way.[1]

We must take the behavior of an animal as it is. It is meaningless to judge it or take a position with respect to it; we can only describe it. Behavior—not conduct—is the word used to designate that psychology which in its scholarly investigations takes its subject matter not from introspection but only from what can be established on the basis of general outward observation. In the interest of the same neutrality the word has also been used in the formation of such technical terms as "behavioral adjustment" and "behavioral pattern."

To be sure, one may also evaluate the behavior of an animal, but this involves applying an alien criterion. The criterion has nothing to do with animal behavior as such.

It is different with respect to the conduct and demeanor of a human being. It is of course possible to describe this too, but description alone in this case is hardly appropriate. Description as applied to human conduct and demeanor is artificial. It can be done, but only by suppressing the immediate and natural attitude which consists in coming to terms with or refusing to come to terms with the conduct and demeanor in question.

It is therefore in the nature of human conduct and demeanor that one takes a position with respect to it. Yet this is not the decisive factor. To take a position could mean no more than that I decide to behave in a certain way, and that the others for their part take a position with respect to my behavior, and that these two things moreover have very little to do with one another. This is not the case, however. It is *with a view to* and

---

1. "The movements of an animal, however different they may be from those of another animal of the same species, are simply those of *the* ape, for example. The *species* alone is regarded as the operative criterion." This is explained by the fact that the animal's relation to its own nature is unbroken. With respect to its natural movements the animal is not "free," in contradistinction to man whose relation to his own nature has been broken and whose movements therefore are free. "Man, however, is always 'conducting himself' in some way insofar as he finds himself in situations which involve claims upon him as a person or self." Hans Lipps, *Die menschliche Natur* (Frankfurt: Klostermann, 1942), pp. 19–20.

out of consideration for the position which the others take with respect to my conduct and demeanor that I give my behavior the form of conduct and demeanor.

Still one more thing must be added to what has been said. Along with the fact that I conduct myself with a view to the position which a person will take to the manner in which I conduct myself, I—consciously or unconsciously—expect that he will adjust himself to my conduct so that he on his part will conduct himself in ways that correspond to my conduct. What we mean, in other words, is not that the situation between us should consist in our constantly exchanging roles with each other, so that sometimes it is I who through my conduct consider the other person's position with respect to my conduct, the other person making claims upon my conduct, and sometimes vice versa. No, my conduct (as also his) is *at one and the same time* concern for and a claim upon the other person's reaction. In fact the concern constitutes a claim. The notice which I take of a person's reaction to my conduct constitutes an unspoken claim upon him to the effect that his reaction must consist in his taking a definite position with respect to my conduct. Briefly stated, conduct and demeanor correspond to the unspoken claim of other people, just as conduct and demeanor also constitute an unspoken claim upon them.[2] It is self-evident that everything which has been said here must not be understood in a narrow and moralistic sense.

Only to an individuality, a self, can one ascribe conduct and demeanor, because conduct and demeanor correspond to unspoken claims. To be an individuality, a self, implies that something is claimed of me. And this in turn means that the moment something is claimed of me, it is I who must answer for what I do or do not do.

All of this may also be stated in this way that man's relation to his own needs, and for that matter to his own nature, has

2. These two assertions—that we shape our needs, and that we do this in response to the claims made upon us and the claims we make upon others—psychology has combined in its assertion that our needs are socialized.

been broken.[3] Man has come to himself, which in turn means that his relation to the world, to the vicissitudes, and to others has been broken. These are only two aspects of the same thing. Man comes to himself by entering into relationship with things, with his destiny, with other people. To put it more accurately, man takes up those relationships into which his own need and the various natural potentialities of life place him. To have an attitude or show an attitude or adopt an attitude—these are what distinguish man from the animal; the animal simply is what it is in and as a part of its habitat.

This is true not only with respect to man's needs but also, for example, with respect to his passions. Passions as such are not peculiar to man. An animal also possesses passions—to a degree the same passions as man. The peculiarity of man in this matter—of every person as an individuality—is the manner in which his passions are, to use Lipps's expression, shaped by his attitude. That which characterizes man is therefore not his passions as such but his attitude which gives shape to his passions.[4]

Eros and Ethos

When we characterize a person's passion, feeling, affection, or whatever it may be as "spontaneous," this must not be construed to mean that his relationship to them is unbroken. A person's passions, feelings, and affections are always shaped by his attitude—or lack of attitude—toward them, however much he may give way to them.

3. See p. 68, n. 1.
4. As an example Lipps mentions laughter (*Die menschliche Natur,* p. 20). He says that we know a person by the manner in which he laughs. Laughter reveals what a man is because his attitude determines how he laughs. Laughter may be cold, pinched, stupid, ordinary. We can be moved by a person's laughter. It reveals the level of his existence. Usually it is the overtones of his laughter which we hear. Lipps quotes Nietzsche as saying that a person who roars in laughter degrades himself below the animal. The reason a person's laughter is so revealing is because the release it affords signalizes, one might say, a general lack of restraint. Genuine laughter may on occasion be drowned out by some coarse outburst which overflows in the most unembarrassed manner. Roaring laughter is engaged in only by those who are entirely devoid of that which enables a person to laugh. In order to be able to laugh, a person must know what it means to be deeply related to others. On the other hand, those who have no sense of being thus related to others are, as it were, dependent upon that lack of relationship which bursts out in roaring laughter.

Our broken relationship to our own nature or, to state it differently, the attitude—or lack of attitude—with which we enter into those relationships into which, for example, our passion, feeling, or affection places us depends, as we said before, upon those claims which we ourselves make upon others and which they make upon us. Spontaneity is therefore not destroyed by the mutual claims we make upon one another. If spontaneity and claim were mutually exclusive, it would be impossible to speak of spontaneity in connection with human existence.

What has been said up to this point, however, is not yet adequate. The relationship between passion, feeling, and affection on the one hand, and the claim on the other hand, has been described as something external. But the claim does not come to us only from the outside. It has, so to speak, become an integral part of the passions, feelings, and affections and has endowed them with their human character—just as the passions, feelings, and affections have been incorporated into our behavior, thereby transforming it into conduct and demeanor. Because the claim is, so to speak, an integral part of the passion, feeling, affection, conduct, and demeanor, it is not therefore incompatible with spontaneity. An illustration at this point may help to clarify the matter.

What is the difference between the purely erotic relationship and the love relationship in its real sense? The erotic choice of another person is determined by the sexual attraction and beauty of his or her psychophysical makeup. This is not a deliberate but a spontaneous choice. It is a matter of falling in love.

However, in a purely erotic relationship a person does not love with his total self. This does not mean that he or she is not completely enraptured by the other; people do not fall in love only to some limited degree or with reservations. What it means is rather that a part of the person has, so to speak, not become involved. The infatuation involved in erotic love, however captivating, is enmeshed in an emotion that lacks authen-

ticity and has something alien about it. What one was formerly
committed to and familiar with is not renewed but renounced.
Only the unfamiliar encountered by the uncommitted is intri-
guing. The past is relinquished in the interest of something different and strange. There is no continuity. The obsession, the
lover imagines, will continue; its existence is a matter of wishful thinking.

The purely erotic relationship is one of "fire, not love." The
difference between love and the purely erotic relationship is a
recurrent theme in D. H. Lawrence. Regarding Ursula Brangwen and Anton Skrebensky he says in *The Rainbow:* "Daring
and reckless and dangerous they knew it was, their game, each
playing with fire, not with love. . . something was roused in
both of them that they could not now allay. It intensified and
heightened their senses, they were more vivid, and powerful in
their being. But under it all was a poignant sense of tran-
sience. It was a magnificent self-assertion on the part of both of
them, he asserted himself before her, he felt himself infinitely
male and infinitely irresistible, she asserted herself before him,
she knew herself infinitely desirable, and hence infinitely
strong. And after all, what could either of them get from such
a passion but a sense of his or her own maximum self, in contradistinction to all the rest of life? Wherein was something
finite and sad, for the human soul at its maximum wants a sense
of the infinite."[5] When Ursula and Anton met again after his
stay in Africa, their association with one another was one hopeless attempt by means of passion to force their way through to
the fulfillment of love. Only through the delusion of the first
few weeks did they succeed in a fashion because she related
herself to a man whom she had herself created. But when
the delusion was gone, their relationship became imperceptibly
—because there was no lack of brilliant experiences and joys—
but increasingly determined by the fact that he possessed

5. D. H. Lawrence, *The Rainbow* (New York: Viking Press, 1961), p. 301.

neither soul nor person in which she could lose herself. He had "no background." But since her desire for the fulfillment which only love for another self can give was unabated, she was seized by frenzied passion. In a frenzy which had turned into inconsiderateness she determined through physical passion to produce what only love can give. Through a passion which had grown cold from desperation she was determined to break down the wall between herself and fulfillment through love, with the result that they were instantly dead to one another and disappeared forever from one another's lives.

The outcome, so far as Anton was concerned, corresponded to the person he was, and it was not without irony. Because Ursula's love had run aground on his lack of soul and person, his lack of "background," this lack became to him an incomprehensible, dark terror from which he tried to escape through marriage with another girl.

It will not do, therefore, to ignore or deny that falling in love is in some sense or other a part of the purely erotic relationship. If it were not, the person involved in such a relationship could never be mistaken. But he frequently is mistaken —and precisely because love and the purely erotic infatuation, although they are not the same, resemble each other to such a degree that they can be confused.

In what, then, does the real love relationship consist? The answer is that when the sexually and erotically conditioned relation to another person is called love, this is because the object of one's love is the other self. Hans Lipps expresses it in this way: that when one loves *something* in the other person, his characteristics or beauty, it is entirely because he loves the other person himself and consequently sees this something in a particular light. Love enables one to see, even as it also makes one blind to the other person's weaknesses. Love is unconditional and ignores factual reasons why it should not love. Therefore, the person who loves is, so far as he is concerned,

committed in love with his total being. There are no reservations.[6]

Due to the sexual drive and the erotic infatuation, love is a
desire for fulfillment. By this we are not saying that love consists in gaining possession of the beloved. In the event that the
desire for fulfillment is not realized love does not die; it becomes
an unfulfilled, unhappy love. Possession of the loved one is not,
says Lipps, a condition for love but only for its fulfillment.

We noted before how we can overaccentuate the difference
between the purely erotic relationship and real love by too
simply equating the former with a purely sexual relationship
and by denying the infatuation. Conversely, the difference can
also be overaccentuated in the opposite direction. We can spir-
itualize real love in such a way that its fulfillment tends to
ignore its erotic content, which if we are talking about love
between the sexes is fully as unreasonable. The love relationship is no less erotic than the purely erotic relationship. Quite
the contrary. The fulfillment of the sensual is never more complete than in one's love for the other self. Superficially it might
appear as though the sensual fulfillment would be greatest if
the relationship were purely erotic. Love understood as love for
the other self might seem to inject a spiritual and disruptive
element into the relationship. In his descriptions of love
Lawrence insists that the opposite is true. Only in his love for
the other self is a person a single, unified, and vital force, and
this he must be if his sensual fulfillment is to be most fully
realized.

The two relationships resemble one another to such a degree
that they can be confused. Love is erotic, and the erotic is not
without infatuation. And still there is an important difference

6. In this respect love is different, for example, from pity, which is something
we never show to the other person as person or self but only insofar as he has
suffered some misfortune. Hans Lipps, *Die menschliche Natur,* pp. 126–128.

In Freiherr von Gebsattel's article, "Allgemeine und medizinische Anthropologie des Geschlechtslebens" (in *Die Sexualität des Menschen,* ed. Hans Giese
[Stuttgart: Enke, 1955], p. 5) we read that personal love transcends erotic love in
that it gives form to the longing which characterizes erotic love.

Hans Giese expresses the idea that the lover knows the other person in his
or her originality, just as he knows himself, i.e., as person. ("Die Sexualität im
zwischenmenschlichen Kontakt," op. cit., p. 231.)

between them. That the two resemble each other and yet are different is evident in the disillusion and disappointment experienced by a person who because of the infatuation involved in it mistakes the purely erotic relationship for a love relationship.

Whether a person is able to differentiate between the two, however, is not a moral question. This depends upon something entirely different, upon the absoluteness of his expectations.

Now, it is not only the nature of love that it loves the other self; love also represents a claim upon that other self. To this someone may object that if this is the nature of love, it is superfluous to speak about a claim. However, it is not superfluous, because, as was said earlier, spontaneity and the idea of a claim are not mutually exclusive. The objection overlooks the fact that the claim has been a factor in giving love its form, that it has been incorporated into love, and has determined its nature. This is why passionate love is always shaped also by the person's attitude or lack of attitude, by his expectation or lack of it.

And it is clear that the nature of passionate love expresses itself as a claim. If it is the other self who is loved, then love for that self can be fulfilled only if that person really is a self. But in the love relationship the other person is a self only when he himself loves in return. Therefore, it is precisely when passionate love is most intense and most demanding that it insists unconditionally on allowing the other person to be a self and to remain free. Love itself demands this. Otherwise it could of course not be fulfilled, inasmuch as a person, precisely in his passion, is satisfied with nothing less than to be loved in return with a passion which in its very nature is spontaneous and free. The claim asserts itself in the absoluteness of the expectation, including the expectation of reciprocal love.[7]

7. There is, then, no contradiction between the nature of passionate love and the claim that its fulfillment depends upon the other person's spontaneous and free reciprocal love. In fact, passion is not one thing and the claim something else in the sense that passion is only the occasion for a claim which normally has its source in something other than passion. On the contrary, love itself is a claim, and it is a claim precisely in its passionateness. The passion and the claim are not incompatible but mutually supportive of one another.

There is a tension between love's erotic desire to fulfill itself through possession and the claim which insists that fulfillment depends upon the other person's free reciprocal love. In the event that love is not returned, passion still wants its love fulfilled even though the other person does not contribute to the fulfillment. The passion has not been able to endure its own tension. It has conquered the love which involves love for the other self. By ignoring the absence of the other person's reciprocal love the erotic relationship, on the contrary, is fulfilled through a callous kind of sexual gratification, an erotic fulfillment which ignores the other person as a self. In seduction love is reduced to a mere erotic relationship.

How completely the claim is nonetheless incorporated into passionate love, and the degree to which the claim is compatible with the spontaneity of passionate love is seen in the fact that the passion diminishes if the claim is weakened. The more exclusively erotic a relationship becomes where love for the other self plays no role, the more insecure the passion becomes, and the more it comes to be dominated by a cold and unfeeling comparison of the psychophysical form and beauty of successive sex partners. Passion gives way before such comparison. The less the other *self* is what is loved, the more he or she is eyed. If both partners have an understanding with one another that their relationship has nothing to do with real love, passion is already on the way to destroying itself. It dies and can be revived only through jealousy—or by a new partner.

It is characteristic of passion that it threatens love through its desire for fulfillment through possession; such desire threatens to turn love into a mere erotic relationship. However, passion at the same time protects love from becoming something merely erotic; the absoluteness of its expectation insists that the other self be loved and rules out all comparison.

Because passionate love contains a claim, the person loved can remain a self. In its passionateness—and precisely in its passionateness—love can be said to be "true." On the other hand, in the purely erotic relationship one can obviously not be a self, because the purely erotic relationship contains no claim.

It makes no sense therefore to speak of the purely erotic relationship as "true."[8]

The Changeableness of the Social Norms

The content of the claim contained in love between the sexes is determined by tradition. It changes from one cultural period to another, from one nationality to another, and along with this change in the content of the claim the character and form of love change as well. The conception of love which has been set forth here, and which is characteristic of our day, has not always prevailed. The emotional pattern—to use an expression from psychology—changes also in the case of erotic love.

In discussing how great the changes may be we shall point to three elements in marriage and family life: (1) the biological phenomena; (2) the psychic and particularly the emotional content whereby the biological phenomena are experienced and to which they give rise; (3) the legally, morally, and conventionally sanctioned cultural form and institution in which the biological phenomena and the psychic content exist.

The biological phenomenon in which marriage centers, both as regards its psychic content and as a morally and legally protected institution, was, for a primitive people like Israel for example, procreation. According to Johannes Pedersen, the psychic content of marriage was entirely the propagation of the tribe. This determined the relationship between husband and wife. The husband was the one who ruled because it was he who carried on the tribe and had his life in it; the wife was his helpmeet. This did not mean that his relation to her was despotic or devoid of affection. But within a relationship which indeed had an intimate and affectionate character it was in fact the husband who had the authority.

Corresponding to this psychic content of marriage was the

8. In the style of his day and in his humorous manner the Danish philologist and bishop, Peder Erasmus Müller, says: "One does not speak of true or pure erotic love but of true and pure love. If a suitor were to pledge his sweetheart eternal erotic love, she would probably not believe him, even were the pledge made under a moonlit sky. She would feel that he had chosen an unnatural expression, and she would think, quite properly, that his feeling was artificial."

institution of polygamy. When a husband lived in marital relations with several wives this was not a matter of unbridled
sensuality. It was based upon the fact that the preservation of
the tribe was the most important thing. Given this view of marriage, there could really be no limits to the husband's efforts to
propagate offspring. If he was not content with his marriage to
free women, he was at liberty to beget as many children as he
wished with slave women.[9]

Corresponding to the psychic content and the institutional
form of marriage there were the legal, moral, and social regulations designed to protect it. We may cite just a few examples:
A wife who entered into relations outside of marriage was
originally punished with death, inasmuch as she was primarily
her husband's helpmeet in providing him offspring; it was his
tribe that she was to increase. The husband, but not the wife,
had a right to dissolve the marriage, usually in the case of the
wife's barrenness. It was the husband's parents who took the
initiative in arranging the marriage, since marriage was a matter
of tribal rather than individual concern.

While it is not possible to sketch the history of the institution of marriage in Western culture, it may nevertheless be said
that by the beginning of our era the view of marriage was
already in process of being changed. For example, at the same
time that adultery was still being condemned on the ground that
it violated the husband's right of ownership over his wife, it
was now also being condemned as evidence of unbridled sensuality. The view of marriage had already become more complex.
It was no longer primitive. The indomitableness of the sex
drive had become a problem. One might perhaps say that marriage, both psychically and as a morally and legally protected
institution, had come to center in two biological phenomena:
in addition to the matter of procreation there was now also the
fact of the indomitable character of the sex drive. Marriage

9. It was primarily male children that were desired since it was they who
directly continued and maintained the husband's tribe; the girl's role was to help
in the development of a tribe other than her own. See Johannes Pedersen, *Israel:
Its Life and Culture*, I-II (London: Oxford University Press, 1964), pp. 60–81.

therefore came to be regarded as having two purposes: begetting children and protecting against immorality. This came to characterize the church's view of marriage.

This change can be attributed to ascetic ideas, though it must be added at once that such ideas have never been generally accepted or gone unchallenged. Indeed, two opposite lines of thought have always held each other in check. On the one side is the ascetic view that sexual union is debased by lust and concupiscence; sexual union must therefore take place only with the avowed purpose of begetting children. On the other side is the line of thought which grows out of faith in God as Creator. Marriage is a part of God's creation, and therefore a blessing.

But it is clear that of these two opposite lines of thought it is the ascetic view which came to predominate. The view was that marital life is merely permitted, that the Christian is permitted to marry if he is unable to remain continent. Under the pressure of ascetic thinking marriage was reduced to a device for combatting immorality. It was condoned on the grounds that it has its blessings, namely, children, family life, and avoidance of fornication. Marriage has always been threatened by this ascetic kind of thinking—but, be it noted, only threatened. The idea that marriage is a blessing was never lost sight of. Had this been forgotten, the idea of creation would have given way to a gnostic dualism—which did not happen except in certain heresies.

But this is not all. Marriage also came to be viewed as a figure of Christ's union with the church and thus as a sign of an invisible blessing, that is, a sacrament. Where Christian marriage came to be regarded as a fellowship centering in the faith, together with the life and works of faith, it followed that marriage consists above all in mutual fidelity.

However, this did not change the idea of the qualitative difference between celibacy and marriage. The idea persisted that as a sign and figure of fellowship with Christ the life of the monk and priest was more exalted and worthy than that of marriage.

That which characterizes the church's view of marriage is its realism, evident in its recognition of the indomitableness of the sex drive. We meet it also in Luther's writings. Luther always takes the biological facts into account in his treatment of marriage, divorce, and the monastic life. In his characteristic manner he says that just as a man is unable to decide not to be man, so he cannot decide to be without a woman. That a man must have a woman and a woman must have a man is something that lies beyond our power to decide. It is more necessary than to eat and drink, than to sleep or be awake. It is implanted in our very nature, and where we try to impede its working that nature will nonetheless have its way—in fornication, adultery, or onanism. Sine the sex drive cannot be assuaged, marriage enables us to avoid fornication. Marriage is a place of refuge. Its purpose is therefore twofold: to beget children and to enable us to live a sexually moral life.

Some of the conventional, moral, and legal regulations and laws which Luther urged for the protection of marriage derive from his respect for the biological facts. For example, he hoped that it might become customary to marry early—the boy at twenty years and the girl at fifteen or eighteen. He quoted the saying that to rise early and to marry early have never been regretted by anyone. He repudiated the canonical law which prescribed that a man who had had sexual relation with his wife's mother or sister was, while continuing to live with his wife, to be prohibited from having sexual relations with her. Luther says this is as ridiculous as laying fire and straw next to each other and forbidding them to burn.[10]

At the same time, as is well known, Luther repudiated the ascetic feature in the Catholic church's view of marriage, and he did this partly on the basis of the indomitableness of the sex drive. Its indomitableness testifies to its having been created in man by God. It is a creation of God. Therefore, if this creation

10. Luther's respect for the biological facts is evident also in what he recognizes and what he refuses to recognize as grounds for divorce. He says that impotence, infidelity, and malicious desertion are grounds for divorce, while wickedness is not. It is libido which constitutes marriage, and libido is not destroyed by wickedness on the part of the marriage partner.

is present in priests, monks, and nuns, they have the duty to ignore their vows of abstinence. They have neither the power nor the right by their vows to hinder God's creation in them. In this connection Luther overthrew the Catholic church's hierarchical distinction between marriage and celibacy. He allowed no station in life to be superior to marriage in the sight of God. In itself the estate of celibacy is greatly inferior.[11]

Still, Luther's breach with the ascetic thinking of the Catholic church was not complete. He was not able to accept fully the implication of his insight that the indomitableness of the sex drive testifies that sexuality is created by God. He did not see that sexuality, like any other need, assumes a particular form in a person's life. He spoke of sexuality in a rather undifferentiated manner. He was not able to distinguish between the indomitableness of the sex drive and its selfish form; instead he equated the two. He declared libido as libido to be sinful.

But how can the indomitableness of the sex drive at one and the same time be regarded as a testimony to God's creation and as sin? In explanation of this contradiction Luther differentiated betwen sexuality as procreative instinct (*instinctus procreandi*) and sexuality as concupiscence (*libido*): Understood as procreative instinct the indomitableness is a sign that the sex drive is created by God. Understood as concupiscence it is a sign that the sex drive is sinful.

Luther did not see that it is the individual person who determines the form of sexuality. As a result, in his thinking its form is determined by the institution of marriage. But this is expecting more of marriage as an institution than he had a right to expect. An institution is not able to determine the form of sexuality; only the individual himself can do this. At any rate marriage can do this only in the most outward sense, namely, that it can restrict sexuality to the married state and prevent fornication. But if we combine the elements in Luther's con-

11. That a person is better able to preach and minister the word of God in the unmarried state is another matter. But this does not make celibacy *in itself* superior to marriage. It follows that only the exception, only the person who has been specially called by God to do so, should abstain from marriage in order better to serve the gospel. No one else should presume to do so.

ception, namely, that the sex drive as such is sin and that marriage as an institution has the function of determining the form of sexuality, then we arrive at his well-known but unfortunate description of marriage as a "hospital for sick people." This notion implies two things: first, that if a person remains true to his marriage, God bears with the sinfulness of his sex drive; second, that marriage prevents a person from falling into the more grievous sins of fornication.

The weakness of Luther's view is related to his conception of love. This does not mean that Luther regarded marriage simply as a purely sexual arrangement for begetting children and for protection against fornication; he also thought of it in terms of affectionate commitment. It means rather that there was not sufficient content and richness in his love concept to enable it to purge out the ascetic feature of the traditional view. This could be done only by an entirely new conception of love, such as we find in poetry. But this was foreign to Luther.[12]

There was not sufficient content and richness in Luther's love concept to enable him to see that sexuality always assumes a particular form. He was not able to differentiate between the indomitableness of the sex drive and the selfish form which the individual always gives it. The question was foreign to Luther whether the sexual instinct, which in an irresistible manner drives a person toward the opposite sex, is a desire to be loved in return with the same passionately free and spontaneous love which he himself has for the other person, or whether it is a selfish desire which is unimpeded by the partner's lack of reciprocal love. There was no room in Luther's love concept for the insight that libido as such is always dominated either by the desire to be loved in return or by a selfishness which does

12. We see this, for example, in the manner in which he repudiated the traditional prohibition against a Christian marrying a Turk, a Jew, or a heretic. Luther contended that if a Christian may eat, drink, sleep, walk, ride, speak, and trade with a Turk, a Jew, or a heretic, he should also have the right to marry her. A heathen is fully as much a man or a woman as were Peter, Paul, and Luke.

Therefore, we do not find in Luther's writings the difference between erotic love and love of neighbor which Kierkegaard, for example, develops in his *Works of Love*. Luther equated the two. Love for the neighbor is, within marriage, the same as conjugal love (*die Brautliebe*).

not at all care whether or not there is reciprocal love. Consequently it was not necessary for Luther to differentiate between the indomitable sex drive and the form in which a person expresses it. But in failing to make this differentiation he introduced another differentiation, namely, between the indomitableness of the sex drive as a procreative instinct (which testifies that it has been created by God) and the indomitableness of the sex drive as concupiscence (which means that it is sin) —as if the sex drive and its indomitableness could exist in any other way than as concupiscence!

Luther's view was by and large adopted by German pietism, though with certain modifications. We shall call attention only to the modifications.

Though the view was retained that sexual life as such is not sinful, the indomitableness of the sex drive was not, as in Luther, viewed both as a sign of its having been created by God and as a sign of original sin; for pietism it is a sign only of original sin. It follows that it is the Christian's duty to moderate and control his sexual desire. It is not to be suppressed; indeed, this is impossible. But it must be tamed. If the Christian succeeds in doing this, God winks at its presence in marriage.

In other words, there is no suggestion in pietism that sexuality is incorporated into a love for the other person and that it receives its form from this love. In fact nothing is said about the forming, the shaping of one's sexuality. The sex drive is rather to be moderated and controlled. A corollary of this is that the sinfulness of sexuality is not the form which a person gives it through his selfishness and callousness toward the partner, but its inherent animality, which is tolerated so long as it is held in check. A person is able to humanize his sexual desire, as he ought, only by moderating the sex drive but never by forming or shaping it in a particular manner. To do that requires a love concept with content and character.[13]

13. This is no solution. And, of course, the Separatists and Zinzendorf were not satisfied with it.

This churchly view of the relationship between the sexes was not the only view—not even in the Middle Ages. In poetry, ever since the twelfth century, we meet an entirely different view. An emotional revolution has taken place. The relationship between the sexes has become filled with feeling and passion. Courtship is dramatized. Women are idealized. We are presented with an entirely new ideal of life. Life worth living is filled with love and feeling.[14] The expectation with respect to the love relationship is for nothing less than fulfillment of life.

We shall take up here only one point in the poetry from which the new conception of love is derived: the woman who is loved is usually a married woman. The theme of the ballads of the troubadours is mainly their love for the wife of a count, who was often their host. If we go beyond merely an analysis of the poetry to inquire about the historical data suggested by its literary content, we will have to explain how the count reacted to all this. To say that love was something purely platonic is hardly satisfactory. The hopes expressed in these ballads, especially those of the early troubadours, are sensual hopes. Jeanroy refutes the idea that through the agony of unsatisfied love the troubadours were seeking sensations and feelings unsurpassed for intensity and uniqueness; such subtlety of thought was strange to the man of the Middle Ages.[15] Others have tried to explain these love ballads by maintaining that the whole thing was nothing but an act and a pastime, that the troubadour wrote solely for the purpose of demonstrating his skill, that it was simply a matter of literary style. But these explanations too are hardly satisfactory; it is inconceivable that in his ballad the troubadour was not also giving expression to his feelings.

14. In the second stanza of Bernart de Ventadour's poem, "La puissance de l'amour" we read: "Surely the person is dead whose heart knows nothing about the sweetness of love. Such a person is nothing but a bother to others. May God not hate me to the extent of allowing me to live for one month or even for one day if I should turn out to be one of those annoying beings who have no interest in love." Alfred Jeanroy, *Anthologie des troubadours* (Paris: La Renaissance du Livre, 1927), p. 24.

15. Alfred Jeanroy, *La Poésie lyrique des Troubadours,* Tome II (Toulouse: Edouard Privat, and Paris: Henri Didier, 1934), p. 95.

If we view this question in the light of the church's thinking, as sketched above, then we come upon a special problem. As was said, the woman who is loved is a married woman; hence the love here expressed amounts to adultery, a breach of the marriage relationship. But this is not to be understood in terms of adultery as we normally understand it. We are prone to connect such a breach of the marriage relationship with changing erotic relations, with promiscuity. But this is not what is involved in this Provençal lyrical poetry. The love extolled here is something entirely different from infidelity. Ideally speaking it is a love which is binding for life; its essence is fidelity.

But, we must ask, how then can a love whose essence is fidelity be reconciled with adultery? The answer is that this could be done very easily where marriage had nothing to do with love. There was no love involved in marriage such as could make the breach of marriage a matter of infidelity. A wife could not be said to be faithless in relation to her husband because it was not love which bound them together. The wife could be unfaithful only in relation to her lover—by giving herself to another lover. For this reason the husband was never the rival, though rivals did frequently figure into the love affair.[16]

Jeanroy describes the contradiction between the troubadour poetry and the church's conception in the following manner: The poetry of the troubadours came into being in a society which had been thoroughly Christianized and in which the purest morality was preached by an autocratic clergy who watched over every last detail of the lives of the people. It was therefore a society in which family ties were exceedingly strong and in which civil law placed the woman in a most humiliating position. Consequently Provençal poetry overthrows the social customs and ignores the church's thinking. It glorifies a love

16. According to Jeanroy, the husband is occasionally mentioned, but always in a rather banal fashion and never with either hate or fear. The troubadour may have feelings of melancholy but is not agitated as he looks up at the tower where his beloved is sleeping with her husband. It is, however, only the earliest troubadours who make mention of the husband. Very soon the husband ceases to be mentioned at all. No one is interested in him. He is a supernumerary who may be ignored. Ibid., pp. 109–110.

which in its hopes at any rate is bent on adultery, and this is the only kind of love it glorifies. At the same time it makes the husband subservient to his wife; it makes him her plaything or slave.[17]

With reference to our problem it should be added that the contradiction is *not* that the church demanded that love have its existence within the frame of marriage, while the troubadours glorified love outside of marriage—as if the church and the troubadours were in agreement about what love is but disagreed about whether it is to exist inside or outside of marriage. This was not the situation.

It would be more accurate to say that for neither the church nor the poets was there any connection between marriage and love.[18] The church made no such connection for the simple reason that it had no love concept. The significance of marriage, its reason for existing, so far as the church's thinking was concerned, was something entirely different from love. Marriage was an arrangement for the begetting of children and for protection against immorality. It was a symbol of Christ's relation to the church, and an institution based on religious and sacramental fidelity.

Not until the twelfth century did poetry occupy itself with love, and the reason why love came to be equated with adultery is that poetry adopted the view prevailing in the church, namely, that marriage is something which has nothing to do with love. Given the notion that marriage exists for the purpose of begetting children, of coming into possession of property, and of avoiding immorality, and that its spiritual content consists in its sacramental character—given these notions, it was next to impossible to introduce love of a passionate and deeply emotional character. The church's view of marriage

17. Jeanroy, *La Poésie lyrique des Troubadours,* Tome I, p. 62.
18. The *Realencyklopädie für protestantische Theologie und Kirche* (Albert Hauck, ed., 3rd ed. rev. [Leipzig, 1896–1913], 5:189) points out that for Clement of Alexandria, "even as for the Greeks, marriage has nothing to do with sexual love." The same can be said with respect to the troubadours' view of marriage.

practically suggested that love seek its object elsewhere than in the marriage partner.

Therefore it is not correct to say that the difference between the views of the church and of poetry was that the church stood for marital fidelity while the poets stood for infidelity. By no means. The two had different understandings of fidelity and infidelity. The fidelity which the church demanded and in the name of which the church forbade adultery was a religiously and sacramentally based fidelity. Marriage was a fellowship centered about the Christian cultus and about the Christian faith and life, and it was a sign of Christ's union with the church. On the other hand, the fidelity which the poets demanded had to do with love understood as passion and deep emotion. Likewise, the church understood infidelity to mean the breach of the marriage relationship whereas the poets understood it to mean a desertion of the loved one; it never occurred to the troubadours to equate adultery with infidelity.

The poets' conception of love was that which prevailed among the nobility. And for a long time, far into the eighteenth century, the idea prevailed that marriage and love have nothing to do with each other. In his account of the difference between the view of the Puritans and of the Cavaliers, Levin L. Schücking says that even in the eighteenth century aristocratic society had no appreciation of family life. Family life was considered prosaic and a detriment to love. The loved one was thought to be degraded by marriage. The Cavalier could indeed be sensitive and considerate, but this was when he was out to win the love of a woman and when the relationship was of a romantic character. To be sensitive and considerate in marriage, however, was regarded as weakness.[19]

Love as the fulfillment of life came to be understood differently in the course of time. The ideas of the troubadour poets moved within a very narrow compass. The lover's physiognomy

19. Levin L. Schücking, *The Puritan Family: A Social Study from the Literary Sources,* trans. Brian Battershaw (New York: Schocken Books, 1970), pp. 129 ff., esp. p. 140.

had very few features, and they were always the same. This was also true of the woman; Jeanroy says that it might well have been the same woman who was loved by all of the troubadours. The Middle Ages had no analytical sense.[20]

It was entirely different in romanticism around the turn of the nineteenth century. Here the emphasis was mainly on the person and on the capacity for new experience. Accordingly, love is a psychic fellowship. Each individual can be fully supplemented only by one particular individual. Only with a particular woman and no other can a man be fused into a unified being. But how is he to find this particular woman? Not by leaving it to fate, trusting in "love at first sight." Not at all. In fact he is warned against this. Instead he must develop his own individuality, and as he does this, he gradually develops a more and more accurate picture of the one and only individuality who is able fully to supplement him. And when they marry, their purpose is to shape their marriage into a well-planned work of art. Their respective individualities and peculiarities do not repel them from each other. On the contrary, it is only by the aid of love that their distinctive characteristics are developed.

Connected with this was an insatiable desire to communicate oneself to and be entertained by the other person. The theme was inexhaustible since it was the finest nuances of one's own state of mind which were to be described by the friend or loved one—in order that he in turn could be entertained by a recital of the sentiments and feelings of the other. In conversation and in writing a person absorbed himself in his own individuality and in that of his loved one with a view to the growth and development of each. It was of paramount importance to understand and to be understood.[21]

20. Jeanroy, *La Poésie lyrique des Troubadours,* Tome II, p. 106.
21. This led to a sentimental self-reflection which when it was a subject of conversation expressed itself in reduplications. For example, Friedrich Schlegel speaks repeatedly about enjoying his own enjoyment. For Schlegel, that upon which one has reflected is combined with the ecstatic. He distinguishes between deliberate love, which we ourselves bring about, and experienced love with which we are passively overwhelmed. And he defines ecstatic love as a religious

While the view of love as fulfillment of life was originally and for centuries found only in the upper classes, it is general today. It is portrayed—and vulgarized—in the most suggestive and intensive manner night after night in movie theatres throughout the world. Likewise every newspaper and almost every novel declare that the experience of love is the only thing which makes life worth living. Marriage today is at least not in want of a love concept. This, however, raises new problems.

The Modern View of the Relationship between the Sexes

There is agitation today for a freer and more natural relationship, by which is meant that prior to marriage persons in love should be permitted to have erotic relations without any thought of eventual marriage and, of course, without having children together. This freer and more natural relationship sometimes also means that married couples might mutually agree not to demand fidelity but allow each other occasionally to fall in love and have erotic relations with a third person. But is there not an inner contradiction in this modern view of the relationship between the sexes?

The modern view is often advocated in preference to the patriarchal view whereby the wife is the husband's property, and virginity is conventionally a condition for her attaining to that most coveted position, a "marriage in purity and honor." It is a question, however, whether this argument for a life of promiscuous erotic relationships is not refuted precisely by the love concept which is characteristic of our day and on which we pride ourselves.

As we said, love today is experienced as fulfillment of life. Love is love for the other person. It is a matter of fate insofar as it can be fulfilled in relation to one and only one other person. This conception of love has been fixed by tradition. One component of it derives from romanticism, another goes back

experience. Experienced love is an experience of infinity, an experience in which one is identified with the divine. The presupposition of this identification with the divine is a religiosity of infinity in which the difference between creator and creature has disappeared.

to the Middle Ages. But entirely apart from the historical inter-play between these two componets, and the question of how far the conception may go back in time, one thing is certain: never has the love concept been so influential in determining our outlook on life as it is today.

But as we just said, the question is whether this love concept can be harmonized with the argument for promiscuity. Will not a life of promiscuous erotic relationships sooner or later make the person concerned come to think that he or she is not able "really" to love? Precisely because infatuation is interwoven in a mood and is something other than love, and is therefore a passing phenomenon, the recurrent experience of it must in-creasingly confirm the realization that the disposition for "real" love is lacking. Must one not therefore choose between love and promiscuity?

But then is choice even a possibility here? For the fact is that whoever chooses always chooses also for the other person, and what right has he to do this? Indeed both partners may be agreed that love in the real sense is out of the question for them and that their erotic relationship is not binding upon them. But might it not easily happen that for one of the part-ners this relationship will develop into a real love relationship? This is a very real possibility since according to the conception of love which prevails today the erotic relationship and love for the other person are very closely connected.[22] But where this does not happen, can the more or less casual erotic connection avoid confirming the other person in his or her realization that he or she lacks the ability to love?

To include in present-day thinking with respect to the rela-tionship between the sexes both the idea of love as fulfillment

22. As a consequence of our modern conception there are very real possibili-ties of conflict when one partner enters the relationship for the purpose of creating and being filled with love while the other partner regards it as an exclusively erotic relationship.

As Helmuth Schelsky expresses it, in the promiscuous erotic connections there is a need for monogamous love. This is why the casual erotic relationship always carries with it the risk that in it one may in fact meet the one and only who has been destined to be his love mate. "Die sozialen Formen der sexuellen Bezie-hungen" in *Die Sexualität des Menschen,* ed. Hans Giese (Stuttgart: Enke, 1955), pp. 263–265.

and the idea of promiscuity as the only natural and free life is self-contradictory. Men have always fallen short of the prevailing conception of love. There have always been rebels. We have never been without conflicts. But what is perhaps distinctive of the view held today is that it suffers from an inner conflict if we allow it to contain both the expectation of a unique experience of love and promiscuous erotic relations. Such a view results in many and painful conflicts. The more passionate and fateful we consider love to be and the more it has the character of fulfillment, the more absolute is our expectation of it.

The contradiction between love as fulfillment and the idea of promiscuity may also be stated in a slightly different way. Those who contend that a life of promiscuous erotic relations is the only natural and free life refuse to acknowledge that the indomitableness of the sex drive inevitably gives rise to problems. They admit its indomitableness, but they do not admit that it can cause problems. But then the question arises whether indeed there is or can be any view of love and sex that is free of problems—except of course the primitive view such as that held in ancient Israel, which is clearly not a possibility for us. In our view of the relationship between the sexes we have never been farther removed from primitive thinking than we are today. What can be farther removed from the primitive than a love which is regarded as fulfillment and is predicated upon an individualism pressed to such a limit that the fulfillment is to be attained in the company of the one and only love partner?

Denis de Rougemont points up the problem when he says that promiscuity derives from our modern concept of love. The theme of western European poetry is not love so much as passion. But passion is incompatible with happiness. It is kept alive only through unhappiness. Passion is deepened by suffering. Therefore, in preference to the harmonious life, one chooses that which is painful. One is possessed by a craving for the beautiful and desirable catastrophe of passion. The theme of the Middle Ages novel *Tristan and Isolde* is the separation of the lovers from one another in the name and for the sake of passion. Tristan and Isolde do not actually love one another; they are attracted to one another by love's passion, its obsession, and its ability to transport them beyond good and evil. The one desires the absence of the other more than his presence, because passionate love is sustained only by opposition. Hence love and death belong together.

Denis de Rougemont makes a convincing analysis of the love concept of our day. He regards it a vulgarization of Tristan and Isolde. One expects some kind of revelation or other from such unfortunate love: that it will alter his life and enrich it with great joys and unforeseen experiences, that it will offer adventure and risk, and make him a person to be envied— which is more than marriage can offer. And hence one must find a new love-object. Thus one solves the problem of the ecstatic love concept with infidelity. *"Passion wrecks the very notion of marriage at a time when there is being attempted the feat of trying to ground marriage in values elaborated by the morals of passion."*[23]

To Helmuth Schelsky the problem of promiscuity is a result of monogamy. People everywhere have come to expect great things from the love relationship. Thanks to the erotic clichés of modern journalism and propaganda, the expectation prevails in all classes in a coarse and standardized form. But it is monogamy which has enhanced that expectation in terms of passion and experience. More than in any other form of marriage the monogamous marriage is filled with feelings and demands and expectations. The primary reason for marriage is therefore the expectation of love—and it is this expectation which in marriage is disappointed. Since, however, one continues to harbor the original expectations of love, these expectations—disappointed as they are with marriage—lead to a need for erotic experiences outside of marriage. "Because strict monogamy tries to concentrate and restrict the partner's sex activity within

23. Denis de Rougemont, *Love in the Western World,* trans. Montgomery Belgion (New York: Pantheon, 1956), p. 286 (italics by de Rougemont).

the frame of marriage, it calls into being those very motives which lead to a breach of the marriage relationship."

Schelsky raises the question whether we should try to remove the dilemma by slackening the moral demands and adjusting our laws, training, and education to correspond with the conditions that actually exist and that way alleviate or avoid the social and psychic conflicts which result from the dilemma. He answers the question by saying that such a solution is only partly correct. At any rate there is one thing we must not forget, namely, that there is always a contrast between norm and reality when it comes to the social formation of sexual life. And values which have been established in a cultural tradition ought not to be given up simply because they are increasingly difficult to live up to. As long as the erotic experience is given primary importance in our expectations of marriage, that is to say, as long as the middle class form of marriage exercises its influence on our society, the moral ideal to which it corresponds cannot be set aside.[24]

Social Norms with Respect to Power, Wealth, and Equality

We shall refer now to an entirely different example of the changeability of social norms. Just as the structure of family life changes, so also the structure of society changes, and therewith come changes in political responsibility as well. We have touched upon this earlier in connection with the distinction between the radicality and the limitlessness of the demand. But we shall take it up here from a different angle.

For the sake of clarity it may be helpful to take a very concrete starting point, namely, Luther's position with regard to the Peasants' Revolt, a position which people today find difficult to understand. We today are able to follow Luther when he speaks about how irresponsibly the princes conduct themselves, not only occasionally but routinely. We understand him when he says that the princes are generally the greatest fools and most arrant knaves on earth and that one must always

24. See Helmuth Schelsky, loc. cit.

expect the worst from them. But we are not able to follow him when he denies to the oppressed peasants the right to rebel. We cannot understand it when he intimates that economic inequality and oppression, even when it is utterly unreasonable and includes serfdom, never justifies active resistance. What did he mean? Space will not allow an adequate explanation; there are many ramifications to this question. I shall therefore ignore the various explanations which have been offered, with the exception of one which serves to clarify the problem before us in our present context.

If it is so difficult for us to understand Luther's view, one reason—and only one—is that he shared the feudal view regarding the relationship between wealth, power, and equality, a view which is entirely different from ours. In feudal society power was predicated on wealth. Power was not a private possession, but a possession one had by virtue of his public office. Property and wealth were privileges which were necessary for the exercise of public power. Extensive holdings together with the income from such holdings were necessary for the sake of effective maintenance of power. Consequently there were limits to what a prince or a lord could give away of his holdings without irresponsibly weakening his ability to take care of his public office for the sake of which he had been endowed with the wealth in the first place.

Feudal society did not invent privileges as a way of distributing goods in as capricious a manner as possible or as a way of making economic inequality as great as possible. According to the feudal conception privileges existed in order to make it possible for the privileged person to exercise his office. Privilege was not to be bestowed arbitrarily and gratuitously upon any Tom, Dick, or Harry. Tax exemption or tax relief for the church and the knighthood, for example, was regarded as necessary if they were to carry out their responsibilities.

That the princes used their privileges to amass wealth for themselves far beyond the needs of their office is another matter. To use privilege for the sake of oppression was an abuse worthy of protest. But the abuse did not justify a demand for greater economic equality. Except among a few of the fanatics, the idea of equality was unknown in feudal society. Economic and social equality would mean the obliteration of all differences among the public offices; it would undermine the government. There was a constant struggle against abuse of the inequality and privileges, but not for their abolition.

In short, in feudal society there was no thought of equality except among the fanatical social revolutionaries. To make oneself the spokesman for economic and social equality in feudal society was tantamount to an attempt to remove the difference between government and people, since wealth was in fact essential to public power. Without economic resources there would be no possibility of exercising authority. To champion the cause of equality would be to promote a utopian reorganization of society.

We shall now return to our starting point: Luther held that economic inequality and oppression can never justify rebellion. One reason—and only one reason—for this stand was that his thinking at this point was shaped by the feudal view. He was completely dominated by the idea that all men are unequal and that this inequality is to remain. He repeatedly emphasized that the secular realm cannot endure except there be inequality between persons, so that some are lords and others are subjects. But inequality in point of power presupposes economic inequality. In other words, economic inequality was an essential part of the social order. For this reason what in the final analysis was only an exaggerated inequality or abuse could never in Luther's estimation give one the right actively to resist the authorities.

In our capitalistic society the situation is entirely different. Here wealth bestows power—private power to exploit and oppress one's fellow citizens. Therefore, it is not fanatical to fight for economic and social equality. On the contrary, it makes good sense precisely because the power which one person has over another person by virtue of his economic superiority is not a public but a private power. In fact it not only makes good sense but in the very nature of things it is necessary. The situation is this: In our capitalistic age, society is so arranged that we depend upon mutual competition as one of the most important mainsprings of individual activity and initiative. However, in order to be able to compete, people must be equally situated. It makes no sense to talk about competition between privileged and unprivileged people. Competition presupposes equality, and in principle demands the abolition of privileges.

However, competition results in inequality. The able and talented—and sometimes the selfish and unscrupulous—person wins and thus comes to enjoy a privileged position in the ongoing competition. Competition presupposes equality but results in inequality. It presupposes the abolition of privilege but results in increasing privileges. Therefore, simply in order to maintain itself, competition needs control; legislation is required which will constantly restrict and at least to some extent abolish the results of competition. The economic inequality must be restricted and the privileges reduced—and precisely in the interest of competition, lest competition be destroyed by its own results. But since competition is such a predominant factor, one of the most important political problems is that of economic equalization. Everything depends upon economics. Man is first and last *homo oeconomicus*. Briefly stated, the struggle in the capitalistic society for economic equalization and social equality is anything but fanaticism. The word "privilege" has the sound of arbitrary and unjust favor since it has nothing to do with a person's office and is not necessary for the performance of official duties.

But we can go a step farther and describe yet another difference between Luther's time and ours. The conception of fanaticism is not what it once was. In Luther's day it was fanatical to discuss the structure of the social order; this was something fanatics did but no one else. Luther did not dream of raising a question about whether the prevailing structure of society could be replaced by another and better structure. What he fought was all forms of abuse within the prevailing order, but not the prevailing order as such. This orientation was connected with his view of the relationship between Christianity and the social order—another time-conditioned relationship which also is subject to change. To this subject we shall return directly.

As concerns the difference which we are discussing at the moment, it is very apparent what it is all about. To us today it is the social order itself which is under discussion. We operate —not to say juggle—in the most casual way with such entities as capitalism, liberalism, socialism, and communism. The question regarding the social structure is the order of the day. In a sense, it was just the reverse in Luther's day. In the sixteenth century the subject of discussion was the form of government. Should it be a monarchy, an aristocracy, or a democracy? The social structure as such was not discussed; that was fixed. People were content simply to point out that the social structure of western Europe was different from that of the Turks. In the twentieth century, however, the situation is largely reversed. It is the political structure that is fixed—at least in theory; no one today dares to be in favor of anything other than democracy. But there is controversy concerning the social structure; we argue about whether it should be capitalistic, socialistic, or communistic.

The point is not that in the Middle Ages people had different notions than we have today about the advantages and disadvantages of the different political structures. The point is rather that the very concepts in terms of which they conceived the relationship between people and government were different from ours. Admittedly they too had opinions about which form of government was best. They did not support the democratic form; every intelligent person at the beginning of the sixteenth century supported the aristocratic form. But the categories in which they conceived of political order were different from ours.

In order to set forth in a fairly clear manner the changed view of the relationship between power, wealth, and equality we chose as our starting point Luther's denial of the right of resistance. But in this matter of the right of resistance there were, as we said before, many other things involved—which is why we think entirely differently about it today than did the Reformers.

If we ask whether there are no limits to the injustice which a government can inflict and still be the government, the answer is clear. May not injustice on the part of the authorities be so great that the roles are interchanged, so that the nominal government is in reality the rebel, whereas those who outwardly are classified as rebels are in reality the true government? To raise the question is to answer it in the affirmative. From 1933 to 1945 the roles were in fact interchanged in Germany. The unsuccessful assassination attempts and *coup d'état* were legitimate attempts to procure a legitimate government in Germany.

However, it is clear that a situation like the one which prevailed in Germany between 1933 and 1945 was unknown to the Reformers. Both the character of the injustice on the part of the authorities and the character of the resistance were radically different in the situations to which Luther and Calvin had reference when they refused to allow active resistance against the government.

The injustice of the government which occasioned the Peasants' Revolt at the beginning of the sixteenth century was, according to Luther's idea, an injustice on the part of the authorities for the sake of personal gain, for the sake of adding to their own holdings at the expense of their subjects. The injustice which the German authorities inflicted during the years between 1933 and 1945 was much worse; it was an attack upon justice itself and upon the very trust between people without which life is impossible.

This is the difference. In relation to the peasants Luther maintained that the princes were to continue to be the government inasmuch as they had violated justice only in the interest of the government's covetousness. It was not the system of justice as such that was being tampered with and about to crumble. As long as the government's attack upon justice is for the sake of personal gain it is, one might say, a local situation and does not affect the foundation of justice itself. And insofar as it is not the foundation of justice itself which is in jeopardy, Luther warns against revolution, using the practical and political argument that the worst tyrant is still tenfold better than mob rule, since the worst tyrant after all serves to maintain the orders of life.

In the view of Luther and Calvin there are no limits to the injustice which the government may commit and still continue to be the government. They stated this view very categorically, because like everyone else they did not know how limited their own experience was. Had they known this, they would have spoken less categorically. Only a later generation, standing in a completely new situation with an entirely new outlook, is able to see how limited a past generation's experience was and to modify its categorical judgments. This is precisely the case with our generation in relation to the Reformers with respect to the matter under discussion here.

But the character of the resistance is also different. What Luther witnessed was that the peasants rebelled because they suffered injustice with respect to their own persons and property. What he had never seen, however, were people opposing a criminal government, not because of injustice to themselves personally but for the sake of justice itself, for the sake of the nation and its people. But this is precisely what we have seen. We have seen unsuccessful attempts at assassination and *coup d'état* to which people were driven, not because they themselves had suffered injustice, much less wanted to seize authority. They were driven to these acts by a sense of responsibility. It was not necessary for them to justify their resistance, because the reasons were perfectly obvious. They were driven to opposition, not by an ideology, nor by a desire for a particular form of government, for example, a democracy instead of a dictatorship. No, they were driven by a fundamental purpose, namely, that men's life together with and over against one another might not lose all of its humanness. In short, the point at issue was not people's *right* but their *duty* to resist.

Thus also with respect to the character of the resistance there was a difference between that which Luther witnessed and what our generation has experienced. The Reformers knew something only about people rebelling because they had suffered injustice or because of their being impelled by some ideology such as that of the Anabaptists. Our generation, on the other hand, knows something about people having been driven to active resistance by a sense of responsibility, of the kind we expect to find in the government.

The statements made by the Reformers have validity only in the light of their particular experience, gained in the situation in which they found themselves. Detached from that situation and applied to our situation, their statements are false because our situation is different from theirs.

The Social Norms and Secularization

As already pointed out, if Luther was not disposed to discuss the social structure, this was due to his conception of its dependence upon Christianity. We do not share this conception today. Secularization has intervened between us and Luther. If we are to take a closer look at the matter, it will be helpful for the sake of clarity to select here too a concrete point of departure, this time Luther's position with respect to heresy. His view of heresy caused him a great deal of difficulty, and this difficulty throws light upon our problem.

In the beginning, in 1522–1523, when a strong reaction set in against the results of his preaching in several German lands, Luther's position was perfectly clear. His enemies among the princes insisted on determining the religion of their subjects. This gave Luther occasion to develop his view concerning heresy trials, and his view on this score is very clear: Heresy is a spiritual phenomenon which cannot be destroyed with iron or fire or drowning. It cannot be counteracted at all with power or sword but only with the word of God. Heresy is a matter of the heart, and the heart cannot be controlled by force. The most one can accomplish by force is to compel the mouth to speak a lie.

This was how Luther viewed the matter in 1523 when he was the defendant against charges brought by the papal princes. But after 1530, when it was he who was charging the fanatics with heresy, he no longer held this view. Now he regarded it absolutely necessary that overt heresy be punished as blasphemy. He continued to insist formally—but only formally—that heresy is not to be punished. His position was that only blasphemy, not heresy, is to be punished. The fact was, however, that he regarded all overt heresy as blasphemy, on the grounds that it is overt.

This is not to say that Luther's view changed simply because his role was changed from defendant to plaintiff, that it was a purely opportunistic change. This was definitely not the reason for the change. There was another factor which contributed to the change, namely, his conception of the connection between Christianity and the social structure.

Why did Luther consider it necessary to punish heresy? Because it is the responsibility of the government to protect God's honor. He says very plainly that the princes are not only to protect the property and lives of their subjects; their primary office is to prevent blasphemy. The secular government is to promote not only man's physical welfare but also and primarily God's honor. Is this duty a religious obligation or a political necessity? Such a differentiation was undoubtedly foreign to Luther for the simple reason that to his way of thinking the social structure was dependent upon the people's religion. If a Christian people were to become a Turkish people it would not only receive a different faith, a different religion, but also a different social structure. And we are not to forget that this connection between faith and social structure was for both Luther and his contemporaries a matter of common observation. If a papal territory or a Lutheran territory became Anabaptist, the people received not only a different church but also an entirely different society. This is why the Anabaptists in a great many instances were treated as insurrectionists, and why the opposition against them raised no theological problems. This was the issue in connection with their teaching that

Christians cannot hold an office involving military duty, or have any government other than the servants of the gospel, that Christians are not to own property, and that they must leave their wives if the wives refuse to submit to rebaptism. It was, in other words, the intimate connection between faith and social structure which made the government's task of serving God's honor at one and the same time a religious duty and a political necessity. These two objectives constituted a unity which is strange to our day.

This assumed and inevitable unity of faith and social structure is expressed by Luther in a number of different ways. It is on the basis of this unity that he levels a number of arguments against heresy, for example, against false teachers who seek protection from the very society which they try to destroy—be it noted by their purely religious heresy. This can be said only of a society whose structure stands or falls with Christianity. Hence it is also said that if the heretics were consistent and respectable, they would emigrate and go to a country where the people are not Christian. A person should either honor and obey the laws of the citizens among whom he gets his living or he should pack up and leave.

It was this unity which also determined the position with respect to the Jews who, though they were set down in the midst of Christendom, lived bodily and spiritually outside of it in their ghettos. It was of course unthinkable that Jews could hold office in the secular realm.

This unity was also involved in Luther's religious justification of the extraordinarily strict manner in which he demanded that the class system be maintained. Here he says that God does not want a person to take up a calling or a task according to his own choice and preference. Any obliteration of the class system was repulsive to him, and he expressed himself on this in drastic terms.

Since the principles of order in civil life are borrowed from Christianity, it follows that religion is a state responsibility. The government cannot be indifferent with respect to something which is the basis of all order and authority any more than it can allow the individual citizen freely to decide what his attitude to this basis will be.

These references will suffice. They serve to show how two concerns collided with each other, and how Luther was caught between them, pressed to offer one fictive solution after the other. From one point of view it is the government's responsibility—a religious duty and a political necessity—to protect God's honor and to punish all forms of overt heresy. From another point of view it must be maintained on the basis of the content of the gospel that no one can or should be forced to believe. The very nature of the gospel is such that anyone who accepts it must do so freely.

One fictive solution was that heresy involves a matter of the heart which, in contrast to all other matters of the heart, does not need to express itself in either word or deed. The fictive character of this conception can best be understood if we keep in mind the different positions Luther took in different situations. In 1523 he knew as well as his opponents that there are very definite external, physical actions which are so intimately and permanently related to faith that faith will die if it does not express itself in these actions. When Duke George of Saxony issued among other things the decree that all New Testaments were to be surrendered, Luther replied that anyone who obeys this decree and surrenders his New Testament denies God; not a single page must be surrendered on pain of the subject's losing his salvation.

It became another matter, however, when Luther had to take a position with respect to the fanatics. To be sure, people may be as heretical as they choose. "Each one can by himself learn and believe whatever he chooses. If he chooses not to listen to God then let him listen to the devil." The government has no right to punish a person for the belief which he has in his heart. No one can or must be forced to believe. However, the heretics must keep their heresy to themselves. If they either publicly or secretly spread it to others, they are to be punished, because heresy in the heart becomes blasphemy when it is spoken. That is to say that though both heresy and faith are matters of the heart, Luther made this distinction between them that so far as heresy is concerned, there is not one single outward, physical action, such as confession or rebaptism, in which it must express itself in order not to die. Here he was obviously wrong, because in this respect there is no difference between faith and heresy.

Other fictive solutions followed from this one. Why is not the unexpressed heresy blasphemy? Does not the silent heretic also blaspheme God with his heresy—in his heart? And should not the government also punish such blasphemy if it is able to detect it? And since it does not punish secret blasphemy, is it because it does not want to try to force a person to believe or is it simply because it is unable to detect it? Was not Calvin consistent when he wanted a man punished for thoughts which the man had not so much as uttered in a single word or revealed in a single act? In the very strange case of Jacques Gruet in 1547 the authorities were for once able to track down a person's most secret thoughts through an unfortunate coincidence. Jacques Gruet had what subsequent developments proved to be the tragic habit of writing down his thoughts on paper in order to remember them better. During a search of his house, when he was under suspicion in connection with an entirely different matter, his secret thoughts were thus discovered. Calvin held him to be innocent in the matter regarding which he had been suspected, but from a letter which Calvin wrote to Viret in Lausanne we learn that he still wanted him punished—because of his thoughts. Jacques Gruet was executed. Calvin could be consistent because the idea of the freedom of the gospel was foreign to him. Luther, on the other hand, knew this freedom, which accounts for his inconsistency.

Let me mention yet another fictive solution of the conflict occasioned by Luther and his fellow Reformers. Again and again they emphasized that punishment for blasphemy is not the responsibility of the preaching office but of the government. The means with which the preachers have been entrusted for combatting heresy is the word alone and not physical power. However, the preachers employ that same word in urging the government to punish overt heresy, and it is often underscored that also in a matter such as this it behooves the government to listen to them. In this manner the preachers succeeded at one and the same time in punishing the blasphemy of overt heresy while refraining from forcing the faith upon anyone. They could do this by assigning the two irreconcilable duties to two different offices.

Briefly stated, all of these fictive solutions testify that in the conflict of interest between the freedom of the gospel and the religious-political task of the government to protect God's honor it is the latter which takes precedence over the former. But how does one arrive at a solution which is not fictive and in which the freedom of the gospel is not shortchanged? The answer is that the view of the social order and structure had to be secularized. Men had to become clear on this, that Christianity does not determine the social order. Gradually they did become clear on it, thanks to an interplay of various factors. The historians contend that it was due to the decline of religiosity, to the relativization in all areas of thought, and not least to the discovery gained from the religious war in France that, if worse comes to worst, two different confessions can exist side by side in the same territory.

Secularization had to take place before the idea of the freedom of the gospel could prevail. And for that matter the idea of the freedom of the gospel may have been one of the factors which brought on the process of secularization.

The Problem of Historical Relativity

We know from history that our mutual relationships, both in family and in the political sphere, and their institutions and norms are constantly undergoing change. Their content is relative. Does this mean that everything is tottering? Many people assert this to be the case. It is obvious, they say, that what is good in one period is bad in another and this fact destroys the difference between good and evil. How can there be anything obligatory about the good, they ask, if that good is something that is only good *today* in contradistinction to what was good yesterday and what will be good tomorrow? They believe that a relativization based upon the historical evidence attesting the changeableness of morality and order can only result in the dissolution of morality and order. And they think that the only alternative is an unchangeable structure in our particular mutual relationships and their institutions. It should be possible, they say, to distinguish between that which changes and that which is eternal in the orders of family and political life. This is the old question of the difference between *lex naturae* and *lex positiva*. By attempting to tie in with the metaphysical tradition in western European culture they hope to clear up the mess into which the relativization threatens to plunge us.

It appears to me, however, that they are addressing an imaginary problem. This can perhaps best be shown if we look at it from the standpoint of logic. What we are talking about is a conclusion with only one clear premise. This is the way we usually reason in everyday life. And we usually get by with it because the other premise necessary to the conclusion is correct even though we are not aware of it.[25] It is different, however, with respect to this imaginary problem. Here the premise of which we are unaware, and which is necessary if the conclusion is to be sound, is wrong.

What is the substance of the conclusion? What does the abbreviated syllogism look like? The known premise says: We learn from history that the morality and order we know today have not always existed; and the conclusion says: Ergo, our morality and order too will totter. Differently stated, the premise and the conclusion assert that when we learn that that which is good today was bad two hundred years ago, then we are no longer in duty bound to do that which is good today. There is yet another premise, however, of which we are unaware but which we must take into account if the conclusion is to be correct. This other premise says that we can as a matter of course and at any time do away with our morality and order and replace it with another. More adequately stated,

25. Cf. L. Susan Stebbing, *A Modern Introduction to Logic* (London: Methuen & Co., Ltd., 1953), pp. 83–84.

the suppressed premise says that historical knowledge gives us such power over ourselves and one another that we are able to replace the content of our particular mutual relationships and institutions with an entirely different content. Historical insight into the fact that civil marriage, for example, had a different meaning two hundred years ago should enable us to master ourselves and our tradition to the extent that we can relinquish the content of marriage today. Stated most succinctly, the suppressed premise, without which the conclusion is wrong, tells us that historical knowledge makes us sovereign in relation to our life and tradition.

But this is untrue. The suppressed premise is mistaken. We are not able to effect such a replacement. The changes we are able to accomplish in this respect are extremely limited. We are in the power of the psychic content of our various particular relationships and institutions, a content which they had prior to our growing up in them or even getting into them. This is true as regards all of them: whether it be love relationships, the relationship between parents and children, or the political order of society. It is simply beyond our power to alter these norms, at least to any great extent. For example, the psychic content of the prevailing love concept and its distinction between good and evil constitutes a part of our very selves. Our disposition, our individuality, our personality, and whatever other part of our makeup we might want to mention have simply been constituted and shaped by this content. Thus it is the traditional content of our various relationships with one another that controls and determines which action is evil and which is good.

This can be illustrated by reference to the relationship between eros and ethos. Through love an individual comes into such a relationship with another person that the individual is in many and decisive ways in his power. One way in which this may happen and which is implied in the passion of love is that it may be up to the individual to determine whether his relationship with the beloved is to be an erotic relationship that is not binding or a love relationship that is binding. In other words, the claim which is contained in the erotically conditioned, passionate love and which determines its character and form, decides what it good and evil, decides what will protect and what will exploit the other person—for the simple reason that the prevailing love concept also controls the other person. On the basis of the love concept which we have in common and on the basis of the claim which has formed it each person knows the other's expectation, as he also knows the conflicts to which he subjects the other if he ignores his expectation. How a person is to protect that other life which has been delivered into his hands is something he already knows from the traditional claim which is contained in the passionate love and which has given it form.

It is self-evident that exploitation of the other person today is not one whit less evil just because one knows that two hundred years ago they had a different conception of the love relationship than we have today. A person simply cannot, by referring to the change which the love concept has undergone in the course of history, weaken the power which the prevailing love concept has over the other person. One cannot, through historical knowledge, diminish in the slightest the other person's expectation—which has been determined by the prevailing love concept—and in that way make one's exploitation less evil.

Generally speaking, the difference between what is good and what is evil in my relation to the other person is and remains absolute, regardless of how relative the norms may be which determine what is good and what is evil. In the other person's life as well as in my own the norms which, historically speaking, are relative are absolute in the sense that we are unable to replace them. The historical knowledge that what is good today was evil two hundred years ago does not make the good today one iota less imperative for us.

But all of this means that the suppressed premise is wrong which says that historical knowledge concerning the relativity of the norms should give us the power to change them. Therefore, the conclusion is not sound which says that the morality and order of our day are tottering because history testifies that they have not always existed. In other words, the relativization resulting from the historical insight into the changeableness of our ethos is not as dangerous as we imagine.

It of course makes no sense to speak of the changeability of the radical demand. Its distinction between good and evil is assumed to be fixed: eternal, metaphysical, or however one may wish to express it. We shall return to this later. But, we ask, was not this demand first uttered at a particular point in human history? Indeed it was. But once the demand has been heard, we cannot imagine a person to whom it does not then address itself in the sense that it ought to be heard now as well as in the past.

One more consideration should be added. If it is not yet clear, particularly to those who are afraid of relativization, how impossible it is to replace one set of norms with another, then it will become clear if we look to the relativization itself for help. To return to the example we have been using, the love concept has come to be of such a character that again and again it causes painful and insoluble conflicts. At the same time we know from history, as we have said, that our love concept changes. It came into being at a particular time in the course of history. Prior to its coming into being we were therefore exempt from conflicts of the kind which afflict us now. And so we ask: Can we not, then, dispense with the love concept? What should hinder us from dispensing with it if it is in fact changeable? But the moment we raise the question it is clear that this cannot be done. Knowledge concerning the historical relativity of the love concept is of no help to us. It does not solve the bitter conflicts or end the unhappiness they bring. In other words, we cannot get rid of the traditional love concept. In fact we cannot get rid of the traditional content in any area. If we were to lose the tradition in which we were reared and which has shaped us, we would lose ourselves. We can belabor the tradition, we can be critical of it and correct it: we can and should judge and criticize it. But we are not able to replace it.

In the course of history the psychic content has changed. But within an individual person's own lifetime it remains largely unchangeable, in a certain sense absolute. There is no return route. In other words, the premise which we did not see when we were facing the danger of the relativization becomes obvious to us when we ask whether the relativization can help us. The moment we raise the question we realize that it is a purely rhetorical question.[26]

26. Helmuth Schelsky's view is in line with the view presented here, though he states the matter somewhat differently because he has a different problem in mind. The view to which he addresses himself holds that it makes no sense to regulate sexual life socially, inasmuch as history shows how differently it has been regulated; since it has been regulated in different ways at different times, we might as well give up the idea of regulating it at all. Schelsky objects that the stated reason has nothing to do with whether or not sexual life should be regulated. The idea that the regulation of sexual life is not justified has nothing to do with historical relativism. Such relativism does not imply that every regulation of sexual life is out of order. It only implies that the social regulation differs from time to time. No, the point at issue is something entirely different from historical relativism; it is biological absolutism. The idea that most social regulation of sexual life is unjustified is due to the fact that a biological dogmatism has replaced a religious-metaphysical dogmatism. By absolutizing the "natural" we allow biology to pose as the social norm. The idea that the sexual relationship should be permitted to develop as it pleases is deduced from the biological variability and plasticity; the historical relativity is enlisted only as a secondary argument. The biologism of our day consists in this, that the social regulation of sexual life, which after all does have a disciplinary significance, is regarded as something "unnatural," while the variability of the physical—including the pathological—dispositions is considered to be a social right. The nature worship of our day overlooks the fact that nature in all of its significant forms is only what man makes it to be. Consciously or unconsciously, the biological orientation tends to endow the concept "the natural" with a normative demand, thereby destroying the social regulation of sexual life which until now has been the basis of our culture. Since regulation of the sexual relationship is a social responsibility, it is subject to historical change and is dependent upon the cultural decisions of society. This social responsibility must be undertaken precisely in the face of the biological variability of the sexual relationship, which in and of itself affords no solution.

5.

The Impossibility
of "Christian" Ethics

The Invisible Relation to the Radical Demand

A person's relation to the radical demand is and remains invisible. We have been reminded of this especially by Søren Kierkegaard. Selflessness can never manifest itself in an action so directly that an outside observer would be able to see it and testify that the action was in fact carried out in obedience to the radical demand. Selflessness is a matter between the person himself and the demand, a matter which to the bystander can only be the object of conjecture or trust. It is not possible to see from the action itself whether it was carried out unselfishly or from egoistic motives. The appearance is the same whether the action is carried out indifferently, or out of a desire for adventure, or out of a need to appear righteous, or in obedience.

The radical demand does not obtain simply within the framework of a particular institutional relationship among men. It applies rather within all the relationships men have with one another. It is implicit within all of them, demanding in every instance that a man care for the other person. There is no particular action which is peculiar to the fulfillment of the demand, nor does the action have an appearance which is peculiarly its own. The radical demand gives no detailed directions concerning the actions and conduct through which the other person is to be served. A person must use his own experience and insight, his own judgment of the other person's situation and of their mutual relationship. And, not least of all, he must use his imagination to determine whether the other person is best served through certain words he may speak or through his remaining silent, through certain actions he may take or through his not acting at all. The radical demand does not bypass a person's own insight, experience, judgment, and imagination. It only indicates whom he is to serve through these abilities, namely, the other person rather than himself.

Since the demand is radical it can never be realized directly. There is always a gap between a person's relationship to the demand on the one hand, and the actions and decisions implied by that relationship on the other hand. It is not that a person's actions and decisions are not affected by his relationship to the radical demand. His relationship to the demand will certainly manifest itself in his concrete outward life—and for this there is ample opportunity. The point is simply that these manifestations never have the character of a realization of the demand; they are only actions and decisions induced by the person's relationship to the demand. In appearance they are similar to actions and decisions of totally different provenance.

What the bystander can evaluate is therefore only the effect and propriety of the action. What he can see is the appearance of the person's conduct. And what he can learn concerning the action is its objective and rational basis. But he cannot know whether the action has been carried out in obedience to the radical demand.

The only thing to which a person himself can point with respect to his action is therefore its objective goal and basis. If he claims to have carried out some action or other at the prompting of the radical demand, there is reason seriously to doubt his claim.[1]

---

1. Possibly someone will argue: Here it is said that a person's relation to the radical demand is invisible, undemonstrable. Earlier it was said that in order to observe certain social norms a person must want to do the same things that the radical demand requires. How can these two assertions be reconciled? In those instances where a person's observance of the social norms is predicated upon obedience to the radical demand, can we not assume that he has probably been living in obedience to it?

True, if his observance of the social norms can be demonstrated! But this is

In other words the demand is, as it were, refracted through a prism in a variety of ways. In the first place, we might mention our various unique relationships with one another—as husband and wife, parents and children, employer and employee, teacher and student. The demand is refracted through the psychic content of these relationships, and since the content of these relationships differs from one nation to another, from one time to another, the refraction takes place in a great variety of ways. Care of one's spouse is different in monogamy than in polygamy, just as child care calls for different actions within the patriarchal family and social structure than in family and social life today.

It is important that these various relationships not oppose the demand but point in the same direction that it does. Through each one of them—each one in its own way—the individual holds something of the other person's life in his hands. Each of the relationships is a particular form of the fact out of which the radical demand comes. Or stated differently, it is not within our power to determine whether we wish to live in responsible relationships or not; we find ourselves in them simply because we exist. We are already responsible, always, whether or not we want to be, because we have not ourselves ordered our own lives. We are born into a life that is already ordered in a very definite way, and this order lays claim upon us in such manner that as we grow up we find ourselves bound to other people and forced into responsible relationships with them.

Further, the demand is refracted by the concrete situation. That is to say, it is refracted through a person's more general experience of and insight into the psychic content of the particular relationship of which the situation is a part. Also it is refracted through his understanding of the other person's con-

---

precisely what cannot be done when everything depends upon one's judgment. Only in instances where judgment does not enter in, because the instructions of the social norms are precise and detailed, can their observance be demonstrated. On the other hand, the more one must depend upon one's judgment, because the social norm is unable to give definitive instructions, the more difficult it is to demonstrate whether or not the norm has been observed.

crete situation, an understanding which is shaped not least of all by imagination.

At the same time, however, the demand is also refracted by a person's own nature, and his nature does not point in the same direction that the demand does. Indifference and apathy make a person unimaginative. Self-assertion and a desire to get ahead distort the fact from which the demand emerges. The fact that one holds the life of another person in his hands is used as an occasion for taking advantage of him. In exploiting the other person one uses both his general insight into the nature of human relationships and his own special understanding of the other person's concrete situation. And at best all kinds of other motives have a way of getting mixed up with the will to obey the demand. Briefly stated, while the radical demand is furthered when it is refracted by the unique relationships in which we live our lives, it is hindered in its course when it is refracted by our nature.[2]

But it all adds up to the fact that a person can never be entirely sure that he has acted in the right manner. As surely as the demand is refracted by our insight and humanity, so surely do we act upon our own responsibility. And as surely as our nature opposes the demand—and all too often replaces broad-mindedness with narrow-mindedness, imagination with unimaginativeness—so surely do we live and act always in an uncertainty which is our own fault.

The Impossibility of "Christian" Ethics

The task which we assigned ourselves in the beginning is to characterize in purely human terms the attitude to the other person contained in the proclamation of Jesus, quite apart from any consideration of its religious setting. This we have now tried to do in various ways, for example, by the help of several distinctions. Before continuing we should perhaps ask, enroute so to speak, whether the attitude we have tried to

2. It is the fundamental idea in Luther's ethic of vocation which I have been trying to express here, though without employing either his detailed development of it or his language, both of which were shaped—more than in the case of many of his contemporaries—by the medieval class society in which he belonged.

describe, primarily with the help of a distinction between the radical demand and the social norms, is always identical with the attitude to the other person as we find it in the proclamation of Jesus. Are there not in his proclamation additional directives about how we are to care for the other person? Is not the silence of the demand to some extent broken in his proclamation?

No, precisely not. It is characteristic of everything that Jesus said—so far as it has been transmitted to us—of every story and parable, of every one of his answers in conversation or argument, of every concisely formulated utterance, that it is a proclamation of the demand which in itself is silent. This is the intangible in his proclamation, that which foredooms all efforts to systematize it. Jesus' proclamation contains no directions, no rules, no moralizing, no casuistry. It contains nothing which relieves us of responsibility by solving in advance the conflicts into which the demand places us. All of his words speak about the one demand, but not with as much as a single syllable does he break its silence.

What his proclamation does say about the demand is that it is God's demand. And because it is God's demand it speaks through the silence and not through anything the other person might utter or through those norms which we have agreed will best serve our mutual welfare.

And it is precisely for this very reason that the demand is radical. God demands only that which he himself gives. This is why in the proclamation of Jesus the demand sets no limits for itself. Every word and every deed which might be of help to the other person are given to us, because life itself with its possibilities for communication through word and deed is a gift. Therefore, if we place limits upon the demand so that its requirements of us may be within reason, we do so—Christianity would say—because we deny that life with all of its possibilities is a gift. What we do not owe God we do not owe our neighbor either.

The demand is intended to insure that our consideration of what is to be said and done will not be diverted from the

other person, whose life is to be cared for, and turned instead
to exultation over our own word and deed. The demand is
intended to insure this because exultation is incompatible
with gratitude. Also, the demand does not refer us to some
kind of divine instruction with respect to what is to be said
and done, thereby helping us skip over the matter of our own
responsibility, our own reflection and effort together with all
the attendant possibilities of error and failure.

The proclamation of Jesus never concerns itself with our
relationship to the other person as determined by kinship or
nationality or as morally, legally, and conventionally regulated
and secured. Jesus constantly polemicized against using religion—the relation to God—as yet another kind of regulation
and protection in addition to the familial, national, moral,
legal, and traditional regulations and protections.[3]

If the demand, understood as God's demand, could be
spelled out in detail, then what God would be giving to man
would be not our life with all of its possibilities but merely
certain ideas, a world view—a theology if you will. And the
demand would in that event be purely an external matter:
that we use these ideas or that world view or theology without any responsibility on our part, without any investment of
our own humanity, imagination, or insight.

3. It seems to me, therefore, that Rudolf Bultmann and Friedrich Gogarten, for
example, are supported by the proclamation of Jesus in their contention that the
social and political orders are not religious but secular entities.
    Many and perhaps most Protestant theologians nonetheless decry the process
of secularization. Among other reasons for this, the main one is probably their
infatuation with Christianity as an ideology, because it is of course clear that an
ideology is to be used to regulate and protect social and political life. What
other purpose could an ideology have? If the ideology is religious, this regulation and protection are, so to speak, of the second power: a regulation and
protection in addition to the familial, social, moral, legal, and conventional
regulation and protection which, it is assumed, are not adequate in themselves.
To be sure, the Protestant church does not go all the way with this view, thanks
to Luther (and in my own country to Grundtvig), but the Roman Catholic
church does. The Roman Catholic church has a fully developed Christian
philosophy with the help of which it can counter every tendency toward secularization. It appears to me that the essential difference between Catholicism and
Protestantism today is their respective positions with regard to secularization.
    In order to avoid a common misunderstanding, it should be said that secular
thinking has nothing to do with the thesis of *Eigengesetzlichkeit*, the autonomy
of society. To think in secular terms is not the same as to give things priority
over persons.

Christianity, whether as church or as theology, whether in politics or in morality, has nonetheless often taken the idea that the demand comes from God and employed it as a means of breaking the silence of the demand. Men have sought, not in their own name but in God's, to know more about the demand than that which is contained—unarticulated—in the fact that in trust or in mistrust the other person's life has to a greater or lesser degree been delivered over into our hands. We pretend to possess a divinely attested knowledge of what is to be said and done in the given situation and of what our mutual relationships ought to be. We have thus turned God into the legal, moral, and political reason for what we should say and do. We break the silence, often in a very noisy and self-opinionated manner and with an unbearable and loquacious sense of superiority.

Therefore, whether it be a matter of taking a position with respect to marriage laws and the rearing of children, or deciding whether the purpose of punishment is vengeance or crime prevention, or determining how society is to be organized, the Christian must make his decision on exactly the same bases as those upon which anyone else decides. The person to whom the Christian message is the decisive truth about his existence will not find in this message specific Christian arguments for any particular view of marriage, child rearing, the purpose of punishment, or the political or economic structure of society. He must support his view of these matters like everyone else, using arguments which make sense to non-Christians as well as Christians. He must use reason, insight, and human considerations in clarifying the questions for himself, just as he must appeal to the other person's reason, insight, and human consideration, with no thought about whether that person is a Christian or not. Christianity does not endow a person with superior political or ethical knowledge. Political and ethical exclusiveness among Christians is a nuisance—the idea that there are laws governing people's lives which only Christians understand, and that there are reasons which are intelligible only to Christians.[4]

The reasons for this have already been touched upon, but we shall discuss them a little more fully. According to the proclamation of Jesus, the point of God's demand is that in his reflections a person takes as his point of departure not his own well-defined interests but that which serves the other person's welfare. This is why the gospel cannot be adduced as an argument. It would be outrageous pharisaism and an arrogant denial of fact if a person were to try to buttress the position he holds with respect to some political or ethical problem with the claim that he has arrived at this position by considering not his own interests but those of the neighbor. In asserting such a claim he would be trying to make his relation to the radical demand—which is and must remain a hidden relationship—a perfectly obvious fact which he would invite an unconcerned bystander to observe and measure.

It will undoubtedly be argued in this connection that when we enlist Christianity in the solution of some particular political or ethical problem, it is not our own personal relation to the Christian message but the message itself which is decisive. This, one would think, is highly objective. However, if we consider the matter more closely we shall see that there is some doubt on this score.

Since the presumed objectivity is rooted in a radical message, it would enable the Christian whether he speaks or remains silent, whether he acts or refrains from acting, to do so with absolute certainty. In other words, no room would be left for his own responsibility with respect to the decisions he makes. The wisdom, insight, and love with which we are to act are then no longer our own; they belong to the message itself. We ourselves are then not really involved; we exist only

4. The only political parties to which the Christian cannot—for specifically Christian reasons—belong are therefore the so-called Christian political parties. And if he happens to belong to a party which calls itself Christian and if he is in agreement with its political views, he can at best support only its politics, while repudiating its attempt to give its politics a Christian basis; he must constantly work to do away with this mixing of politics and Christianity.

to carry out, only to realize and apply, the directions which have already been given—without any personal involvement, without very much reflection, and without ourselves having to make any decision. If we deceive ourselves into thinking that the radical can be realized immediately and applied directly, then the insight requisite thereto is not something of our own which we exercise in great uncertainty; it belongs rather to the radical and is a matter of perfect certainty.

But then Christianity has been ossified into an ideology. To adduce the Christian message as an argument, with no thought given to our own relation to it, is to change it into useful ideas and principles. To the degree that we ignore our own relation to the message and employ the message as a given entity in support of a particular standpoint—to that degree we have distorted it into a manageable ideology. The confession which we owe our neighbor turns out to be a matter of proselytism, an organized thrust in the advance of a particular church. The other person then becomes the object of some cause which is to be promoted. The services which we individually owe our neighbor are turned into group activities of a particular church and thereby reduced to a means for ecclesiastical mission. The Christian becomes interested in the power, honor, and influence of the church. The church establishes itself as a special front among the people; it assigns itself the task of organizing and collectivizing the confession and the services in order to make them effective. We tend to fear that they might be ineffective if they are only the confession and service of the individual Christian, that which he owes to every neighbor among the people with whom he lives.

The radical is then no longer something given in and with the fundamental fact that the other person's life is in one way or another delivered over into our hands; it has been shifted instead to the sphere of actions, standpoints, and solutions. But as soon as the radical is understood as a definite goal, the goal takes precedence over man. When the goal is made radical, it becomes more important than man and leads to coercion—to coercion carried out with a perfectly good conscience since after all it is undertaken for the responsible purpose of realizing the radical.

As we have said before, care of the other person's life never consists in our taking over his responsibility. But if this is to be avoided, we must understand—precisely because the demand to take care of the other person's life is radical—that the words and actions, the standpoints and solutions through which we are to care for the other person's life are in themselves definitely not radical. If we were to shift the radicality to the words and actions, to the standpoints and solutions, these would become more important than the person they were intended to serve, and they would leave no room for the exercise of our own responsibility.

If one asks how it comes about that an entire system or ideology can be structured out of a demand which after all is silent, the answer is contained in what has just been said: It is the result of shifting the radicality to the actions, standpoints, and solutions. This means that in reality we take our own experience, insight, and imagination—which are necessary if we are to act, if we are to take a standpoint and find solutions—and we absolutize them. This means in turn that for lack of imagination and insight on our part we absolutize the standpoints which presently prevail in contemporary laws, morality, and convention—or which prevailed in New Testament times. But since the psychic content of the law, morality, and convention which prevailed in the Mediterranean world in New Testament times was the first prism through which the demand in the proclamation of Jesus was refracted, the actions, standpoints, and solutions which came out of that refraction are not absolute. Nor is that to be construed as absolute which represents a refraction in terms of present-day law, morality, and convention.

Usually the ideology is in fact deficient and the system inadequate. To try to make a case in the matter of political and ethical questions by appealing to the Christian message always leads to an oversimplification of the problems whereby the decisive considerations are lost sight of altogether. The

Christian is left sitting with many considerations which are as correct as they are meaningless, as beautiful as they are banal, while he turns over all of the real difficulties to the non-Christians. The moment the absurdly correct and beautiful considerations are tested by the concrete political and ethical questions, that which we earlier called refraction takes place, and then the Christian and the non-Christian are equally helpless.

It also has been known to happen that people—forgetting that our relation to the radical demand is invisible—make the demand itself into an outward, manageable principle that is supposed to be able to operate as a magical principle and solve all problems. The result is that the demand becomes nothing but a cliché.

No one is more thoughtless than he who makes a point of applying and realizing once-delivered directives. His claiming that the directives are radical really makes no difference. Thinking and imagination become equally superfluous. Everything can be carried out very mechanically; all that is needed is a purely technical calculation. There is no trace of the thinking and imagination which are triggered only by uncertainty and doubt.

6.

The Protest Against
the One-sided Demand

The Protest in the Name of Mutuality

In his own way each one of us protests vigorously against the demand. We defend ourselves by arguing: There certainly should be a limit to what is demanded of me! I too have my rights! Why must I set aside all personal considerations, even very modest ones, out of consideration for someone who has nothing whatever to do with me and, strictly speaking, does not even belong to my world? Who says that the other person's life is of more value than mine? Why must every cultural and moral judgment of him be ruled out? After all, we do place limits, in fact very sharp limits, upon what can, as we say, be "reasonably" expected of us.

However, we do not stop with just making such immediate and purely personal protest. We also seek to give it justification: Why isolate the fact of my holding the other person's life in my hands from his holding my life in his? The fact is that we are both delivered over to one another, and that this deliverance is therefore mutual! This admittedly implies a mutual demand that we care for one another's lives, but it can never imply a demand which excludes all mutuality![1] We thus justify our protest in terms of mutuality. The viewpoint of mutuality is to be used for regulating our mutual life and for

---

1. To be sure, in any particular case where the deliverance is one-sided, the idea that the person to whom the demand is made also has his rights is not relevant, but it could be relevant to other cases in which the roles are reversed.

moderating the demand in such a way that he who has been placed under the demand also receives his due.

The Outlook on Life and the One-sided Demand

The protest in the name of mutuality leads us to a further characterization of the demand or, more correctly stated, a further characterization of the outlook on life with which the demand stands or falls. According to this particular outlook, life and all that it contains has been given us, and we therefore possess nothing to justify our making a counterdemand upon another person; in view of the fact that we possess nothing which we have not received, we cannot make counterdemands.

A person is a debtor not because he has committed some wrong but simply because he exists and has received his life as a gift. The demand that he take care of the other person's life roots in the very fact of his indebtedness for all the different potentialities he has himself received: intelligence, speech, experience, love, and many others. A person need not have committed a crime against another person in order to be indebted to him. It is enough that he has received his own life as a gift, so that nothing which he possesses, his success, his equipment, his advantage, makes him sovereign over his own life.

In other words, the demand which invalidates the mutuality viewpoint does not arise exclusively from the fact that the one person is delivered over to the other. This demand makes sense only on the presupposition that the person to whom the demand is addressed possesses nothing which he has not received as a gift. Given that presupposition, the demand is the only thing which makes sense.

Given the fact that life has been received as a gift, it is impossible to deny the demand. However, both can be denied, both the demand and the idea that life is a gift. In fact if a person denies that his life is a gift, he must also deny that the demand for unselfishness rests upon him. If his life has not been received as a gift, he is sovereign in his own life, and then it is only reasonable that he should make his reasonable counterdemands. Conversely, if a person refuses to acknowledge any demand for unselfishness, he thereby also refuses to acknowledge that his life has been received as a gift.

On the other hand, if he admits that life and all that it contains has been received as a gift, it is not possible at the same time to deny the demand implied by the fact that one person is a part of the other person's world. It is impossible to refute this reasoning, because the life which we have received implies from beginning to end that we belong to one another's world. Others are a part of the life we have received; they constitute its content. Any other life, a life in isolation, is humanly speaking unthinkable.

In order to avoid misunderstanding it should be added that a person may very well dispute theoretically that he has received his life as a gift while in fact he does accept it as such. Similarly a person can theorize in grand fashion about accepting his life as a gift while in fact he lives as if it were all his: not a gift but his due.

From the question concerning the one-sidedness or mutuality of the demand we are led also to another theme: We can take no credit for our life. We have only been entrusted with the task of managing it by assuming responsibility for what we are and what we have. We have not called ourselves into existence. Does this mean that our life has been given to us? Does it suggest that life is to be lived in gratitude for our having received it? That is the question.

From this understanding of life in which the demand is rooted we learn at least one thing about what the demand means and what it does not mean: Care of the other person's life can never consist in words or deeds which prevent his discovering that he has received his life as a gift. Our care of his life must never support him in his ingratitude or aid him in oppressing others, thereby denying that his own life is a gift.

It was brought out in earlier chapters that the circumstances of the situation determine what will best serve another person. In advance it is not possible to say wherein care of the other person's life will consist. The demand is silent. Only one thing can be said, inasmuch as it is implied in the demand itself. Care of the other person's life never consists in our assuming his responsibility for him, and thereby making ourselves the master of his will.

One thing more can be said, because it is implied in the demand's own outlook: Care of the other person's life can never consist in words or in silence, in action or inaction which would hinder him in understanding that his life has been received as a gift. Otherwise there would be no difference between goodness and wickedness.

Controlling Existence by Way of Theories

If life is given to us, not once and for all but in every moment, it follows that we have it for the purpose of delivering ourselves over to it. If it is a gift, it has been given in order that it be lived in confidence to it. And the trust in the other person which we always have from the very outset, and which in a fundamental way belongs to human existence, is based upon and goes hand in hand with the confidence in life which comes with the gift itself. Life exists to be lived as something unfinished, in the sense that we can never be done with fashioning our relation to the other person. The one-sidedness of the demand expresses the fact that we receive life in order that we should in confidence surrender ourselves to it. In contrast to this, every moral theory based on the viewpoint of mutuality is an expression of our desire to have control over existence.

But, one might ask, does not the desire to control our existence find support also in our thinking and knowing? After all, the purpose of thought and knowledge is to have done with something, to finish it in order to get on with something else.[2]

The answer is that our thinking and knowing can have done with things in very different ways. They may solve the ethical

2. Hans Lipps, *Untersuchungen zu einer hermeneutischen Logik* (Frankfurt: Klostermann, 1938).

question by means of a theory so handy and incontrovertible that the fresh reflection demanded by every new situation will turn out to be nothing but the application of a theory already thought out. The thinking called for in the new situation is then almost entirely a matter of calculation. The basic reflection has been carried out once and for all; it has been reduced to a theory. This is indeed the case as regards the moral theories built on the viewpoint of mutuality.[3]

The one-sided demand also requires that a person do some thinking and arrive at knowledge of what he will do. But our thinking and knowing do not, because of the one-sided demand, take on a different character; they still consist in attempting to have done with something. By his decision and action, arrived at through thought and knowledge, a person puts to rest whatever the problem may be in the concrete situation. This is not to say, however, that the solution once reached in the particular situation is now a theory which he can apply to each new situation without having to go through the rigors of basic reflection once again. Not at all! There is in fact no handy, ready-made theory. Certainly the directive of the one-sided demand is anything but that. In a sense the demand forces us to start afresh in each new situation precisely because it provides no explicit directive. This is why in order to become clear about what will best serve the other person we must use imagination quite as much as calculation. There is nothing with which to start, nothing to be simply applied. Moreover, the one-sided demand contradicts our own desire.

3. This is true also of a moral theory such as that of utilitarianism, even though the question concerning the one-sidedness or mutuality of the demand here plays no role. The fresh reflection demanded by the new situation consists in calculating the sum total of pleasure or pain resulting from the various possible actions. Although the calculation can become quite complicated when the most remote results are taken into account, this does not alter the fact that the thinking involved here has in fact the character of outright calculation. In calculating, all that a person has to do is to apply the theory. His existence is subordinated to his thinking. However, as was said before, there is this peculiarity about utilitarianism: it has no mutuality viewpoint to accommodate the theory to our nature. Time after time, in fact, the calculation of the sum total may turn out in favor of the other person. Utilitarianism therefore, while it may be admittedly handy and incontrovertible in theory, is not so in practice; man's will upsets it. Utilitarianism therefore poses a special problem which, however, we shall not discuss here.

We do not consent to its directive. Indeed, our objection to it is so radical that each new situation forces us seriously to reflect upon whether the directive, so lacking in mutuality, can even be valid. Our objection is so emphatic that in every conflict between concern for the other person and for ourselves what is really at stake is the one-sided demand's understanding that we have received our lives as a gift.

The difference, then, between the one-sided demand and a moral theory based on the viewpoint of mutuality is not a matter of different theories. It is possible to construct on the bases of the mutuality viewpoint theories which can be used for ordering our existence. On the other hand, the demand which sets mutuality aside intends with its outlook on life to disclose to us the purpose of our existence before we set about ordering it for ourselves.

One more thing must be added. We said before that no moral theory can be constructed on the basis of the one-sided demand; it cannot be used to control our existence. Nevertheless, we do try to clarify for ourselves the content and character both of the demand and of its outlook and to formulate what we believe we have learned in this manner.

But all knowledge regardless of its content, every formulation regardless of what is being formulated, can very easily suggest that through such knowledge and formulation we have gained control of the thing in question. There are two reasons for this. First, because, as already mentioned, through knowledge we hope to have done with something in order to get on with something else. Second, because in settling upon a certain formulation as authoritative, we are apt to set aside our own position with respect to the matter formulated.

Therefore, as long as we try to know and to formulate the demand and its outlook, there will always be a tension between knowledge and formulation on the one hand, and the demand with its outlook on the other hand. The tendency inherent in knowledge to regard its object as something mastered, and the impulse implicit in all formulation to leave out of the picture one's own relation to the object formulated, gain the upper hand over the demand and its outlook. Although the demand and its outlook are a judgment upon us when through our knowledge we set them aside and in our formulations ignore them, our knowledge and formulations nonetheless triumph over the demand and its outlook. The emphasis is shifted from the content of the demand and its outlook to our knowledge and formulation of them.

The Protest in the Name of Suffering and Death

A protest against the one-sided demand's outlook is also made in the name of suffering and death. A person whose fate has been good to him may have no difficulty in accepting the idea that life is a gift. But can the person whose life has been mostly suffering, possibly indescribable suffering, accept it? Can a person accept the idea that life is a gift if his world has been left empty by the other person's death or if he is tormented by hopeless and painful disease?

We are not concerned here with the spectator's protest against the idea that life, including suffering and death, is a gift; his protest is only of a theoretical character. What we are concerned with is the unfortunate person himself, who asks whether in order to be relieved of his despair he would have preferred never to have known or possessed what he now has lost. It is he who wonders whether in order not to have known suffering he would wish that life had never been given him.

If the death of a loved one is the cause of his suffering, the unfortunate person will, if his mind has not completely snapped, answer in the negative. He would not choose never to have known the person in question if such a choice could have meant escape from the pain of now losing him in death. His despair will not bring him to wish that the person whose death is the cause of his despair had never been an essential part of his life. He will not curse life because of death.

Despair does not prevent the unfortunate person from accepting his life as a gift. On the contrary! By his having been a living part of the unfortunate person's life, the person now lost through death enabled the unfortunate person to accept his life as a gift. And it continues to be a gift. This fact is not altered by despair over the other person's death. The unfortunate person prefers the burden of despair to having never known and loved the person whom he has now lost.

For a person in utter despair to wish that the other person had never been a part of his world would be the same as to try to minimize that person's importance in his life in order to make his own despair endurable—in fact in order to circumvent his despair. It would be the same as to curse the content and the joy which the other person brought into his life.

When the unfortunate person does not desire to escape his misfortune in this way, however, this is not a case of his own achievement, because in despair he is incapable of either reason or achievement. The greater the despair, the more determined he is that he would not have wanted to be without the other person in his life. This defiance of despair is not deliberate. It is a defiance which the unfortunate one cannot avoid. That which here stands its ground and asserts itself is his very life, life in its character of something received as a gift.

It is only the spectator, not the unfortunate person himself, who thinks—speculatively—that death is incompatible with life understood as a gift. The thing that makes us dispute that life is a gift is not death or suffering; it is our own desire to be worshiped, our own will to power.

But there is a world of difference between the suffering caused by the death of a person who was a part of one's life and the suffering of physical and mental illness which one must bear alone. If the illness hinders the development of a person's abilities and powers, if the pain prevents him from entering into the experiences of life, other people must supply an indispensable and living part of his existence if life in its character of something received as a gift is to hold its own through all the suffering.

7.

The Radical Demand
and Natural Love

The Two Components of the Ethical Demand

The ethical demand consists of two elements. First, it receives its content from a fact, from a person to person relationship which can be demonstrated empirically, namely, that one person's life is involved with the life of another person. The point of the demand is that one is to care for whatever in the other person's life that involvement delivers into his hands. Second, the demand receives its one-sidedness from the understanding that a person's life is an ongoing gift, so that we will never be in a position to demand something in return for what we do. That life has been given to us is something that cannot be demonstrated empirically; it can only be accepted in faith— or else denied.

But the content of this understanding or outlook is of such a nature that whether a person accepts it or refuses to accept it is determined only by the manner in which he actually lives in this involvement with others. If he uses the involvement as an occasion for taking care of the other person's life, it is evident that in faith he accepts his own life as an ongoing gift. If, on the other hand, he exploits the involvement to his own advantage, he clearly denies that his life is an ongoing gift.

There is, therefore, the closest possible relationship between the two elements comprising the demand. Despite the fact that the demand receives its content from empirical life situations which can be demonstated, it receives its one-sidedness from an outlook on life which is of a nonempirical character.

Natural Love and the One-sided Demand

The one-sidedness of the demand, the exclusion of the mutuality viewpoint, raises the question concerning the relationship between this demand and natural love. Has the demand already and as a matter of course been fulfilled by natural love in those relationships which natural love has itself created and in which it belongs? Or does the demand have nothing to do with natural love? Is it an unimportant linguistic accident that the word "love" is applied both to the human relationship determined by inclination and passion and to the relationship or, more correctly stated, to the demand which in the proclamation of Jesus is called love for the neighbor? The question must be stated precisely: Is natural love characterized by a mutuality that makes it incompatible with the one-sided demand?

Where natural love prevails between two people, the lives of both are successful—insofar as natural love and its actions are determinative of people's success. This is always assumed. When we care for the other person's life, it is not only that person's life which succeeds, but our own as well. If parents take care of their children and bring them up wisely, there is a good chance not only that the children will succeed but that the parents will also. Their relationship with their children will be successful. Stated differently, a person is himself a participant in the success of the other person, because by caring for the other person's life he helps himself to become successful. When we counsel ourselves or one another we therefore appeal in one and the same breath to that which best serves both ourselves and the other person.[1]

1. This is true not only with respect to natural love but in a sense also with respect to our observance of the legal, moral, and conventional regulations. The situation is not that either the person who obeys the law and the moral regulations is successful or that the other person for whose benefit the law and the regulations are being obeyed is successful. No, both are successful. If the land is governed wisely, the result is not only an order of security and prosperity that benefits the citizenry, but also success for the politicians. Therefore, we think and judge and act very largely in conformity with the more or less coherent complex of prevailing social norms. And we do so without any further thought—out of habit. The person who obeys the laws has a stake in the life of all other persons who are successful because of his obedience. Even in cases where

However, there is no room for the idea that the care of the other person is motivated exclusively by a concern for our own success, and that our concern for his weal or woe is only a means to that end. This idea is excluded because by virtue of our love for the other person he constitutes a vital part of our own life. His success or failure is an essential part of our own success or failure. His success or failure affects us directly, not just by way of certain objective and material relationships. The other person is in such a real sense a part of our world that it is in fact awkward to refer to him or her as "the other person" rather than as one's child or spouse. The action to which natural love moves a person is therefore motivated by the fact that it serves both his success and our own. These two concerns simply cannot be separated from each other.

We cannot say, then, that through natural love a person does what he does only for his own sake, and that it is only a fortunate turn of circumstances if what he does also benefits the other person who is the object of his "love." Neither can we say that care of the other person is exclusively motivated by concern for his weal or woe, and that any benefit we ourselves might derive from it is purely accidental. Natural love is precisely natural. Both motives—that one's own life and that of the other person may be successful—belong together. To the degree that parents are motivated by natural love, it is both for their own sake and for the sake of their children that they conduct themselves as they do. This is also true if, for example, they find themselves in economic straits and therefore deny themselves in order to be able to help their children get ahead. Through their self-denial they themselves succeed; apart from it they would not succeed. If they were

an action in conformity with the social norms results only in something with which we are not pleased, we can nonetheless well afford to support the action inasmuch as failure to do so would result in sanctions against us. In other words, not only in the case of natural love but also in the case of our observance of the social norms the same action benefits ourselves as well as the other person.

However, there is this decisive difference that in the observance of the social norms motive usually plays a subordinate role. As already pointed out, the more precise the regulations the less important is the factor of motive on our part with respect to the benefit which the other person may derive from our obedience.

not willing to deny themselves, they themselves would be worse off, because for the rest of their lives they would suffer from seeing how poorly their children are getting on in life.

People are bound to one another, among other things, through love, sympathy, and solidarity. By love and friendship they are bound together in a spontaneous way, whereas in solidarity they are bound together more through cooperative endeavor and common circumstances. But whether these ties are formed spontaneously or socially, it is these ties which constitute a person's existence. This is why every time one cares for another person in love, sympathy, or solidarity, he is himself rewarded through the maintenance of those relationships in which a person has his life and which constitute his existence. The more intensely and comprehensively a person binds himself to other people spontaneously and socially, the more he will see that a selfish life lived at the expense of others is empty and unsuccessful, and the more he will refrain from that kind of life.

But the deeds of natural love are not on that account to be equated with deeds done for the sake of a cash return. On the contrary! It makes a great difference whether that which benefits a person is seen as the maintenance of the relationships in which he has his life or whether it consists in the idea that "one good turn deserves another." If I help a person perhaps at every conceivable juncture, but always in a loveless manner and only because one good turn deserves another, that person does not belong to my life as an indispensable part of it. On the contrary, the two of us are of no concern to one another. Whether my favor to him is of help to him or not is in itself of no interest to me—so long as I receive his favor in return. He is only somebody who does me this favor, nothing more.

We are thus referring here to two very different relationships. Doing everything for the sake of receiving some return means in effect a relationship based upon the demand for mutuality. We use the word "mutuality" deliberately in order to point up the incompatibility between such a relationship and the one-sided demand.

On the other hand, it is not helpful but confusing to speak of mutuality in connection with natural love, where both persons benefit from the deed done by one for the other out of love. That I should benefit in return is of course not a condition or requirement that I attach to my love for the other person; it simply follows, so to speak, because indirectly the other person is a vital part of my own life. For this reason it is hard to see why natural love should in this respect be regarded as contrary to the one-sided demand.

Then too, there is the fact that the outlook upon which the one-sided demand is predicated, namely, that a person's life is an ongoing gift, is never more evident than in natural love. Indeed, it is precisely when a recipient of our natural love becomes a part of our own life that we understand best that life is a gift. The understanding of life as a gift becomes so real to us that even the death of the other person cannot alter it.

Natural love and the one-sided demand have a common outlook. What is peculiar to natural love is that it takes for granted the outlook of the one-sided demand—apart from the demand itself.

When, then, does the one-sided demand address us? When the other person whose life we are to care for is not a part of our own life which we have received—or, more correctly stated, when we do not wish him to be a part of it. It is when we regard him as something entirely other than a gift because he is a bother and an inconvenience to us. The demand that we nevertheless take care of his life is therefore directed to us on the presupposition that our own life has been given us as a gift. To state it in anthropomorphic terms for the sake of clarity, the demand concedes as it were and is sufficiently realistic to recognize that the other person is too much of a bother to be able to help in making our life a gift received. He is anything but loved. Nevertheless, the demand says to us that precisely because our life was given us and since of ourselves we therefore are nothing and possess nothing, we are therefore to take care of the other person's life. In other words, because we do not want the other person to be a part of our life, the demand places our own outlook in jeopardy. Through the demand we are, so to speak, asked whether we intend to make ourselves masters of our own life to the point of deciding for ourselves who shall and who shall not be a part of it, or whether we will accept our life as a gift in order to use it for taking care of the other person's life.

In the case of natural love the one whose life is to be cared for and the one who turns his own life into a life received as a gift are one and the same person. The care of the other person's life is therefore an inevitability which renders the demand superfluous.

We have said that there is no mutuality in the fact that where natural love prevails, both persons prosper through one and the same deed. But is not natural love's craving for reciprocal love incompatible with the one-sided demand, particularly since this craving for reciprocal love could hardly be more intense than in natural love? A person wants to be loved by the other with the same passionate love with which he himself loves. He expects the reciprocal love to be as spontaneous and free as his own. A person craves reciprocal love for his own sake.

It is of course quite possible to contend that the craving on the part of passionate love for reciprocal love is the same as a craving for mutuality. But then one must add that there are two different kinds of mutuality which have nothing to do with each other.

Usually we speak about mutuality in such a manner that the more the idea of mutuality dominates our relationship with others or, more accurately stated, the more the relationship is dominated by the ulterior thought of mutuality, the more we will hold ourselves in reserve, the more we will keep ourselves outside, the more we will guard against our being swept along with it, the more we will make the relationship purely a means for getting out of it what we can. A relationship which consists in "one good turn deserves another" is not worth maintaining for its own sake but only for the sake of the returns we may derive from it. Hence the relationship is characterized by a strained and guarded watching of one another. Indeed, it consists in this and nothing more. It is simply a case of lying in wait to see whether the return favors are forthcoming, and whether they appear promptly and in sufficient amounts.

It is precisely the opposite in the case of passionate love. By nature—that is, because of the passionate character of love—a person is through love drawn toward the other person. In its longing for the other person love is intentional. By virtue of its passion it carries man along with it in order that he may exist in love. Likewise, through the same passion, he craves fulfillment through the other person's reciprocal love. However, this craving is not in the nature of a counterclaim in return for his love. On the contrary, the reciprocal love is desired as an unearned happiness. If it were of the nature of a return favor it would be worthless or, differently stated, it would be absolutely meaningless. The desire for reciprocal love as such is therefore not incompatible with the outlook presupposed by the one-sided demand. Therefore, there is nothing in the desire for reciprocal love which violates the idea that life is a gift.

Does this mean, then, that natural love as such is by nature unselfish? Unselfishness means that in whatever concerns us, in whatever we do, in whatever stand we take, we think not of ourselves but of the other person—in spite of the fact that it would be quite natural to think rather of ourselves. If we do think of ourselves rather than others, we are not transgressing certain social norms; neither are we in danger of being slandered, much less of having sanctions placed against us. Strictly speaking, unselfishness means that although we have every right to think of ourselves, we do not do so.

But in that sense natural love is not unselfish. Natural love is not in the dilemma of having to think either of itself or of the other person. According to its very nature it does not find itself in that situation. Love always has reference to the other person; it is a case of being drawn to him. This is its very nature. Natural love as such is therefore by nature neither selfish nor unselfish.

Loneliness

Pursuant to our description of natural love we should perhaps digress and give some attention to an equally common and false idea regarding loneliness. It is characteristic of our day that we speak about loneliness in a very undifferentiated manner, though loneliness in fact means several things, or at any rate two things.

There is one type of loneliness which is admittedly frightful. This is when a person's world has become or continues to be empty. There is no one whose life he touches and no one whose life touches his. There is every reason to call this kind of loneliness frightful.

However, it is a mistake to speak of loneliness as frightful if by loneliness is meant the circumstance that one person's feelings cannot be shared by another. We meet this common misunderstanding even in such a perceptive philosopher as Moritz Schlick: "Here lies the source of the final, awful loneliness of man, from which there is no escape, because each individual, each consciousness is enclosed within itself; so that its feelings can be only its own feelings and can never be felt also by another."[2]

There would be more reason to call this, so to speak, epistemological loneliness a blessing rather than a curse inasmuch as it is the condition for all love. The strangeness which results from one's inability to feel the feelings of another constitutes a continuing incitement to love. Precisely because the person whom I love is unable through his feeling to know my love, I must constantly testify to it. If he were able, even for a moment, to know my love as well as I know it myself, it would be unnecessary for me to express it. A strange stagna-

2. Moritz Schlick, *Problems of Ethics*, trans. David Rynin (New York: Dover, 1962), p. 175.

tion would set in. The love which desires to declare itself
would become meaningless.

But this is not all. For me to experience and to know a person's love for me as fully and completely as he knows it himself would be tantamount to my loving myself as he loves me.
But what would this mean other than that through the cessation of the epistemological loneliness—if we may use this
designation—his love would be tantamount to narcissism? And
this would be too much of a good thing. All my joy and thank-
fulness over his love would vanish. Hence it is not loneliness
of this sort but its cessation which is frightful.

To speak in an undifferentiated manner about loneliness—
including the epistemological loneliness of feeling—as a curse
is not only thoughtless but harmful. It drives one to try to
resolve the loneliness and its curse by analyzing one's feelings
and then telling some other person all about them. The "curse"
might be at least partially resolved or alleviated in this artificial
manner. Love's desire to declare itself is replaced by a self-
analytical communication of one's own lonely love feelings.
This takes place through the inexhaustible analytic conversation which picks the psychic content apart into small bits of
sentiment and resentment. The conversation proceeds by way of
suggestions, hints, suspicions, and in the worst cases by clever
witticisms. Many novels are cut of such literary cloth.

Love is threatened by this sort of thing. It may not even
survive such stubborn banalization. It will perhaps be unable
to endure this confusing of its desire to declare itself with
exhibitionism.

The purity of love consists in its outgoing character. The
epistemological loneliness is anything but frightful. It is in
fact forgotten in love's intentionality: in love's movement and
declaration—which it conditions—the epistemological loneliness is a blessing in our life. If we think of it as something
unfortunate, we are no longer at one with love's intention but
on the verge of isolating ourselves within our own feeling.

Love between persons, therefore, does not consist in knowing one another to such an extent that one is in no sense a

stranger to the other. On the contrary, love between persons is kept alive precisely by the element of strangeness in their relationship. Without this strangeness love will perish in trivialization. That the other person is a vital part of my life, therefore, does not mean that I feel his feelings, but it does mean that his destiny concerns me—concerns me in my own way.

The Inadequacy of Natural Love

To continue where we left off earlier, it was maintained that the one-sidedness of the demand is not at odds with the fact that natural love wants to be loved in return and the fact that the lives of both persons are benefited through the same deed. Another matter is that natural love always receives its shape—whether dispassionate, passionate, or sentimental—from the self.

Dispassionate selfishness means that in whatever a person does or in whatever happens to him he has himself in mind, though for no objective reason. He is concerned about what he himself can get out of it, what role he may get to play, or how he may exploit the situation to his own advantage.

Judging by the terms just used to describe it, dispassionate selfishness is clearly both subjective and confused behavior. Tacitly yet clearly, the terms used define dispassionate selfishness in contrast to concern for the success of a given cause, in contrast to consideration for the other person as the only objective and unambiguous attitude.

Dispassionate selfishness is not inconsiderate. It is simply petty, dull, truncated. The dispassionately selfish person is a mystery to himself, a mystery which may develop into hypocrisy.

Natural love is in many different ways shaped by dispassionate selfishness. It can be dominated by a vain desire to be worshiped. If this desire is not met, the person tries in vain to extricate himself from the relationship—through resentment and its mysteriousness. He asks the impossible, namely, that the relationship should at one and the same time have the character of natural love and love for a return favor.

Or, in spite of the fact that natural love has been received as a gift and that here more clearly than anywhere else life is seen to be a gift, we nevertheless regard natural love and its deeds as our own achievement. We try to make ourselves masters of our own lives, and we live and reason as though we ourselves had produced our natural love.

But the more natural love is viewed as testifying to our own superiority, the more it is in danger of being destroyed. The more that a sense of our own merits causes us to take credit for the deeds of natural love, the more externalized the relationship becomes.

Rightly viewed, self-righteousness conflicts with natural love. It is at pains to reduce the relation to the other person to an extraordinarily good opportunity to say to itself, to other people, or to God: I have done my duty! I cannot be blamed for anything! The temptation of natural love to think of its own meritoriousness and superiority threatens to choke it. Just as in the relationship dominated by the adage "One good turn deserves another," the other person exists only for the purpose of assuring me that I get my return: beyond that he is of no further concern to me. The other person exists only to provide me with my meritoriousness; beyond that he is of no interest to me. This is the outcome if self-righteousness gains the upper hand in natural love.

Passionate selfishness never takes into consideration the other person.[3] But this does not make for improved insight into itself. Passionate selfishness either fails to face up to its inconsiderateness and looks in all other directions in the hope of finding excuses and ameliorating circumstances, or else it runs amuck and in its passion loses control of itself.

3. Perhaps the word "selfishness" is used in everyday speech primarily with respect to its dispassionate form, while the preferred word for the passionate, inconsiderate, and even brutal form is "egoism." Though the difference is not carefully observed in popular usage, "selfishness" probably means devoted occupation with oneself, while "egoism" refers more to inconsiderateness and disregard for every reasonable concern for the other person.

Sentimentality is a threat to natural love. It is not that the other person is not a vital part of the sentimental person's life. It is rather that the sentimental person is not content to live in that dependence. Instead he draws it into himself, introverting it in order to be able to observe it. Instead of just depending he seeks to taste the dependence. He wants to feel sentimental happiness at knowing that his own vital happiness is dependent upon the other person's vital happiness. But such redoubling of happiness is impossible. His sentimental happiness can exist only as a parasite on his vital happiness, threatening to consume it. And when he wants to feel sentimental unhappiness through his dependence upon the other person's unhappiness, he finds that this too is not possible. It loses the point and becomes powerless. Indeed, it is perverted into a sentimental happiness at being dependent upon the other person's vital unhappiness.

It follows that the sentimental person does not want to be alone with his own sentimentality. He wants the other person —upon whose happiness and unhappiness his own happiness and unhappiness depend—to be with him in introverting the dependence. He wants both of them to contemplate their dependence, and to exchange the redoubled sentimental happiness of their mutual dependence by an inexhaustible emotional entertainment of one another.

Occasionally the other person resists this immodesty and its stifling banalizing and defends himself against having all vitality sucked out of a living dependence in his life. In the end he may defend himself by destroying his dependence.

It is remarkable that human relations which cannot be destroyed by vice, crime, or unprincipled conduct can be destroyed by such an innocent thing as sentimentality. While the criminal or depraved person maintains contact with the person who suffers on account of his misdeeds, the sentimental person, while elaborating all of his virtues, remains isolated in his own loneliness, and never does understand why the contact has been broken with that other person with whom he only wanted to share everything.

Natural love may also fade and eventually disappear, or it may turn out to have been an illusion. The consequent conflict is all the more painful.

And if the natural love does not cease, and if the conflicts in the internal relationships in which natural love belongs do not gain the upper hand, the relationship is invariably exploited as an occasion for walling oneself off from the world, from the outsider.

Natural love is biologically, psychologically, and sociologically conditioned. There must be erotic excitement, for example, or the other person must be one's own child, one's own flesh and blood as we say. Or there must be psychic harmony. The intensity of these factors varies greatly. It extends all the way from the sexually potent natural love to the more or less weak sympathy for those who are supposed to be the beneficiaries of our efforts, and to the solidarity created by common circumstances and interests.

However, the relationship between love and its natural basis is anything but unambiguous. The natural basis conditions love—and destroys it. To mention a single example, in the relationship between parents and children the biological basis of the relationship, namely, that the children as their parents' flesh and blood belong to their parents' world and life, can be used to the detriment of natural love. Unfulfilled ambitions on the part of the father or mother can be transferred to the son or daughter. The son, then, is not to live his own life; he is to relive his father's life, but at a level of brilliance not attained by the father himself. The father makes the son's life his own, and the mother makes the daughter's life her own. They sponge on their children's lives and do everything they possibly can to hinder their children's independence. The very fact implied in natural love, namely, that the other person's happiness and unhappiness directly determine one's own life, is exploited to distort love into covert self-love.

Through natural love a person comes into such a relationship with the other person that the latter in many and decisive ways is delivered over to him. Therefore, when natural love in one way or another fails in its own relationships, a conflict arises between consideration for the other person and consideration for oneself. In that conflict the demand asserts itself, radically and one-sidedly, to the effect that the other person's life is to be cared for at one's own expense.

Precisely what he must deny himself in the given situation depends upon his outlook on life. What the life is which he must lose in the given relationship is determined by his understanding of what success in life means.

If the conflict is caused by resentment, it is his own self-esteem and vanity which are to be given up. If the conflict arises because the parents will not allow their children to become independent of them, then it is their own—unfulfilled—ambitions and dreams of success which must be given up, because these ambitions and dreams are causing them to live at their children's expense. If the conflict is due to our constantly emphasizing that we have done our duty, then the outlook which must be given up is the notion that we are the masters of our own lives.

Stated differently, the point of the radical and one-sided demand depends upon our expectations of life. The content of the demanded unselfishness is determined by our ideas of what success in life means, insofar as these ideas conflict with our care of the other person's life.

The difference between good and evil therefore does not depend upon whether what a person does benefits himself or not. It depends rather upon how he understands his own life. If we understand our life to consist in amassing wealth, making a career, or attaining honor, distinction, and power, then our life will be successful only through a cold, calculating policy of never doing anything without receiving something in return. In that event there is nothing in our outlook which will prevent us from living at other people's expense.

On the other hand, in the measure that other people belong to our life in such a way that their happiness and unhappiness directly influence our own happiness and unhappiness—in that measure we are urged by our life and our outlook to care for their life. If in so doing we ourselves should benefit to whatever degree, this does not mean that we are evil—provided the benefits accruing to us actually derive from the benefits received by those who constitute so vital a part of our own life.[4]

The Destructive Demand

The idea which has been presented here is that if natural love did not fail in its own relationships, the one-sided demand would not assert itself in these relationships. At least two objections will be raised against this idea. The first objection is to the effect that since natural love makes it possible for our own expectations of life to be fulfilled in the process of our taking care of the other person's life, then natural love must be incompatible with a demand which is one-sided.

In reply to this objection it should be said that one-sidedness can mean two different things. The one-sidedness of the demand means that in the struggle between my expectations of life and my care of the other person's life it is the expectations that must give way. Does the one-sidedness mean then that I must have no expectations at all?

If this were the case, then our expectations of life would be judged by the demand not on the ground that the fulfillment of them entails conflict with care of the other person's life, but simply on the ground of our having them in the first place. We would not be judged by our ideas about what a successful life must encompass, ideas which drive us to live at the other

---

4. To use an expression from Jakob Knudsen's chapter on "Reward": "Everything demands a reward. Without it nothing happens" (*Kristelige foredrag* [Copenhagen: Gyldendal, 1956], p. 118). The difference between selfishness and unselfishness does not depend on whether a person demands a reward for what he does or dispenses with all reward for his actions. Everyone, whether he is selfish or unselfish, in fact demands a reward for everything he does, because psychologically there is no such thing as an unrewarded deed. The difference between selfishness and unselfishness is determined rather by the kind of reward a person demands.

The word "reward" is not altogether fortunate. In everyday usage it does not have the breadth of meaning that Knudsen attaches to it. Instead it is usually understood in the narrow sense of a return favor.

person's expense. The demand's judgment would fall upon our life simply because we want it to be successful, regardless of how we understand success.

This would mean that the demand no longer arises out of the fact that I hold the other person's life in my hands. It would arise out of an entirely different fact, namely, that I entertain some expectations of life, that I hope my life will be successful and fulfilled. The fact upon which the demand is based has thereby been replaced by a different fact, and as the fact has changed, so also has the demand. The point of the demand now is that a person be willing to give up his life altogether, sacrifice it in every sense of the word.

If the destiny of the other person still plays a role in the demand, then it must mean that existence is so arranged that he is not able to live at all except by the sacrifice I make. What the other person needs then for the care of his life is my self-destruction and self-annihilation. On the other hand, he derives no joy from being loved with a love which draws him into the life of the person who loves him with a natural love.

Care of the other person's life, then, does not require that I, inspired by my natural love, try to determine what will best serve him. It would require something entirely different. The task which the radical demand, thus understood, imposes upon me is to discover the situation where I can be certain that my expectations will be disappointed, that my own life will fail—and that a more painful demise could hardly be imagined.

But this is not all. If my own life cannot in any sense succeed but can only fail due to the fact that the other person's life is to be successful through my having taken care of it, then the other person cannot belong to my own world as a vital part of it. This has two strange consequences. First, the unselfish deed comes to be the loveless deed. A person can act unselfishly only where natural love is lacking or has been killed. Second, in the acute conflict situation where the one person can live only at the expense of the other, it now becomes actually possible to fulfill the radical, one-sided demand.

For this, one is not dependent upon his nature; instead one's nature is to be surrendered. The demand, therefore, can actually be obeyed—but only in the death instinct of desperation in which a person loses his nature.

The Wickedness of Man and the Goodness of Life

We turn now to the second objection to the idea which has been set forth here. Someone will say that when it is maintained that the one-sided demand would not assert itself if natural love did not fail in its own relationships, then we are operating with natural love as an imaginary entity. But the only love we know anything about from our own actual existence is a natural love to which we have given our own self's selfish form; any other kind of love is pure speculation. In other words—to put it in philosophical terms—to speak about natural love in the manner of this discussion is to hypostatize it.

This is entirely correct. However, I do not see how it can be avoided. If someone wants to call it speculation, then it is a speculation which is essential to ethical reflection. And as for the charge that it is a case of hypostatization, this is admittedly inadmissible in psychology, but so far as I can see unavoidable in ethics.

We cannot avoid distinguishing between natural love and the selfish form in which it actually appears. We may compare natural love with the trust which is a fundamental part of human life. In both cases it would be absurd to say: This is my own achievement! That would be as absurd as to say: It is through my own achievement that I exist at all! It is as true of natural love and of the trust which in a fundamental sense belongs to human life, as it is of our very existence: we cannot take the credit ourselves. As little as I can take credit for my own existence so little can I take credit for my natural love. It is not due to some achievement on the part of parents that their children's happiness and unhappiness constitute a part of their own happiness and unhappiness. If it were an achievement on their part, it would not be love, inasmuch as it is in the very nature of natural love to recognize that the other person has been given as a gift. It is the same in the case of trust. It is not my doing that I show trust and surrender something of myself. The trust which concerns us here is precisely the trust without which none of us can at all exist.

For this reason trust and love also contain an understanding of the fact that our life and the person who is the object of our love have been given us as gifts. From this understanding or outlook on life—however unconscious—trust and love cannot be separated. They are distorted when I take credit for them myself, regarding them as my own achievement. If I take credit for the fundamental trust which I show, it atrophies: I begin to make calculations, taking into account all possible eventualities and all the time keeping the way clear for retreat—even as love too is stifled when it is turned into a matter of my own meritoriousness. This makes our trust guarded; we hold ourselves in reserve instead of surrending ourselves—even as we endow love with our own self's selfish form.

But the opposite of what we have just said about trust and love is true with respect to reservation and selfishness. I am myself the cause of my reservation and selfishness; they are indeed my own achievements. Abstractly considered, we can of course deny this. We can maintain that we are as much the cause of our trust and natural love as of our reservation and selfishness, albeit not in the same way or with the same results. We can insist that I cannot help my reservation and selfishness, because this is the way I was created; and since I did not create myself I cannot accept the responsibility or the blame for how I am. But the result of such abstract argumentation is that "my" thoughts, "my" actions, "my" feelings are no longer mine; they could be mine only if I could take over my own life, so to speak, through being the cause of and assuming the responsibility for who I am and what I do. In short, I become nothing.

Clearly, there is no analogy here. This is evident in the fact that we cannot understand reservation as a received life potential any better than we can understand selfishness as something we have received along with life itself. This would be possible only in a perversion which knows that it is perverse.[5]

We must therefore generally maintain that our expectations, experiences, reactions, feelings, and thoughts vary. Some of this variation is caused by ourselves; some of it is not.

Where then is the difference to be found? Not in psychology! Mistrust is just as much a psychological disposition as is trust, and hate is no less a passion than love.

Neither is the difference to be found in nonmetaphysical ethics. In nonmetaphysical ethics it is quite possible to insist that love is something good and hate something bad. But the moment we go on to maintain that we are *not* the cause of our love and that we *are* the cause of our hate, we have gone beyond the bounds of nonmetaphysical ethics.

Seen from the viewpoint of psychology and of nonmetaphysical ethics, the distinction involved here is a metaphysical distinction inasmuch as it contains an understanding of human existence in its totality. Inherent in the insight that trust and love are not of our making is the understanding that life as a whole, our very existence, is a gift which we have received. Theologically speaking, it is a distinction which assumes that man was created and has been placed in an ongoing relationship with his creator.

To show trust and to surrender myself, to entertain a natural love is to be good. In this sense goodness belongs to our human existence, though we ourselves are evil. Both these affirmations need to be taken in full seriousness. Often this is not done, for example, when it is said that there is "at least some good" in a person. To this we must reply; No, there is

---

5. To be the cause of something can be variously understood. To maintain that I am myself the cause of my trust and my love is a self-gratulation that stifles both trust and love. On the other hand, to be the cause of the reservation in which my trust is stifled, and of the selfishness with which I infuse my love, is to assume responsibility for my own life.

Correspondingly, to know that I am not the cause of something can also be variously understood. Not being the cause of my trust and love is to accept life and the other person as gifts received. To deny that I am the cause of my own reservation and selfishness, however, is to refuse to take over my own life; it is to become nothing.

not! The notion that there is "at least some good" in a person amounts to subtracting something from the evil and adding it to the goodness of a man's account—as though trust and natural love were not given man as a gift but are his own achievements and can be credited to his account.

However, nothing can be subtracted from man's wickedness. The self brings everything under the power of its selfishness. Man's will is in its power; addressed to our will, the demand to love is an impossible demand.

Nor can anything be added to the goodness of human life. The goodness is there. It exists, but in advance, always in advance—among other things through the realities of trust and love.

If the radicality of the ethical demand makes a person's guilt radical, is it even permissible to speak of the goodness of human life? Does not the idea of the goodness of life diminish the radicality of guilt?

No. Precisely the opposite is the case. A man is evil when he exploits the goodness he has received, destroying it for the sake of his own advantage.

If we deny created goodness out of a theological zeal to underscore the radicality of guilt, the result will be the opposite of what is intended: The individual will be excused, because whatever his guilt, it can never be as serious as that involved in perpetually destroying the given goodness of life.

Or, stated in other words, what we spoke of a moment ago as a man's personal "account" is really his will, and the radicality of guilt consists in the fact that it is the human will which is selfish and evil.[6] But this is something we can accept only if we acknowledge that human life is good. The will is evil only if its wickedness consists in its overcoming the goodness of human life.

---

6. "Man without the Spirit of God does not do evil against his will, under pressure, as though he were taken by the scruff of the neck and dragged into it, like a thief or footpad being dragged off against his will to punishment; but he does it spontaneously and voluntarily." Martin Luther, *On the Bondage of the Will,* trans. J. I. Packer and O. R. Johnston (Westwood, N.J.: Fleming H. Revell Co., 1957), p. 102.

Natural Love and Love of Neighbor

Natural love does not originate simply in the fact that the other person's life is more or less dependent upon our care. Something more is required. There must also be an erotic relationship, or the other person must be one's own child, or there must be a situation of psychic harmony.

What is demanded of us, therefore, is that our nature be of such a character that the sheer fact that something of the other person's life is in our hands creates love for that person not because he is biologically or sociologically or in some other manner related to us, but solely because our own life has been given to us. As in the proclamation of Jesus, the neighbor is the stranger and the enemy. The difference between natural love and love of neighbor is that natural love is biologically and sociologically determined.

The similarity between them is that they have a common outlook on life. This is why, despite the difference between them, natural love teaches us something about love of neighbor. It is no accident that the same word is used in both instances; in both cases we speak of "love." When through the exercise of natural love a person becomes a vital part of our life, it is easy to see that our life has been given us as a gift. This should be just as easy to see when a person comes into our life who is dependent upon us, regardless of how strange or hostile he may be. For out of the acceptance of our life as a gift—out of living life as a gift—spring the works of love.

8.

Compromising
the Demand

The Problem of Compromise

Why does care of the other person's life require love? To use a term in the proclamation of Jesus, why is love of neighbor the content of the demand? Because love alone corresponds to the fact that something of the other person's life is delivered over to us. Only love is able to measure up to the demands of this fact. A person runs a risk in having a part of his life depend upon us. And because our life is temporal, if we fail him—that is, if instead of caring for him we exploit his dependence upon us—the damage is irreparable. Only love can protect him in the face of this risk.

Where natural love was once present but later vanished, it cannot be re-created by the demand. And where there never was love, the demand cannot bring it about. As mentioned earlier, what is demanded is nothing less than that love come into being through the sheer fact that a life has been placed in my hands, a life which is not a part of my existence by virtue of sex, kinship, or friendship. We do not possess such love, and if we do not possess it we cannot create it. The one-sided demand fails to get through to us.

But occasionally a particular situation comes to a head. In our resistance against the demand this situation becomes a claim upon us, a claim so strong that we cannot wrest ourselves out of its grasp. The claim does not transform us. It does not create a love which fulfills the demand. But it happens occasionally that, in the grasp of the claim, we act in the manner we would naturally act if we did possess the demanded love. Though we

151

do not possess love, we do the deed which love would have us do, albeit for all sorts of other reasons.

We may do it because of a fear born of the conviction or vague feeling that there is something in our life we cannot escape, or because of a pride which cannot face the possibility of life being made worthless, or because of a fierce and frantic hatred of men who oppress others. Or we may do it out of self-righteousness, in order to be able to say to ourself or to God: I have done my duty! Or it may be that we want to win the respect of some third person who is observing our conduct. Or perhaps we simply do not want to be cowardly, dishonorable, insincere, or irresponsible. We may also be motivated by a particular outlook, a metaphysically grounded generosity as in the case of Spinoza, a lyrical joy over life's beauty and adventure—or a fixed and handy ideology.

Though love may be absent, the demand remains. The deeds that a person knows within himself love would have him do are therefore constantly demanded—which cannot be said of the reasons why he will eventually do them. These various reasons represent the individual's compromise with the demand. He compromises through what he does out of fear or self-righteousness, through what he does for the sake of his own attitude or outlook. In short, it is meaningless to demand the reason why a person without love nevertheless does the works of love, whether it be because he does not dare to do otherwise or because he does them cheerfully. That would be a new demand which would have nothing to do with—and would therefore ignore—the fact out of which the ethical demand itself arises. If a person does not wish to entangel himself in illusions concerning his own position, it is essential that he not confuse his compromise of the demand with the demand itself.

Is this not where the matter of responsibility belongs, responsibility as understood by theology and by the philosophy of existence? If it is true that love is the content of the demand, then to act responsibly is not to obey the demand but to do what one believes love would have him do, only to do it for a different reason.

There are almost no limits to the talk about "responsibility" these days. Perhaps people use the term in order to avoid using the word "love"—which would be quite understandable in view of the sentimental overtones that word has received. But perhaps this is also due at least in part to the fact that Kierkegaard has discredited the spontaneous life. Fear of spontaneity has so gotten into the theologian's system that he cannot allow the demand to be anything as spontaneous as love. It must involve a more reflected attitude, a responsible attitude in which the person does not lose himself in a love which is turned outward, but reflects upon what love indicates he should do, and in this reflection keeps himself under control.

Understandable as it is, however, that the word "responsibility" is preferred to the word "love," it may represent in fact a compromise with the demand. The tacit reasoning is as follows: That which is demanded cannot be something spontaneous. Love for the neighbor is demanded. Ergo, love for the neighbor cannot be spontaneous but must be a matter of responsibility. In other words, people can substitute the word "responsibility" for the word "love" because they regard it as more important that love is *demanded* than that *love* is demanded.

The relationship to the demand varies with the reasons that obtain for obeying it. The demand is present and asserting itself whenever a person who is without love does nevertheless, out of a sense of responsibility or out of fear, what he believes love would do. Through the sense of responsibility we are aware of its authority, and the fear is a fear of authority.

The demand is distorted through self-righteousness, because self-righteousness completely forgets that it is love which is demanded. We deceive ourselves into thinking that it is a matter of outward actions in which we do not ourselves need to be at all involved. We imagine that if only the actions are carried out, we may ourselves remain uninvolved in them—or even be opposed to them. Self-righteousness inevitably reduces the demand to the judicious and mutual consideration which current morality and prevailing legislation require.

The demand is present in a similarly remote and unrecognizable way when the motivation is a matter of attitude, character, or the opinion of some third person. Duty, personality, and self-righteousness constitute a single motive complex.

Finally, the demand disappears altogether if the motivation is an outlook on life to which we relate ourselves aesthetically.

It is self-evident that we can distinguish between motives only in the abstract. In actual life they are interrelated. They both reinforce and offset one another. This is precisely why one becomes involved in reflection.

The Sharp Contradiction

The demand which calls for the ethical decision is that we are to live our life as something which has been given us as a gift. This demand comes to us because we want to be sovereign in our own lives. But thereby we have brought ourselves into a sharp contradiction.

If obedience to the demand were merely a matter of managing the gift, whereby our receiving life would be one thing and our managing it another, there would be no contradiction. But this is not the case. The demand does *not* mean that since life has been given us as a gift, we must manage it in such and such a way. In that event the demand would consist of regulations about how it is to be managed, which is not the case. On the contrary, what the demand tells us is that each of us is to live by continually receiving his life as a gift. Receiving life is not one thing and managing it another.

But this makes the contradiction evident, because while every attempt at obedience consists in managing our life— whereby we separate the managing from the receiving—the meaning of the demand is that we are to live life by continually receiving it. In a sense, our attempts at obedience actually work against the demand, for every attempt at obedience is an expression of that which the demand opposes, namely, the will to be sovereign in our own life. By willing to be sovereign in our own life, by refusing to receive life as a gift, we place ourselves in a sharp contradiction: every attempt to obey the demand turns out to be an attempt at obedience *within the framework* of a more fundamental disobedience. In other words, what is demanded is that the demand should not have been necessary. This is the demand's radicality.

Stated differently, the ethical decision arises when the situation in which a person finds himself confronts him with a challenge. But while he can meet this challenge through courage, character, honor, a sense of duty, a feeling of responsibility, or an outlook on life, he cannot through love meet the challenge of love. Why not? Because love exists only in a life which is acknowledged to be a gift. This constitutes love's spontaneity. Either love is something which a person receives, and then, so far as love is concerned, the situation calling for decision cannot arise; or a person knows nothing about love, and then the situation of decision does arise, without his being able to meet its challenge.

Nevertheless, he finds himself involved in the necessity of making decisions, and then he probably does what 'he believes love would do. However, he has thereby transformed the situation into a challenge to the courage, attitude, outlook, or whatever it may be which might also result in the same action. But this is not obedience to the demand, because what the demand demands is love. The demand does not, out of consideration for our lack of love, revise its intention so as to make obedience or anything other than love its aim.[1]

---

1. In ethical decision love cannot be confined, as can characteristics, attitudes, and outlooks, to a particular action which should be carried out. Where love is concerned, therefore, the relationship between motive and action is essentially different from what it is in the case of all other motives.

In many situations the relationship between action and motive may be fairly unambiguous. For example: A soldier is asked to volunteer for a dangerous assignment. The situation is, as we say, clear: If the soldier is brave he will volunteer, but if he does volunteer it is almost certain that he is brave, for it is practically impossible to imagine that he would otherwise volunteer.

The relationship between love and action is never that unambiguous. The situation is never so clear that we would be able to say that if a person carries out the action it is because he is motivated by love.

Helpfulness is often cited as an illustration of love, and it may very well consist in doing things which we believe love and its desire to communicate would want us to do, even though we actually do them for all kinds of other reasons. For example, helpfulness may well be used as a means of keeping the other person at a distance; help may be rendered for the sheer purpose of preventing communication. It is quite natural to refer to helpfulness as an illustration of what love is, inasmuch as helpfulness often characterizes love; Jesus did that in his preaching. But helpfulness devoid of communication does not constitute obedience to the demand, as Jesus' preaching also amply attests; to think that it does is to regard as a directive what for Jesus was purely illustrative.

9.

The Ethical
Decision

Decision and Resolution

A person becomes involved in ethical decision because the
situation in which he finds himself demands something very
definite of him. He is the object of an appeal or a challenge, an
appeal from another person or a challenge implicit in the
situation itself. It follows that his decision, in contradistinction
to a resolution or resolve, must be made within a definite time
limit. This difference between decision and resolution calls for
further discussion.

In writing on the theme "No Man Can Serve Two Masters"[1]
Jakob Knudsen describes resolution and the signs of whether
or not there is any vitality in it. Knudsen takes as an example a
person who owns a small piece of property and is considering
whether he should sell it and buy a larger property. If he is in
doubt about whether to make this change, he should not
picture to himself the future because it is dangerous to follow
one's imagination. He must look rather at the present. If there
is vitality in his resolve to make the change, it will be evident
in the fact that his present circumstances lose their glamour
and content and come to seem empty and temporary. If, on the
other hand, after having lost himself in imagination concerning
the future which supposedly would be his if he makes the
change, he returns to reality and finds that every little detail of

1. Jakob Knudsen, *Kristelige foredrag* (Copenhagen: Gyldendal, 1956), pp.
7–12.

156

reality testifies that the imagined future was only a dream—an ugly dream—this is a sign that no change should be made and that the resolution died before it could be born.

In other words, genuine resolution has a maturation period, as Jakob Knudsen's illustration aptly demonstrates. The life blood of resolution is discernment, which in due time will bring it to a state of maturity. Therefore, says Knudsen, "fashioning a resolve always takes patience."

Since it is the individual who fashions the resolve, he can himself determine to give resolution time to mature. This is not true, however, when it comes to the matter of decision. The situation forces him to decide whether he wants to or not, and often on very short notice.[2]

The fact is, however, that decision no less than resolution needs time to mature. It may involve a matter of momentous consequence which alters one's life, giving it a new form and even a new content. Still, there is hardly time for the sorely needed process of maturing. The result is that decision is often characterized by painful tension. And the tragedy of it is that even a decision which may affect one's entire life is made blindly.

The decision should have had time to mature in order that there might have been greater discernment and certainty. Factors which might destroy life's unity should have been noted. Factors which might result in a life beyond the person's abilities or in a narrow existence should have been taken into account. The decision should have had a chance to mature into the one genuine possibility. This is why it is unfortunate that decision must often be made on such short notice, because immature decision is a matter of blind chance: as likely as not the person will make the wrong decision.

Can such immature decision be avoided? Is it possible to avoid blind chance? Indeed it is possible—if decision is

2. The distinction between decision and resolution is generally not observed in everyday speech, but it may be very useful in clarifying the matters under consideration here.

preceded by time for maturing so that one is prepared for his decision.

As a counterpart to Knudsen's example of resolution let us take an example of decision made on short notice. During World War Two people in the occupied lands often found themselves face to face with that kind of decision, more so in countries other than my own where decisions did not have to be made instantaneously. In Norway, for example, decisions often had to be made on the spot. People were faced with the necessity of deciding, whether they wanted to or not, solely in virtue of their occupation or office. Without an initiative on his own part the Norwegian suddenly found himself face to face with the decision either to say "No" to the demands of the Nazis and take the serious consequences, or to say "Yes" and thereby betray his own country; there was no third alternative. On a particular day every Norwegian teacher had to choose between supporting Nazism by joining a Quizling organization for teachers and thus becoming propagandists for Nazism in the schoolroom, or, if he refused to do this, facing the possibility of deportation to a concentration camp. This was the predicament not only of the teacher but also of the journalist, the judge, the union leader, the actor, the clergyman, and many others who simply because of their position or office were placed before this decision. They had to say either "Yes" or "No." There was no third alternative, and there was very little time for deliberation.[3]

But this example also shows that an instant and fateful decision may be predictable—even inevitable—due to the fact that the life and outlook of the person involved are already so unified and integrated that he could not falter. There is a psychic maturity which can make the direction of many an instant decision a foregone conclusion. Even where much is at stake, a person need not therefore necessarily be in doubt

3. The difference between Norway and Denmark in this respect is accounted for by the different political situations in the two occupied countries. In Norway no indigenous government remained to intervene as a buffer between the Nazis and the Norwegian people, shielding the individual citizen in crisis situations from the direct imposition of Nazi ultimatums.

about what is right and about what he will do. The situation
may be "perfectly clear," as we say. Purposes contrary to the
challenge, and desires to avoid risk or inconvenience are not
permitted to develop into matters of reflection and argument.
They have already in advance been beaten down. Perhaps the
whole matter is simplified by the fact that the situation has, so
to speak, been intensified by an expressed appeal. Because of
this expressed appeal, refusal to assume the risk or inconvenience would be tantamount to failure of such gravity as to
be ruled out in advance.

It should be added, however, that though the decision is
clear, time for reflection is not therefore superfluous. The
person does well to "sleep on it," as we say, not because he is
actually in doubt about what he will do, but for a different
reason. In order to remain calm in the face of the risk or
inconvenience involved he must have the conviction that his
decision could not have been otherwise. Unless he is an
adventurer, he will reach this conviction not on the spur of the
moment but only through calm reflection.[4]

Conflict of Duties

In a different situation, however, a person may take the very
opposite attitude. He may be practically certain that he will
not do what he knows he ought to do.[5] What then is the nature
of the process of reflection which is set in motion by such an
"inner conflict"? In the first place, reflection consists in
imagining and picturing to oneself all of the disagreeable
consequences of doing the right thing. But it characteristically
includes also something else. The reason for conjuring up so
many disagreeable consequences of doing the right thing is the
hope of discovering among them at least one consequence

4. Objectively viewed, there are of course several alternatives, but from the
outset it is a foregone conclusion which one will be chosen. At no point, therefore, does reflection have the character of wavering. It is not a vacillation
between possible alternatives. Nevertheless, it is necessary in view of the far-
reaching consequences.
5. This may be because the situation is not intensified by some expressed appeal.
One's own spontaneous initiative is required if one is to do the right thing,
though a person may do the wrong thing by merely doing nothing, leaving
things as they are.

which is not merely disagreeable but from an ethical point of view also doubtful. If one succeeds in finding one such consequence he can in good conscience refrain from doing the right thing. He now refrains from doing what ought to be done, not because it would be disagreeable but because, ethically speaking, it would have unfortunate consequences. Through reflection he has succeeded in turning a clear case into an ambiguous one. One might also put it this way, that through his reflections he has established a case of conflict of duties. In the beginning his duty was clear to him, but since among the consequences of doing his duty there is one which is ethically questionable, it becomes his duty to refrain from doing that which at first he regarded as his duty. Through reflection he has succeeded in bringing duty into conflict with duty. His failure to act has now been camouflaged as a conflict of duties. Choosing the convenient solution has been made as ethically responsible as choosing the inconvenient solution.

It is therefore entirely too simple to say that in the process of reflection one vacillates between doing that which is right and that which is not right. The classic characterization of reflection as a struggle between duty and inclination is therefore inadequate inasmuch as it fails to take into account the real character of reflection. The fact is that when the moral person does that which is evil, he always thinks he is ethically justified in doing so. Only the amoral person does evil and recognizes his action for what it is. In other words, the moral aspect of reflection is its self-deception; the possibility of one's deliberately doing wrong never really enters his mind. Thus a person who is not amoral is necessarily hypocritical. Stated differently, a man can become honest and sincere only as he struggles against his own hypocrisy.[6]

We commonly have the notion that a person has to be a scoundrel to get involved in falsehood and fraud. But this is

6. In order to avoid misunderstanding it should be inserted that the subject under discussion here is decision and its process of reflection. Apart from decision, the morally sensitive person may indeed do that which is wrong and recognize his action for what it is, in which case it is done in an unpremeditated manner—in ill temper, annoyance, hate, or jealousy. However, in the decision which is made as a result of reflection the moral person never admits that he does wrong.

true only in the case of conscious falsehood and in the case of fraud which is punishable or on the borderline of punishable fraud. We imagine that we are normally sincere and honest and that we get involved in dishonesty and fraud only through some conscious and deliberate act. However, this is true only in the case of civil or legal relationships, in the realm governed by *justitia civilis*.

When it comes to the matter of evaluating our own position and actions, judging our motives and efforts and the various arguments we advance in this connection, we are not necessarily in and of ourselves honest and sincere. On the contrary, we can be honest and sincere in these matters only through ruthless self-criticism. Unless we struggle to reach clarity, unless we are consciously determined to refrain from glossing over or dodging the issue, dishonesty and self-deceit inevitably assert themselves. Arguments are used to camouflage our motives. Whatever is disagreeable we push into the background or entirely forget. Unwillingness to have our own efforts underestimated and disinclination to admit error or failure on our part cause us to hide certain facts or to regroup them in such a way that everything comes to be seen in a false light. In short, we arrange things to our own advantage. And all of this is done largely unconsciously. In other words, dishonesty and self-deceit are the normal state, honesty and sincerity are an achievement.

It is at this point that conscience has its function of unmasking man's self-deceptions. Man deceives himself, making himself out to be something which he is not. The point here is not that he deceives other people, but that he deceives himself. He veils himself with a smoke screen of hazy motives, and this self-deception is precisely the presupposition of the unmasking function of conscience. One who in full awareness of his own wickedness injures someone or is brutal in his conduct is an unprincipled person, a person without conscience.

We do not call a person unprincipled if he deceives himself and in his self-deception ascribes his actions to motives other than the motives which really govern him. We call him a

hypocrite, but never unprincipled, inasmuch as he is hypocritical precisely because of a bad conscience. But the unprincipled person is the person who is able to renounce his
self-deception and face up to his own wickedness and ruth-
lessness and remain utterly unaffected.

. Thus conscience is man's openness to exposure and unveil-
ing, the openness which was the occasion for his self-deception.
In self-deception man refuses to face up to his wickedness; he
flees from the judgment of his conscience. In other words,
self-deception is a product of morality. At the same time the
self-deception awakens the conscience and thus brings about its
own exposure through the "bad conscience" with which the
self-deception takes place. To have a "bad conscience" is
therefore the same as to suspect that one's motives are not as
genuine as he himself makes them out to be. Both conscience
and self-deception are therefore forms of a person's openness
to himself. Self-deception presupposes the conscience from
which it flees, and conscience presupposes the self-deception
which it exposes.

All of this must not, however, lead us to think that
conscience is to accomplish its purpose by searching out the
labyrinth of shifting motives or the maneuvers through which
they are explained away. It does not go to all that trouble.
Conscience is no bloodhound. It has no neutral ethical
function. It is not a matter of spying on oneself. Rather with a
rough hand, so to speak, conscience tears everything aside and
points to one's guilt. It is not interested in the technique by
which one has lied himself out of his guilt. In the midst of a
person's self-deception conscience simply exposes guilt, but it
does not map out the course of the self-deception—this it
leaves to the person's own self-observation and other leisure
activity. Conscience goes straight to the heart of the matter—
to his guilt. This is the "intuitive" aspect of the conscience.

Preoccupation with Motives

We have seen that we can make our inaction ethically
respectable by camouflaging it as a conflict of duties. But this is
not the only way it can be done. We can also justify our

inaction by continuing the process of reflection. By continuing to reflect upon the matter we avoid taking action. Although our attitude, outlook, or morality call for action on our part, we fail to act and instead continue the process of reflection—ostensibly in the very name of our attitude or outlook or morality.

But in what does our ongoing reflection then consist? It consists in a preoccupation with questions of attitude, outlook, and morality *as motivations.* Such preoccupation robs them of their power. An attitude, an outlook, a morality becomes impotent when considered as a motivation for action. Preoccupation with the motivation of an action paralyzes one for action, because it forces one to continue to repeat the process of reflection.

If our attitude, outlook, and moral considerations are to function as motivations, we must cease to think of them *as* motivations. Our attitudes and outlook and moral considerations lead to action only if we—for the very sake of our attitude, outlook, and moral considerations—forget our own relation to them. They will lead to action only through a commitment to them, a commitment in which we no longer preoccupy ourselves with our own relation to them. We will act upon a demand only if we forget *how* we ourselves relate to the demand and concern ourselves instead solely with *what* the demand is, and with the outlook on life implicit in it.

The Decision's Claim upon Us

Ethically understood, the decision consists in a person's attitude, character, or outlook being focused upon a particular deed which a person knows he ought to do. If he fails to do it, or if he does any one of a number of others things instead, he is weak, characterless, or untrue to his outlook. From the viewpoint of ethics the question of his courage or lack of courage, his sincerity or insincerity, his faithfulness or his failure with respect to his outlook cannot be divorced from the deed which ought to be done.

Obviously this does not mean that decision is inescapable. Frequently the person does manage to avoid making a decision altogether. As we have indicated, he may do so by way of self-deception, or by continuing the process of reflection. But there is also another way to avoid making a decision: He may ease the situation with excuses, appealing to the manner in which he has conducted himself in the past and in which he expects to conduct himself in the future, and ranking the demanded deed with the things he has done in the past and those he intends to do in the future. His reasoning runs something like this: After all, one paltry act, one failure to act can hardly cancel a whole series of honorable actions or transform all of one's past integrity into unfaithfulness. So, even though I fail this one time, I am in the main honorable and faithful.

This reasoning, however, is hardly an ethical decision. In a twinkle it has transformed the reflection from something ethical to something psychological. Ethically speaking, the question of whether a person wants to be courageous or cowardly, honorable or dishonorable, faithful or faithless cannot be separated from the question of whether he will or will not do the particular thing which he knows he ought to do.

But it is clear that if we relativize that which is at stake and should motivate our actions, that is, if we relativize our attitude, our character, our outlook, we thereby help to set the ethical decision aside through psychological considerations.

Why do we want the ethical claim upon us removed through psychological considerations? Simply because it is a claim! We do not want to be confined. We want to be free from having to make decisions and free from having to do what is to be done. We can have this freedom at any time, but only through unfaithfulness. This freedom is the freedom of paltriness, unfaithfulness, cowardice. This is not easy to accept, and so we try to ease the situation with psychological considerations, reasoning that, after all, we have acted honorably many times before. To act differently this one time should not matter.

This attempt on the part of psychological considerations to replace the ethical claim upon us is of course greatly facilitated by a relativization of the attitude, the character, or the outlook which is at stake and should motivate the action. If we can make a case for the notion that attitude, honorableness, and outlook are after all not absolute, that there are things more important than these, then we have, in the name of a fundamental consideration together with a psychological consideration, succeeded in assailing the stronghold of the ethical decision.

Is it not then possible to relativize everything which is ethically at stake? No, there is one thing which cannot be relativized, and that is a person's understanding that his life has been given him as a gift. This understanding can only be contradicted—by the opposite understanding that one is lord and creator of his own life, in other words, that he has received nothing.

In the ethical decision this understanding and the contradiction of it are by no means of merely theoretical character. If through his action a person gives attention to himself at the expense of the other person, then he is living as though he were both the author and the sovereign of his own life. On the other hand, if he cares for the other person's life, then he is living his life as something he has received. What this ethical decision lays hold on and embodies in the action which is to be carried out is a person's understanding of the fact that his life has been received as a gift. He can avoid making a decision and fail to act only by making himself the other person's evil god. This is the absoluteness of the demand which creates this ethical decision, and this is why all ideas of mutuality and comparison are excluded.[7]

7. Indeed there is, or at least there seems to be, something absolute about all other kinds of ethical decision in which something entirely different is at stake, such as, a person's courage, honor, sincerity, or outlook on life. But more precisely stated, it is apparently the ethical decision's exclusion of every psychological reflection which makes the ethical demand absolute, regardless of what is at stake, whether it be characteristics, attitudes, or outlooks.

It is a question, however, whether the absoluteness of general ethical deci-

The Critical and the Normal Situation

A decision will not likely be in the nature of a claim upon us unless the situation is acute. Justice is being violated every day and we are aware of it. People are constantly being oppressed, and constantly their lives are being ruined. But all this does not affect us because consciously or unconsciously we attribute it to "conditions": that is the way things are. The destruction of human life is so common and undramatic that we come to think of it as inevitable—and in this way keep it at arm's length.

But the situation may become so critical that it is no longer possible to blame the oppression of people on "conditions." The oppression may take on the character of crime; it may even invade one's immediate vicinity. It was out of such a critical situation in Germany that the movement of opposition to Hitler arose. Irrefutable reports of outrageous acts in the occupied lands as well as in the homeland kept accumulating. Lawlessness had come to be the order of the day.

At the same time, however, there were a sufficient number of circumstances suggesting that it was not one's duty to interfere. Those who opposed the regime had not themselves placed in office the men who proved to be criminals. Both before and after 1933 they had been among the opponents of Nazism. Some of them were children at the time of the upheaval, and even now played no role in public affairs. Under the dictatorship individual citizens had no influence with respect to what was happening and were therefore also without any political responsibility for it. In no respect were they involved in the crimes which were committed, and to all appearances they were unable to do anything to correct the

sions, regardless of the issue, is applicable to the specific ethical decision in determining whether a person wants to live his life as something he has received or insists on being his own and the other person's god. Is not this specific ethical decision the hidden absoluteness of all other ethical decisions with respect to all kinds of issues—a person's outlook, his character, his personality? In other words, if we were able to segregate the specific ethical decision from the other decisions, they would revert to relativization. In that case it would not be the ethical decision's exclusion of the psychological reflection as such which makes the ethical demand absolute. But the question whether the demand is absolute or not depends upon *what* it is that the ethical decision lays hold on and embodies in the deed which is to be done.

situation. Revolt in the traditional sense is doomed to failure in a modern, thoroughly organized dictatorship which has all kinds of means at its disposal. And we might add that the opposition movements in Germany and in the occupied countries were in several respects very different from one another. The German opposition movement had no support, either moral or material, from the Allies. It could not count on the sympathy of a corresponding national movement and did not enjoy the protection of a united people. It knew that there would never be anything triumphant about the liberation for which it was working.

All of these circumstances made the situation critical. Inhuman and irrational crimes were perpetrated in the immediate vicinity—crimes the citizens had no part in whatsoever and which there was very small likelihood they could do anything about.

In such a critical situation what moves a person to act at the risk of his life? No one knows, least of all the outsider, and possibly not even the person himself. The only thing one can see is the heroism of the struggle. And the hero himself "does not see the meaning of his life in his subjective attitudes but in the greatness of the cause he promotes, before which he holds himself in the background."[8] What the outsider sees is the goal or objective of the action, its purely factual and rational basis. Even in the case of an unarmed revolt through word of mouth and the fly sheet, as in Munich in the early part of 1943, there was clearly a political objective. It was hoped that some people could be reached in this way, that a movement might be started which would hopefully reach those within the dictatorship who still had a measure of influence, who indeed might even engineer a *coup d'état*. The reason for it all we learn from the accused persons themselves, from their own statements when on trial before the people's court. Among other things, Kurt Huber stated: "As a German citizen, as a German university professor, and as a political being I regard it not only

---

8. Rudolf Bultmann, *Glauben und Verstehen* II (Tübingen: J. C. B. Mohr, 1952), p. 91.

as my right but also as my moral duty to take a hand in helping to shape Germany's destiny, to expose manifest wrongs
and to oppose them. . . . To return to clear moral principles, to
a government of law, and to mutual trust between men is not
illegal; on the contrary, it is the *restoration of legality.* . . .
There is no more terrible judgment upon a nation or a society
than the admission which all of us must make, namely, that no
one feels secure in relation to his neighbor, no father in
relation to his sons. . . . Outward legality has its limits, beyond
which it becomes inauthentic and immoral; that is, when it
comes to be a cover for a cowardice which does not dare to
take a stand against manifest injustice."[9] And he concludes
with this word of Fichte: "You must act as though the affairs
of Germany depended solely upon you and your action, and as
though the responsibility were yours alone."[10]

These words articulate the meaning of political responsibility
in a democratic sense. Political actions and decisions are not
the sole responsibility of government. They are the responsibility of everyone, inasmuch as everyone—in the name
of the idea of the sovereignty of the people, which is
the basis of democracy—shares in the sovereignty. In an
office which affords opportunity to exercise influence, for
example the teaching profession, one has especially great
political responsibility.

All that we are able to ascertain is what a person does, his
objective and why he pursues it. So completely is the silent,
radical, one-sided, and impossible demand incorporated into
the concrete and actual challenge that no one knows how the
action got under way. And the person himself neither can nor
will act out of any other motive than the challenge of the
situation and the greatness of the cause.

Nevertheless, we cannot avoid asking what it is that
motivates a person to risk his life. The only answer we receive
is that provided by our own conjectures and interpretations

9. *Kurt Huber zum Gedächtnis. Bildnis eines Menschen, Denkers und Forschers,*
ed. Clara Huber (Regensburg: Josef Habbel, 1947), p. 25.
10. Ibid., p. 28.

and trust. But this is true with respect to all relationships among men.

The extent of the deviltry and insanity of the crimes must have aroused his indignation, brought his hatred toward the oppressors to such a savage pitch that he became miserable with feelings of shame. The enemy's contempt for his outlook on life raised the question whether that outlook could any longer have meaning if it did not issue in action.

But will a person sacrifice his life out of indignation or hate? Must he not also then lose his composure and act in desperation? On the other hand, if he remains composed and keeps clearly in mind what his duties are and what they are not, will he then sacrifice his life? Will a person sacrifice his life because of the shame of other people's being tortured and murdered when there are sufficient factors to relativize the shamefulness of it? He is not to blame for the difference between himself and those because of whose suffering he is ashamed. He has in no way contributed to their suffering. There is no prospect of his being able to intervene. Does not a person cling to life sufficiently to be able to accept a shame which can easily be relativized?

Even when his outlook implies that he is responsible for the fate of his people and for their prevailing state of injustice does a person sacrifice his life for an outlook? Here it should be pointed out that although by doing nothing and remaining alive he denies his own outlook, such denial is very relative since he has in fact had no hand in actually causing the state of anarchy and would not in any way rectify the situation by dying. A further argument against conspiracy is that there is a serious obligation, and that it may indeed be possible, to preserve existing cultural values through a hopefully temporary state of barbarity.

Strictly speaking, the people in Germany to whom we have referred were not coerced. Circumstances did not force them to act. They took action entirely on their own initiative, even though there was every indication that it would cost them their lives, and in spite of the fact that they might have refrained from acting and from risking their lives without thereby jeopardizing their integrity and their outlook.

We may try to explain a person's initiative in that kind of situation by saying that he knows within himself that if he were not to act, such inaction would make his life worthless. But this is not correct. Such a relativized shame and unfaithfulness as are under discussion here—which are no greater than the shame and unfaithfulness of which we are guilty in normal life—do not make a life worthless. Politically, legally, and morally speaking, it still can have worth.

The question is whether a person in the critical situation acts because, consciously or unconsciously, he understands that his relation to an absolute authority is of decisive importance to his life. Is this a part of the reason why he acts, regardless of the role which his indignation, shamefulness, hate, and his outlook may play? If we call it courage, is it courage in the heroic sense? Perhaps it is rather the kind of courage which Kierkegaard says a person gets from learning to fear the yet more fearful. "In this way a person always gets courage. When one fears a greater danger he always has courage to face a lesser danger. When one infinitely fears one danger, it is as though all other dangers were non-existent."[11]

People are also troubled, despondent, and unhappy under normal circumstances. They are hungry and thirsty, strangers, naked, sick, and in prison (Matthew 25).

The difference between these people and those in the critical situation is only that the difficulty and despondency of the former are not unusual and are not caused by crime, but are normal and due either to fate or to a legally legitimate oppression. They may also themselves be the cause of their plight.

We may not necessarily have contributed directly to the misfortune of other people. We may not have had anything at all to do with it. The parable in Matthew 25 is not about those who had taken food, drink, and clothing away from the

11. Cf. Søren Kierkegaard, *The Sickness Unto Death*, trans. Walter Lowrie (Princeton, N.J.: Princeton University Press, 1941), p. 14.

unfortunates, evicted them from their homes, caused them to become sick, or put them into prison. It is about people who had nothing to accuse themselves of in this respect, but who had witnessed what had happened and who had been aware of the circumstances of the unfortunate. In this respect there is no difference between the normal and the critical situation.

However, in two other respects there is a difference. Action on behalf of those who suffer under normal circumstances need not be hopeless. On the contrary, there is good reason to believe that it will effect the desired results. There is a possibility of their getting out of their difficulty, despondency, and unhappiness. Their plight may not be completely rectified, but it will at least be alleviated. The hungry will be fed, the thirsty will receive something to drink, the stranger will be given shelter, the naked will be clothed, the sick and the prisoner will be visited.

And the action will not be at the cost of life itself. It will, however, entail inconvenience. The fact is, though, that we are engaged in certain projects which we enjoy, and we do not wish to be disturbed. Our life has been established in a comfortable routine, and we do not wish to be inconvenienced. Our attitude has been so adjusted that we know what we will accept and what we will not accept, and if our wishes are not respected, we are not slow to react. Of course, we want to be accommodating and helpful. There are no limits to our "goodness"—except that it must not cost us anything.

Despite the fact that there are good prospects that our action will bear fruit and that it will not entail the sacrifice of our lives, we do nothing. Why not? Because we cling to our desire to remain undisturbed, comfortable, and self-adjusted as tenaciously as we cling to life itself. Therefore we are more than willing to allow ourselves to be dulled by the customary, the perpetual, the undramatic, and the inevitable character of people's plight.

Therefore, if we claim to know that the decisive factor in life is our relation to an absolute authority, such knowledge has no binding effect on us. We close our eyes and ears to this absolute authority because we are afraid that it might interfere. What we are afraid of is that the life which we have circumscribed and reduced to a system might get out of order. In everyday life we cling more to our desire to be undisturbed, and more to our material and spiritual possessions, than many a person in the critical situation clings to life itself.

10.

Science
and Ethics

We disregard the silent, radical, and one-sided demand. It is resisted by our self-assertion and will to power, by our ceaseless concern about what we ourselves will get out of what we do. This resistance is so real that often our falling short of the demand is not so much a matter of our failing to live up to it as of our inability to live up to it except at the expense of our nature. Or, more correctly stated, since in any given instance we can live up to the demand only by going counter to our nature, we distort the demand the moment we attempt to live up to it. Our falling short of the demand is determined not so much by how little we govern ourselves by it, as by the fact that we can govern ourselves by it only by corrupting it. Only out of cowardice can we govern ourselves by the demand to take care of our enemy's life, which has been placed in our hands; obedience to the demand therefore means distorting it into a demand to be cowardly. The demand not to worry can be obeyed only when we are worried about not worrying; obedience to the demand therefore means distorting it into a demand that we be in a state of desperate worry, not just worried in the usual ways. Obedience to the demand that we are not to treat a person according to what he has deserved is possible only to a dispassionate observer, a spectator who pretends to govern himself by the demand but does not actually love the undeserving person. The impossibility of the demand manifests itself most strikingly precisely in the attempt to fulfill it, when

173

a person does what he believes love would do, whether out of fear or out of a self-righteous concern for what he may get out of the deed which is supposed to have been done unselfishly.

Does this mean then that the demand must be regarded as unnatural? Since it can sometimes be fulfilled only in unnaturalness, and then only in terms of outward appearance, must it not be said to be unnatural? No, because the circumstance out of which the demand arises is as natural as it can possibly be: the other person has been delivered over into our hands and life is understood to be a gift—which understanding is the presupposition of the demand's one-sidedness. That the demand can be fulfilled only through unnaturalness therefore means something else, namely, that ethically speaking we exist in contradiction.

But is not the demand canceled by the fact of its impossibility? Can the demand abide its own impossibility? The assumption is that every demand, whatever its content, presupposes that it is fulfillable; otherwise it is not a demand but a meaningless pretense.

But how is this to be understood in view of our being in this contradiction? On the one hand, it is impossible to escape the demand, inasmuch as we cannot dismiss the fact out of which the demand arises, namely, that one person has been delivered over into the hands of another person. We cannot dismiss this fact any more than we can deny that life has been given us as a gift. Our existence is greater than we are; it is superior to us. In fact we constitute one another's world, whether we wish to or not. On the other hand, we distort the demand through that unnaturalness in which alone we are able—only apparently— to fulfill it. The demand is impossible of fulfillment.

Being in this contradiction means two things. First, it means that we cannot speak about this demand which comes to us along with life itself except in anthropomorphic terms. This is implied in the fact that this demand, like any other demand, presupposes fulfillability. This is all the more true here inasmuch as the demand in question must defend itself against our claim that it cannot be fulfilled. We can speak about our existence and the demand implicit in it only anthropomorphically, as about a person who insists that we are wrong in asserting its unfulfillability.

That the demand can be fulfilled is, moreover, the most obvious thing in the world because the fact out of which it arises is the blessing of our existence, namely, that we do not live alone but in company with one another. To disregard the demand would therefore be to disregard this blessing. To ignore the demand would be as absurd as to disregard the blessing of human existence. From the standpoint of our very existence, therefore, the demand is indeed fulfillable. Along with the blessing in which the demand is incorporated, life has provided us with all that is necessary for its fulfillment.

Second, the contradiction under discussion here means that it is not enough simply to assert that we exist in a state of contradiction. One claim is always countered by another. Life's unspoken claim asserts that in and with its blessing it has made it altogether possible for us to fulfill the demand. But this assertion conflicts with our own claim that we cannot by nature fulfill the demand and that its "fulfillment" will therefore only have the appearance of fulfillment. If we were to sacrifice our own self-assertion and will to power, there would be nothing left of us. A fulfillment of the radical demand would be a caricature of the love which the demand speaks about.

But we cannot leave the matter here, nor will it be left here if it is clear to us that the idea of the impossibility of the demand can mean two different things. There is an impossibility which in a certain sense is coupled with life's claim that the demand can be fulfilled, namely, the impossibility for which we ourselves take the blame. We connect life's claim that its demand can be fulfilled with our own claim that it cannot be fulfilled. We do this by blaming ourselves for not fulfilling it, thus conceding that life's claim is right.

On the other hand, the impossibility of the demand which cannot be connected with life's claim is the impossibility for which we refuse to accept blame. We refuse to accept the blame by maintaining that we cannot help it if we do not obey the demand. Refusal to assume responsibility for the impossibility of the demand consists in our refusing to own that our self-assertion and will to power, which cause us to live at the expense of others, are a part of our nature. Hence to claim guiltlessness is the same as to destroy ourselves. In guiltlessness we cease to be.

But it must be added that we cannot concede life's claim that the demand is possible by giving up our own claim that it is impossible. Why not? Because this would be the same as to entertain illusions about ourselves. To give up our claim that the demand is impossible is to become entangled in the pious fraud that self-assertion and will to power are not products of our nature, and that we would therefore be able to overcome them without dying. The result would be a life of pretense and a feigned unselfishness.

Theoretically, these two claims cannot be reconciled—life's claim that its demand, implied in the fact of a person's being delivered over to another person, can be fulfilled, and our own claim, made on the basis of our nature, that it cannot be fulfilled. Theoretically speaking, we must either maintain that we are right in claiming the demand to be unfulfillable and therefore drop it as a meaningless pretense—or we must maintain that life is right in its claim that the demand is fulfillable and therefore drop our own claim to the contrary, including the illusions about our own nature to which we have succumbed as a consequence. Either way, the contradiction is theoretically resolved; that is to say, it is shown to have been not a real problem.

But if our life is, ethically speaking, a contradiction, it is important not to remove the contradiction theoretically. We must then allow both claims, each one in itself correct, to stand side by side. And we ourselves must continue in the contradiction by accepting full responsibility ourselves for the impossibility of the demand.

It was said earlier that we can speak about life and its demand upon us only in anthropomorphic terms. We gave as the reason for this that life must defend itself against our claim that from the viewpoint of our nature its demand is impossible. We may add that life must make this defense in such a way that it transforms our claim to an acceptance of the impossibility as being our own fault. We can remain in the contradiction only by taking a position with respect to it.

Let me add that the theological reason why we can speak of life's demand only in anthropomorphic terms is because through life's demand we hear God's word to us. And, incidentally, I believe that in this discussion I have only been expressing in modern-day language what Luther spoke of as God's word to us apart from Christ.

Nonmetaphysical Philosophy and the One-sided and Impossible Demand

It is clear that the understanding of the demand which has been set forth here conflicts with every form of nonmetaphysical philosophy. This gives rise not to one problem but to several problems which must be distinguished from one another.

An old, familiar, and important philosophical distinction is of the greatest importance here. Descriptions, statements, assumptions, judgments, and similar phenomena are one thing, and they have this in common that they are either true or false. Demands, commands, desires, and the like are something else, and they are neither true nor false. The negative characterization of the demands, namely, that they are neither true nor false, raises the question whether it is therefore an entirely arbitrary matter what attitude we take to them, whether we acknowledge them or reject them.

The immediate answer is that when we acknowledge certain demands this is not a matter of conscious choice, but of our having been reared in the attitudes we take to them. In the very process of growing up we have already taken a position with respect to the demands, and it is only to a very limited extent that we are able to modify that position, not to speak of replacing it with others.

This only means, however, that we are confronted with the same question in a somewhat modified form: Is a change in

attitude purely a matter of a person's subjective, arbitrary decision? If this were the case, a discussion of ethical questions
would be meaningless.

But a discussion of ethical questions is not meaningless. The
fact is, as we shall see later, that every demand contains a
greater or lesser number of assumptions concerning purely
empirical data. The same is true of the position we take with
respect to the demand: it contains certain empirical assumptions. Therefore, disagreement between two persons with reference to their respective attitudes to a particular demand can
often be traced back to different assumptions regarding the
empirical data. If these data are investigated, and if the assumptions of one or both of the two persons can be corrected,
the difference between their respective attitudes often disappears.

Furthermore, we tend to think that our attitudes are consistent. One of the aims of a discussion of ethical questions
therefore is always to point out a contradiction between divergent attitudes.[1]

The range within which a person can take an attitude to a
specific demand—an attitude of rejection or acceptance—is
therefore very limited. It is limited by the milieu. And if we do
not wish to rely upon false assumptions regarding empirical
data, and if we do not want to get involved in self-contradic-
tion, it is still more circumscribed. Nevertheless, the attitude
we take to a certain demand within this limited range is in
principle arbitrary since the demand is neither true nor false.

We may now go on to ask the question which concerns us
in this connection: Does nonmetaphysical philosophy exclude
the acceptance of a demand which abolishes all mutuality and
which is impossible of fulfillment?

In itself it does not! The demand as such does not even come
within the concern of the sciences, since a demand cannot be

1. In his *Ethics and Language* (New Haven: Yale University Press, 1965)
Charles L. Stevenson makes a thorough analysis of the methods employed in a
discussion of normative questions and how they differ from the methods which
obtain in a discussion of purely scientific questions.

shown to be either true or false. This is as true of the one-sided demand as it is of the demand conditioned by prevailing law and morality.

Scientific investigation may make a judgment about whether or not a demand is fulfillable. It may conclude that the demand cannot be fulfilled. But it does not presume to say whether or not it makes sense ethically to speak about an impossible demand.

It is one thing that the nonmetaphysical philosophy does not exclude the idea of a demand which will not admit of mutuality. It is another matter whether such a demand and its acceptance can be content with the place accorded it within nonmetaphysical philosophy. Can the one-sided and impossible demand accept the characterization that it is neither true nor false, and does it make sense to accept it if in principle it is arbitrary? This is the question.

So long as it is a matter of the acceptance of demands which arise out of prevailing law and morality, the fact that they are neither true nor false and that their acceptance is in principle purely arbitrary is not a serious matter. In the first place, legal sanctions and public opinion place rather strict limits upon arbitrary disregard for the demands. Furthermore, the mutuality viewpoint places its own limits upon arbitrariness. And even out of a purely selfish concern I am interested in observing the legal and moral regulations. Stated somewhat differently, that which is neither true nor false is in principle left to our own arbitrariness. Therefore, if it is to endure it must rely upon something else. This is precisely what law and morality do. That their regulations are arbitrary in the sense that it is not possible to determine to what extent they are true or false does not matter. It does not matter because they are protected from all arbitrariness in another way, partly by overt sanctions and public reactions and partly by the less overt but just as effective mutuality viewpoint. You can depend on me—purely for my own sake—not to take advantage of the arbitrary character of law and morality in order to construct for myself a law and morality different from the prevailing ones.

But what about the demand which will not admit of any mutuality? According to nonmetaphysical philosophy the demand as such is neither true nor false. Correspondingly it should be up to a person's own subjective and theoretically arbitrary choice whether or not he will accept it. But does this make sense? Can the one-sided demand exist in such arbitrariness? No, because in this case everything is different. Here there are neither sanctions nor a clear self-interest to compensate for arbitrariness or to render it harmless. In short, a demand which, precisely because it is one-sided, is protected neither by threats nor promises cannot possibly subsist within the arbitrariness to which it is consigned by nonmetaphysical philosophy.

A one-sided and impossible demand, if it is to be accepted, must be true—and in fact it insists that it is true. It not only says what a person *ought* to do; it also says *who* the person is. The respective roles of the sciences and of the demand, therefore, are not that the sciences are to concern themselves with man's reality, and that it is the prerogative of the demand to define the goals of his existence, inasmuch as he is in fact an acting being. The demand also says, as was just pointed out, who man is. This discloses its impossibility.

True, the one-sided demand expresses itself in an entirely different manner regarding man's reality than the sciences do, because it claims to speak the absolutely decisive word. It presupposes—upon this presupposition its one-sidedness depends —that a person has his life and the world in which it is lived only as a gift which he has received.[2]

The same is true in the case of the impossibility of the demand. A demand which is not true would not be able to maintain itself in the face of the knowledge that it is unfulfillable. In order to endure despite its impossibility the demand must place a person face to face with an authority which insists that the demand is fulfillable, and which holds him responsible if in his case it is not.

2. To use the classic philosophical designation: The one-sided demand contains an ontology, a fundamental and constitutive definition of being, namely, that man's life and the world that goes with it have been given him as a gift.

The conflict with the nonmetaphysical philosophy is and remains unavoidable. The demand which sets mutuality aside cannot subsist in the place to which it is assigned by nonmetaphysical philosophy. Its one-sidedness presupposes a power which has given a person his life and his world and which at the same time presents itself as the authority of the demand. This power is invisible, and as authority it is silent because it is transcendent. And the disclosure of a person's existence, which is expressed in the impossibility of the demand, makes all other disclosures inconsequential.

In accepting a nonmetaphysical philosophy we ordinarily give up the idea of a one-sided demand. At any rate the idea is retained only in a weak and opaque form in what we speak of as an altruistic attitude. However, Professor Esbern Lomholt, M.D. takes exception to this. In a lecture on "The Secularization of the Psychic Life" he combines a nonmetaphysical philosophy with the idea that the ethical demand nullifies mutuality. And he combines the two in a way whereby the annulment of the idea of mutuality consists precisely in this, that the demand has no authority. He asks: Does not the demand lack authority precisely because it is silent, radical, and one-sided?[3]

His reasoning is as follows: As concerns the demands which are implied in and conditioned by the social norms, it is clear that they contain an authority before which we will be called to give an accounting. There is a third party, an institution or an authority different from the other person, which law and morality demand that we take into account in the manners they prescribe. So far as the legal regulations are concerned this "third party" is the state. As concerns morality it is other people or public opinion.

However, Lomholt is inclined to believe that the demand which arises out of the fact that we hold something of the other person's life in our hands has no authority. This is precisely its

3. Esbern Lomholt, "Sjaelelivets saekularisering," *Studenterkredsen,* December, 1951 and February, 1952.

unconditional character. Or, if we prefer, the authority coincides with the other person whose life has been delivered over to us, and is not a third party, an institution or some outside authority. This does not mean that the authority is the other person's own more or less expressed wishes and expectations; it is rather his very life. Lomholt's objection might also be formulated as a question whether the idea of an authority in the unspoken, radical, and one-sided demand to which we will be held accountable is not a speculative, a metaphysical reminiscence such as is found in literature or in theological discussion but which does not exist in the actual situation. Is not such an authority ruled out by the very fact that the other person's life judges us when we take advantage of his being dependent upon us?

There is a twofold presupposition in Lomholt's view. First, the sciences do not take a position in relation to a demand as such; therefore, nonmetaphysical philosophy does not exclude the idea of a one-sided demand. Second, the demand which nullifies the idea of mutuality has no authority; in other words, it contains no metaphysical assumptions. Thus in Lomholt's view there is no conflict between the nonmetaphysical philosophy and the acceptance of a radical, unspoken, and one-sided demand.

But is the one-sided and impossible demand really without authority? Does not the one-sided demand stand or fall with the fact that our life together with all that it contains has been given us as a gift? And does not the circumstance that we are not sovereign in our own lives but that life has been received constitute an authority before which we will be held accountable if we nevertheless use our lives to make one counterdemand after the other and to take advantage of the other person's dependence upon us?

In that event the demand does not come from the other person's life, which the demand says we are to take care of. On the contrary, it comes from the authority which has given us our life and has blessed it with a trust through which the other person places something of his life into our hands. And this is why our care of the other person's life can never consist in words or deeds which prevent him from discovering that his life has been given him.

In its silent, radical, and one-sided character the demand is impossible. It is only the demands concerning more or less definite conduct as prescribed by law, morality, and convention which can be fulfilled. But when the demand must itself, so to speak, demonstrate that it is a demand, so that we can speak of it only in anthropomorphic terms, is it not the authority which is asserting itself?

And when a person without love does out of fear what he believes love would do, what else is this than a fear of the authority which has given him life? He fears because instead of recognizing that authority he makes himself the sovereign of his life, indebted to no one.

Science and the Assumptions of Every Demand

We arrive at the same conflict if we use another consideration as our point of departure. As was mentioned earlier, it is not the prerogative of the sciences to deal with the demands as such or to concern themselves with our attitude toward them, with whether we accept them or reject them. But it is their prerogative to deal with those assumptions regarding empirical and demonstrable data which are contained in every demand. It is the task of the sciences to confirm or invalidate these data.

The one-sided demand is no exception. It too contains assumptions regarding empirical and demonstrable data, inasmuch as the demand arises out of the fact that through trust —without which we cannot exist—we are delivered over to one another, whether we wish it or not. It is this fact which the sciences are to investigate, and to invalidate or confirm. And they do confirm it. It is empirically demonstrable that one person's actions and conduct influence another person's disposition and the course of his life. The effects, whether superficial or radical, may be either evident or hidden. If hidden, the cause and effect relationship is made the object of scientific investigation by psychology and psychiatry. This is especially true if it is the psychic constitution which has been affected, affected by phenomena which neither the person himself nor anyone else not trained in psychiatry would dream could have any causal relationship to the case in question. This relationship can only be established scientifically. Up to this point there is no conflict between a nonmetaphysical philosophy and what is said about a one-sided demand.

However, the one-sided demand also contains assumptions whose content cannot be empirically established or scientifically verified, inasmuch as they are of a metaphysical character. And here the conflict is evident and inevitable, as was made clear in the previous section.

Intellectualism and Responsibility

A conflict of an entirely different kind arises when we consider that the scientific method stands or falls with the fact that its object—and this includes everything—is conditioned. With that presupposition a whole set of ethical attitudes and their accompanying feelings, passions, and moods are in danger of becoming illusory, such as, responsibility, guilt, duty, conscience, remorse, resentment, indignation, reproach, and self-reproach.

The situation is that the more insight we get into how determinitive heritage and environment are of one's personality and character, the less indignant we are over his misdeeds, the less we expect of him, and the less guilt we attribute to him. The judge in the courtroom experiences this when the defense counsel describes the defendant's environment, and the psychiatrist experiences it when he becomes acquainted with a person's psychopathic constitution.

A conflict therefore arises between one's insight into the cause of the action and the indignation (or remorse) to which the action gives rise. In light of the cause of the action the indignation and the responsibility and guilt which we attribute respectively to the other person and to ourselves turn out to be illusions. True, they are factually real, but their understanding and interpretation of the action are wrong. They are illusory in the light of our understanding of the cause of the action.

Why is the indignation wrong? Because it implies—so we insist—that the person who committed the act which gave rise to the indignation was in possession of a free will. To judge another person morally guilty, to hold him responsible for what he has done, or to judge oneself guilty and responsible presupposes a partially indeterministic view of the origin of character and personality. Moral judgment, censure or self-censure presupposes the idea of a certain freedom. Consequently the judgment or censure is dropped when we discover in a person's heritage or environment a legitimate cause of his character.

It is not only certain special actions, however, which we believe have been determined either by a psychopathic constitution or an unfortunate environment. We regard every action of every person as being determined. To accept the scientific method is to refuse to exempt anything from scientific investigation, which in turn means that we unconsciously take for granted the ontological conception that there is nothing which is not conditioned.

We therefore recognize the connection between indignation, guilt, and responsibility on the one hand, and free will on the other hand, which has been one of the arguments for indeterminism. However, we do not conclude that a person therefore has a free will. The indeterminist draws this conclusion because he understands and interprets man's existence only from the viewpoint of responsibility and guilt, which in turn justifies indignation over his misdeeds. But we draw the opposite conclusion from the connection between indignation, responsibility, and guilt on the one hand and free will on the other hand, namely, that the indignation, responsibility, and guilt are illusions, as is also the idea of the free will.

We might well ask: Who says that the conflict between the cause of the action and the resultant indignation must be resolved in such a way that it is the cause which is right and the indignation which is wrong? Why must the ontology of the scientific method prevail when it is in conflict with a set of

ethical attitudes? Why not rather the understanding and interpretation implicit in these attitudes?

These questions cannot be answered by the scientific attitude
because the scientific attitude is itself a part of the problem. It
is the scientific conception of reality which is to be determined,
and this is something science itself cannot do. In fact this is
very well understood. It is the individual himself who in a very
personal manner makes that decision. And this he can do—to
use Hedenius's expression—by choosing the morality of intellectualism. He makes the moral decision that in his morality he
will acknowledge no assumptions which he does not believe to
be true—true in a theoretical sense. And the moral phenomena
we have discussed are not true, since our insight into the factors which have determined them abolishes them. The conflict
between intellectual honesty and a whole set of ethical attitudes and reactions, such as, responsibility, guilt, indignation,
and remorse together with their reproaches and self-reproaches,
is decided by the morality of intellectualism in favor of the
former.

Instead of an intellectualistic morality we might advance
what for the sake of brevity could be called a morality of responsibility. It would maintain that assumptions or arguments
which turn responsibility and its attendant attitudes into illusions cannot be true. The sense of responsibility and guilt
should be so convincing that it would demand such a morality.
In passing let it be said that this morality is not necessarily
indeterministic. It might well be compatible with a deterministic conception which insists that a person incurs guilt solely
because he wills the action, regardless of whether the will is
determined or not. It would therefore be the will itself and
not the will's partial freedom which makes man responsible
and guilty. (We shall return to this in the next section.) But
entirely apart from this, would one from the point of view of
an intellectualistic morality be justified in saying that such a
morality of responsibility is dishonest? Hardly, because the
decision we make in the situation of conflict is precisely a

decision and is therefore outside the jurisdiction of science. Whether we choose the one morality or the other, we are dishonest only if we refuse to face up to the difficulties in the morality we have chosen. And here I should say that it seems to me that there are difficulties connected with both kinds of morality. The difficulties in a morality of responsibility are plain. They consist in a conflict with the scientific method and its assumptions.

The morality of intellectualism runs into difficulties which are just as serious, though of a different kind. It maintains that the purpose of the moral judgment, whether of the other person or of ourselves, is to influence, alter, or intensify his or our own attitude. And in a certain respect this makes good sense from the standpoint of a deterministic conception. The ethical judgment is itself a contributing factor. It enters in to help determine the other person's future actions. This is its intention. So far, so good.

However, is this not done by appealing to the other person's responsibility for his conduct and actions, and by calling forth in him either indignation or guilt? Can it be done in any other way? If not, then the ethical judgment of necessity works with illusions.

Possibly it will be objected that no one has said that the ethical judgment must appeal to the other person's indignation or conscience, to his sense of responsibility or guilt feeling. It is to appeal to the ethical phenomena in the other person, phenomena which from a deterministic viewpoint are not illusions, for example, mercy, love, sympathy, patience, and tolerance.

This answer, however, does not remove the difficulty. Our concern is not to create the best possible condition for the development of, for example, mercy and tolerance. Rather, our hope is that through an ethical judgment we might appeal for mercy and tolerance. But does not the appeal which belongs to the ethical judgment bring forth the mercy or tolerance which it is the responsibility and duty of the person concerned to manifest? Regardless of what the ethical judgment appeals to, does not the very appeal of the ethical judgment make that to which the appeal is made something which the person in question *ought* to do or *ought* to have? But to appeal through an ethical judgment to that which someone else or which we ourselves *ought* to do is the same as to appeal to a person's responsibility and duty. If this is correct, then it follows that in order to be a determining factor the ethical judgment must make use of illusions. But this the morality of intellectualism will not allow. Must not the morality of intellectualism then refrain from making ethical judgments? But would it not thereby abolish itself?

In order to point up the difficulty inherent in the morality of intellectualism we might ask: If it demands honesty of itself —and the demand for honesty constitutes its morality—does it not make honesty a matter of one's own responsibility? Is not honesty, by virtue of its being demanded, something which we *ought* to manifest? Bear in mind that we are discussing a demand and not the best possible conditions for the development of honesty. But does this mean that the morality of intellectualism, by demanding honesty, makes honesty a matter of responsibility and duty? Does it mean that the morality of intellectualism appeals to something which, in the light of the determinism which called this morality itself into being, is an illusion? As morality, the morality of intellectualism operates with something which, as intellectualism, it regards as an illusion and which, as morality, it has pledged itself to oppose— but which it is able to oppose only by using it itself.

We said earlier that in the case of the judge and the psychiatrist their indignation diminishes as their knowledge of the defendant's or the patient's heritage and environment increases. It should be pointed out here that in the struggle between the morality of intellectualism and the morality of responsibility the movement is not always in that direction. Just as often it is in the opposite direction because of our starting out with a psychological analysis which changes into indignation. And is it not doctrinaire to insist that the first movement is always right and the last one always wrong?

To take an example, in E. M. Forster's novel, *Howards End,* already referred to in a different connection, Henry Wilcox is described as a person of helpful disposition so long as he can have his own way. According to his ultratraditional—not to say ultrareactionary—view of women, a woman must be beautiful, weak, and helpless—always dependent upon her strong and energetic husband. A good husband is one who is superior and whose help is needed. Ultimately this is because he cannot exist except in a psychic stronghold which he has himself built and secured. Therefore, he cannot well tolerate being in the wrong. And if in the face of incontrovertible evidence he cannot deny his having done wrong, there is at any rate one thing he cannot consent to, and that is to be forgiven, because that would bring his spiritual stronghold to ruin. Rather than suffer the humiliation of being forgiven he will take the consequences of his wrong. And if contrary to his wishes he is forgiven on the spot, he must build up his stronghold with excuses, even if they be of the most banal kind.

Margaret has known this concerning her husband from the very beginning. She has no illusions regarding him but accepts him as he is without trying to weaken his stronghold. And although she neither loses her temper nor becomes passively helpless when difficulties overwhelm her, but on the contrary is a gifted and unpretentious person not unaccustomed to taking the initiative, she nevertheless occasionally accepts his view of women.

But when his character drives him to an unreasonable condemnation of her sister whom she loves dearly, there is a momentary break between Henry and Margaret. The plot of the novel is too intricate to be reviewed here. Suffice it to say that there is a very close relationship between Margaret and her sister Helen. When Henry therefore refuses to consent to Helen's spending a night at his house because she, though unmarried, is expecting a child, a violent crisis takes place between him and Margaret. The whole affair is aggravated by the circumstance that, judged by the moral standard he has laid down, Henry has himself been living anything but a spotless

life. He was unfaithful to his first wife, and he has contributed
to the unhappiness of his former mistress and the man whom
she later married. Therefore, the refrain in Margaret's accusation is that he is not able to "connect" anything.

In one sense Margaret's opinion of her husband is the same
following the crisis as it was before. In his relation to Helen,
in turning down her request to spend a night at Howards End,
and in his reason for turning it down Henry conducts himself
as he always has conducted himself. Margaret has always been
accustomed to his psychic defense mechanism and his very
straitlaced morality. He does not manifest one single new character trait, which she also admits.

In another sense, however, Margaret's opinion of her husband is by a single stroke changed. She judges him and sees
him as he appears in the light of that judgment—something
she has never done before. She sees him now as a traitor to his
first wife, as an inconsiderate and irresponsible cynic in relation to his former mistress and her husband, as a phrasemonger
in relation to Margaret, and a hypocrite in relation to Helen.
She now sees it all in the light of exactly the same character
traits which prior to the conflict were harmless in her eyes.

In what does her changed view consist? It consists first in
something psychological and second in something ethical. The
movement here is from the psychological to the ethical, and to
the reader of the novel it seems right that the movement can
also be in that direction.

Does this mean then that we can view a person's conduct
now psychologically and now ethically but never in both ways
at the same time? Are human conduct and our view of it like
the puzzle picture which, when we have figured it out, we can
view in two ways, ways which are incompatible with each
other inasmuch as we can never see both of them simultaneously—though the puzzle picture, regarded as a physical stim-
ulus, remains unchanged? Maybe this is saying too much. The
psychological can well be incorporated into the ethical. But we
can say at least this much, that probably at no time are the
ethical and the psychological equally involved. Though Mar-

garet's psychological view of her husband was taken up into her accusation against him, and in this way persisted, it was far less important during the crisis than the ethical, and in itself it had no importance.

The Interpretation of Determined Decision

The conflict between the morality of intellectualism and the morality of responsibility is a part of the conflict between nonmetaphysical philosophy and theology. We must understand, however, what that conflict is about and what it is not about. Theology does not defend indeterminism. The debate between nonmetaphysical philosophy and theology is not a debate between determinism and indeterminism, but a debate concerning the interpretation of determined decision.

Theology too recognizes that in making a decision I cannot cut myself off from my past and escape its determining influence. I am not able to get away from my past. Rudolf Bultmann says this very succinctly: "All of my decisions have in fact already been made. I only grasp more firmly what I already am. . . . I always bring my past with me. . . . I am what I have become. At no moment do I have myself in hand. I am not free."[4]

Indeed I do experience something which I call decision. But if I scrutinize it closely I discover that it is an illusion to think that what I experience is really a decision. I merely call it that. What I *experience* is that I break through that which determines me—which is why I call it decision. But upon further reflection I perceive that this breakthrough is an illusion. The way I understand myself in the experience to which I refer as decision is therefore a wrong interpretation, even though this wrong interpretation belongs to the experience itself as one of its elements.

On the falsity of my understanding of decision positivism and theology are agreed. But while positivism is content simply

4. Rudolf Bultmann, *Glauben und Verstehen* II (Tübingen: J. C. B. Mohr, 1952), p. 70.

to declare the fact, the Christian message judges it. Positivism says simply that man is always determined by his past, whereas the theological interpretation of the Christian message says that man has been lost to his past. When positivism says that decision is an illusion, theology adds that man has lost his freedom.[5]

There is a presupposition for the theological judgment: When the Christian message judges the decision illusory this is because it demands real decision. In order to clarify what the positivist and the theologian are agreed upon and are not agreed upon, it will be necessary to distinguish between decision as experienced and decision as demanded (or experienced and demanded freedom). There is agreement about the illusory character of *experienced* decision. Indeed, in the light of the Christian message, the determining influence of our past is seen to be even more certain and the experienced decisions even more illusory. Man is not able to liberate himself; it is simply impossible. The demand to do so is an impossible demand. Every attempt to liberate oneself from the determinativeness of his past only intensifies it. On the other hand, theology and positivism do not agree about whether, given this determinativeness of the past, it nonetheless makes sense to *demand* decision. To positivism (at least in the form of a morality of intellectualism) it makes no sense; the Christian message on the other hand insists on it.

This difference derives from their divergent views of man. To demand that a person make decisions one must assume, as in Christian anthropology, that man is able to act as a unity, out of a personal center. As Paul Tillich puts it, the demand is addressed to the person who should be able to relate to himself, to weigh his motives "and react as a whole, through his personal center, to the struggle of the motives." The appeal is made to the person who is not identical with his motives, but

5. The Christian message passes this judgment upon us because in the measure that a person's decision is illusory our historical existence is unreal. By this is meant that the encounter with the neighbor is not a real encounter if we are too determined by our own past to be able to obey the demand implicit in the encounter.

who from out of the wholeness of his personal center should
be able to relate to them.[6]

On the other hand, the anthropology on which the morality
of intellectualism is based is a psychology which, as Bertrand
Russell puts it, conceives of the person as a series of events
grouped together by laws of causality.[7] In terms of such a psychology it therefore makes no sense either to demand a decision
or to appeal to a person's responsibility. What, then, is the
significance of ethical demands and judgments, which are not
addressed to phenomena which as decisions and responsibilities
are—deterministically viewed—illusions? The answer is that
they are merely contributory factors—hopefully the decisive
factors but nonetheless only factors—which work together
with other factors to determine the conduct of the person in
question. This anthropology therefore also polemicizes against
the idea that man is an integrated whole operating from a
personal center. It admits that it may be natural to conceive of
reflection as a weighing of one's motives or as a struggle between them, but it finds these metaphors misleading. They are
misleading because they assume that the different motives are
simultaneously the objects of reflection; but this is a mistaken
assumption inasmuch as the motives appear successively. A
person can of course interrupt the successive development of
the motives in order in retrospect to unite them in a single
conception. However, the decision never depends upon such
a conception, but always upon the one motive which gradually
becomes dominant. In other words, we may well conceive of
all the motives simultaneously, but we do this only after the
fact, through recollection. The conception of motives is one
thing, the operation of the motives is something else. Their
operation involves the development not only of series of ideas
and thoughts, but also of impulses of movement and action.
Decision is never the result of a conception of motives; it

6. See Paul Tillich, *Systematic Theology* I (Chicago: University of Chicago
Press, 1965), p. 184.
7. See Bertrand Russell, *Religion and Science* (New York: Oxford University
Press, 1960), pp. 138–143, 205–208; and *An Outline of Philosophy* (Cleveland:
World Publishing Co., 1968), p. 171.

always depends upon which motive finally becomes dominant.[8]

However, we must constantly keep in mind what the disagreement is about and what it is not about. Theology does not dispute that decision is determined—which in this context means that theology does not dispute psychology in its scientific description of the process of reflection. When man destroys his own wholeness, gives up being a center, and abandons his freedom, then his decision and action are the result of the motive which in thoughts and feelings is most strongly developed.

The disagreement, however, is about something else. The morality of intellectualism alleges that it adheres to the scientific viewpoint of psychology according to which the human psyche consists in functional relations. Its determinism is therefore *methodological.* On the other hand, the theological case for the determinativeness of decision is based on the *historical* fact that man is constantly destroying the wholeness, the center, and the freedom of his own existence. It therefore makes good sense to demand a decision and an action of the man who is presupposed to be a unity, with a center, and free.

For the sake of completeness it should be added that the determinism represented by the morality of intellectualism is not the only determinism. As mentioned in the foregoing section, in a sense it shares the presupposition of indeterminism that it is meaningless to speak of responsibility and guilt if the will and the choice are determined. However, it does not take indeterminism's point of departure, namely, that it *is* meaningful to speak of responsibility and guilt. And therefore it does not maintain, as indeterminism in fact does, that the will and the choice are not determined. It takes the opposite point of departure, namely, that the will and the choice are determined, and therefore draws the logical conclusion that the responsibility and the guilt are illusions.

Quite common to philosophy in our day is another form of determinism which maintains that in order to be able to say of an action that it is intentional and to judge it either good or

8. Jørgen Jørgensen, *Psykolgi på biologisk grundlag* (Copenhagen: Munksgaard, 1941), pp. 413–415.

bad, it is enough that the person in question could have acted differently *if* he had chosen to do so. The reason our condemnation of a crime is not unreasonable is that the criminal would not have committed it if he had chosen not to. And the reason that it usually makes no sense to condemn a man for being ill is that he would have become ill even if he had wanted to avoid it. Responsibility is abolished not by the fact that a person's will and choice are causally determined, but only if all of his actions are unintentional so that there would be no difference between involuntarily committing a crime and involuntarily becoming ill.[9] In order to speak of a person making decisions and of his being responsible for his actions it is sufficient that he has not been coerced into acting as he did but that he wanted to act as he did. Responsibility and guilt are not illusions just because the will and the choice are determined.

In a certain sense this form of determinism corresponds with the view of Luther and Calvin. When G. E. Moore, for example, says that though the will is determined, the action is nevertheless intentional and for that reason either good or bad, he is in agreement with the Reformers who maintained that the bondage of the will does not abolish man's responsibility for who he is and what he does. Characteristically, therefore, both Moore and the Reformers clarify this by reference to the difference between necessity and coercion. The determination of the will in the sense of causality and the bondage of the will in the sense that without God man does evil—both mean that of necessity man acts according to his own will, but that this necessity does not abolish his responsibility and guilt. Only if he is coerced are his responsibility and guilt abolished. But the will cannot be coerced since to will something is to desire it, be eager for it, and put forth effort to realize it. Only the action itself can be coerced against one's will.

This second form of determinism is compatible with a morality of responsibility. According to this form of determinism it makes good sense through the ethical demand and judgment to appeal to all of those phenomena which the determinism

9. See G. E. Moore, *Ethics* (New York: Oxford University Press, 1965), p. 92.

represented by the morality of intellectualism excluded, such as responsibility, guilt, and conscience.

Nevertheless, we must also direct a critical question to this second form of determinism. It too is methodological. Its anthropology is a psychology according to which the human psyche consists of a series of occurrences held together by laws of causality. This is evident in the fact that the meaning of the ethical demand and judgment consists only in the hope that they might become the decisive link in the chain of psychic occurrences which constitute the person. But is this tenable? Do not the ethical demand and judgment take into account the fact that man was created to be a whole and a center? Do they not at the same time take into account man's responsibility, guilt, conscience, remorse? Is the anthropology which is presupposed by determinism in its methodological character—according to which the person is nothing but a chain of events held together in certain intimate relationships—compatible with the categories of decision and responsibility?

In a certain sense the Reformers' view, though similar to this second form of determinism, is also different from it. Bondage and determined decision for the Reformers are not the same thing. It is man in the totality of his being who is in bondage, while it is the individual psychic occurrence which is determined. While the Reformers therefore assumed that man is a whole, the idea of determinism assumes that man is a chain of psychic occurrences held together by laws of causality.

Ultimately the problem is whether psychology's conception of the human psyche as functional relations is not phenomenologically false.

The Interpretation of the Scientific Reduction

The scientific approach to things takes place through a reduction. All questions except the purely scientific ones are ignored.[10] For a clarification of the problem posed here, it will be

10. "The process of reduction in science excludes in principle certain ways of framing the questions." Freiherr von Gebsattel, "Allgemeine und medizinische Anthropologie des Geschlechtslebens" in *Die Sexualität des Menschen,* ed. Hans Giese (Stuttgart: Enke, 1955).

helpful to distinguish between what we might call a methodological and an ontological reduction.

We shall first take up the methodological reduction. Clearly this has been most widely employed by the advanced sciences in which one research is taken up where the previous one left off and in which phenomena already scientifically established are taken up for further investigation with respect to certain of their relations. But we get the clearest picture of the methodological reduction if we think of those sciences which are in early stages of development and in which the researcher must start at the very beginning. Here we observe the reduction at its point of origin. On the one hand, the researcher must be content to describe the phenomena in terms of everyday language. After all, he must begin somewhere, and he must begin by letting the phenomena have the scope and meaning which they already have in the natural understanding and classification of the world. On the other hand, he is not interested in that understanding itself: an explanation of the natural understanding is not his concern. All that he is interested in are the constant relations between the phenomena. His purpose in describing a phenomenon in the words and expressions of everyday language is only to objectify it for the sake of relating it to another phenomenon.

The reduction then consists in this, that the sciences do not have an independent interest of their own in the natural understanding and its interpretation. More exactly, the reduction consists in their ignoring all the peculiarities of the phenomena except those on the basis of which the constant relationships are established. We may explain the reduction in yet another way: If the scientist arrives at the intended results and it is ascertained that two phenomena do in fact vary proportionately with each other, then he assumes either that the one phenomenon is conditioned by the other, or that both are conditioned by a third phenomenon. With the aid of the theoretical connection established between the phenomena he is enabled to predict the outcome. The scientific reduction may therefore also be defined in this way, that in the sciences the sole interest as regards the objects of research is in what must be assumed concerning them in order to be able to calculate them.

To illustrate: Psychology has no independent interest in how a person understands himself in the experience of guilt. What psychology is interested in is to place the phenomenon of guilt feeling into a presumably constant relationship with another phenomenon, such as an authoritarian upbringing. Psychology pursues the interpretation of the self-understanding only to the extent that it regards it as useful in discovering the phenomena with which the guilt feeling stands in a constant relationship.

It is one thing to interpret for practical and personal reasons the attitude we assume toward other people and toward ourselves, together with the feelings, passions, and moods associated with that attitude. It is another thing to make that attitude with its feelings, moods, and passions the object of an investigation concerning how it varies proportionately with other phenomena.

There is one more element in the methodological reduction which must be expressly mentioned. The scientific description of the phenomena under investigation involves classification of them, whether with words or expressions from everyday language or in terms of precise definitions. This classification, however, is not of interest in and of itself. It only serves the purpose of helping to discover the constant relationships. The classification must therefore constantly be revised until two groups of phenomena are discovered between which there exists a constant relationship. And it is self-evident that what is involved in the revised classification is among other things a replacement of the everyday language classification of the world with an artificial classification. Since the classification of the phenomena is of no interest in itself and must constantly be revised, it follows that the concepts and definitions which scientific knowledge uses to classify the phenomena are artificially created. They are, as we say, purely operational in character.

But this brings us to the question concerning the relationship between the artificially created, purely operational concepts, definitions, and classifications of the sciences on the one hand, and our prescientific, more or less transparent understanding which manifests itself in everyday language on the other hand. Does it make sense to allow these two kinds of knowledge to compete with one another? Or—is there perhaps no other way? Does science always involve also a view of the world and of life? The question may also be formulated differently: How is the methodological reduction related to the ontological? By ontological reduction we mean the claim that only those characteristics of the phenomena which are necessary for ascertaining constant relationships have any reality. In other words, only those properties of the phenomena are real which we must assume in order to be able to calculate them in advance. All other characteristics are creations of our interpretation and are therefore unreal.

Let us begin by emphasizing two things about which all of us are agreed. In the first place, we are agreed that it is not sufficient simply to describe and theorize. For this, our life is too enterprising and too emotionally conditioned. We cannot be content with a merely scientific attitude to things. There must also be some other kind of orientation. Without feeling and interpretation we can neither exist nor act. In the second place, we are all agreed that nothing must be exempt from scientific investigation, not even our attitudes and actions, our feelings and interpretations.

But we must now take up the problem. We are familiar with two kinds of knowledge: scientific knowledge and the knowledge which for the sake of brevity we may call "interpretation," that is, the kind of knowledge which belongs to our enterprising and emotionally conditioned life. For two reasons the relationship between these two kinds of knowledge is an urgent problem.

The first reason is that interpretation can in certain instances be replaced by scientific knowledge. This comes about in the following manner: An attitude together with its self-understanding and the feelings and actions which go with it are made the object of scientific investigation. They are characterized

psychologically. Evidently such a characterization by means of
psychological concepts does not constitute a psychological demonstration of the attitude itself and the understanding which
goes with it. It presupposes the difference between the attitude
and its self-understanding on the one hand, and the psychological
demonstration, in fact every scientific pronouncement, on the
other hand. In other words, interpretation and scientific knowledge are kept separate.

But, we might ask, is this saying anything beyond the com-
monplace that the phenomena which are scientifically investigated obviously do not thereby become science, that a stone is
not turned into science by its being made the object of a
mineralogical description? Really, nothing more than that is
said! Still, it is not superfluous to distinguish between a person's attitude and the psychological investigation of it. Because
the scientific investigation is for its part an attitude, and because the investigated attitude for its part contains a particular
understanding, the one can be replaced by the other. The scientific attitude may on occasion simply assume the place of the
investigated attitude. This is precisely what happens when accusation or self-accusation, which holds the other person or
oneself responsible and guilty, is replaced by a scientific attitude which explains or determines the cause of the action. Not
content to investigate a given phenomenon, science also chal-
lenges it. And, strange as it may seem, science transforms the
phenomenon—into science. This is possible only because the investigated phenomenon and the investigation of it are of the
same kind. Both are attitudes and both involve understanding.
We might also express the matter thus: What Hedenius calls
the morality of intellectualism is possible only on the presupposition that the investigated attitude can effectively be challenged by the scientific morality.

This differentiation between an attitude and the scientific
investigation of it may also at times enter into the psychiatrist's
therapy. The patient, for example, is helped to a scientific understanding of his case, and this is supposed to correct his
pathological attitude. We see, then, that although scientific

knowledge and interpretation are indeed kept separate, they also at the same time very effectively compete with one another.

The second reason why the problem of the relationship between the two kinds of knowledge forces itself upon us is that in our attitude, action, and feeling we cannot avoid interpreting the scientific reduction. This is brought out with poetic force and clarity in Thorkild Bjørnvig's poem, "Samtale."[11] Our feelings are scientifically reduced to internalized reflexes, and our linguistic interpretation of our existence is reduced to imagination. This sober insight into the nature of our feelings is not itself feeling. If it were, it would abolish itself. It is based rather upon a scientific intent to look at things as they really are without any interference by feeling. Likewise the conviction that the linguistic interpretation is pure imagination does not itself purport to be an interpretation, in which case it would abolish itself. On the contrary, it is based upon a knowledge which renounces every interpretation in order not to know anything about things other than what must be assumed in order to calculate them.

But if we seriously accept the idea that our feelings are nothing but internalized reflexes, then there is no sense in our relying upon them. We have no need to await defeat because we are already defeated. And if we seriously accept the idea that our linguistic interpretation of our existence is mere imagination, then our existence is empty. But then what is the issue? Is it mistrust and hopelessness, or is it a scientific and radical intent to live without any illusions, that is, to see things as they really are? The answer is that it is both. As we have said, the scientific approach to things takes place through a reduction. Feeling and interpretation are eliminated and with them all the questions of human existence—with the exception of the scientific questions—which occupy feeling and interpretation. However—and this is decisive—we continue to feel and to

11. See the Thorkild Bjørnvig anthology *Anubis* (Copenhagen: Gyldendal, 1956), p. 15.

interpret; we cannot get around it. And therefore we are not able to refrain from feeling and interpreting the scientific reduction. And translated into feeling and interpretation, its results are mistrust and hopelessness.

We might almost say that the debate between scientific knowledge on the one hand, and feeling and interpretation on the other hand, is a matter of each one trying to follow after the other, because the one which follows has the advantage. Scientific knowledge takes up its position behind feeling and interpretation. It makes our attitudes and actions together with their understanding and feeling the objects of scientific investigation. And through an ontological reduction it declares only those characteristics to be real which are needed for ascertaining the constant relationship and for calculating the occurrence of the phenomena. The rest is declared to be a matter of illusion.

But the interpretation and the feeling in turn take up their position behind the scientific reduction and expose the mistrust and hopelessness which result when feeling and interpretation are reduced to imagination. The scientific knowledge that the understanding which comes from feeling and interpretation is illusory does not by any means destroy that understanding. The understanding is indestructible inasmuch as we cannot but feel and understand the emptiness of that existence and that world which remain behind after the scientific reduction has taken place. As long as we live we continue to feel and to interpret what it means to have our feeling and interpretation turned into illusions.

11.

Poetry and
Ethics

It is very common to discuss the problems connected with the relationship between science and ethics. Not so common, however, is a discussion of the relationship between poetry and ethics, though this too happens occasionally. Moreover, the problems connected with both the ethics-science and the ethics-poetry relationships are intimately related to one another. Particularly when scientific knowledge is seen from the viewpoint of a reduction and when ethical knowledge is regarded as an interpretation, we are led to ask about the relationship between poetry and ethics, because if any kind of knowledge has the character of interpretation, it is that of poetry. The question therefore is how those two kinds of interpretation—the ethical and the poetic—are related.

Statement and Expression

The kinship between conversation and poetry is clear. Regarding this kinship Johannes Pfeiffer, a German historian of literature, says that poetry has indeed divorced itself from all corporeality of human conversation. But, he adds, a peculiarity of poetry is nevertheless that there is something about it which is akin to the corporeal tone and gesture of conversation.

In order to understand what this means we must momentarily leave the subject of poetry and turn our attention to the ordinary conversation with its tone and gesture. And to understand what is meant by tone and gesture we must differentiate between what we might call the "statement," that is, *what* is said, and the "expression," that is, *how* it is said. As concerns the "expression," it is determined by pitch, tonal quality, and gesture. "In comparison with the word which has fullness and precision of meaning, says Hans Lipps, "the gesture has power of expression."[1] To the expressive power of gesture he might have added tonal power—which in a way he also does. Gesture and tone are closely related phenomena. Tone is sound gesture indicating that the speaker is moved or gripped by something. This is why gesture, as Lipps also says, in its tonal quality reaches into the spoken word.[2]

It is not possible to escape the effect of tone and gesture. A person's mood, what he has in mind, possibly in opposition to the rest of us, are spontaneously expressed in his voice and its tonal quality. *How* a person says something aids our understanding of *what* he says and determines the faith we put in his words.[3] A person is far more vitally present in the expressive power of tone and gesture than he is in what he merely says.[4]

As an illustration of what Pfeiffer and Lipps would call to our attention, each in his own way and context, we need only think of a certain experience which we all have had. If we are uncertain of the people about us, if we have a feeling that they are watching us, we are careful not to reveal our uncertainty in any way. In our insecurity we repress our expressiveness. Tone and gesture must not betray us. We determine to rely entirely upon the purely factual content of what we say. In our uncertainty we reveal only as much as we are prepared to defend, and this is usually far less than what is revealed through the expressiveness of tone and gesture. It is another matter that our insecurity may be so great that *it* becomes expressive, for instance, through our gesture of embarrassment, or through a tonal quality of fear or anxiety.

1. Hans Lipps, *Untersuchungen zu einer hermeneutischen Logik* (Frankfurt: Klostermann, 1938), p. 114.
2. Ibid., p. 112.
3. Ibid., p. 114.
4. See Johannes Pfeiffer, *Zwischen Dichtung und Philosophie* (Bremen: Johannes Storm, 1947), p. 108.

We shall now return to poetry and to Pfeiffer's claim that there is something in poetry which is akin to the corporeal tone and gesture of conversation. The kinship—and the difference —between poetry and conversation consists, so far as tone is concerned, in the fact that while in conversation tone is purely corporeal and spontaneous, in poetry it is connected with timbre and rhythm. But what is there about poetry which corresponds to the corporeal gesture in conversation? The answer is that through the use of image and metaphor the poet conjures up a situation which is determined by his attitude. In its spontaneity it reaches into the situation, and this is the linguistic version of gesture. Due to the expressiveness and urgency of tone and gesture the poet speaks as though he were actually confronting us. [5]

Beauty and Precision

But why should that which has been seen and experienced be recounted through picture and metaphor? Why should the expression be tied to timbre and rhythm? The immediate answer is that they meet an aesthetic need. But is this all? If a poetic experience is given poetic expression, is this because the poet has—one might say happens to have—an aesthetic need and talent? Hardly! There is a much more compelling reason. The fact is that there are impressions and experiences which simply cannot be expressed in free form. The sensitivity of impression and the power of experience are too strong for this. A free, unpoetic expression could hardly articulate them. The greater the sensibility and intensity, the more precise the articulation must be, and sometimes nothing but the picture and metaphor, the rhythmic and sonorous expression, can suffice.

If this were not true, if the poetic expression had only an aesthetic purpose, its content would necessarily be limited to things beautiful and pleasant, because it would be perverse to give beautiful expression to the ugly and the hopeless simply

5. Ibid., p. 108.

for the sake of the beautiful expression. The only sober thing to do in such case would be to curb one's aesthetic need.

Therefore, if we regard beauty only as the gratification of an aesthetic need, the field of poetry becomes entirely too circumscribed. Half of what we today regard as poetry and art would be excluded. Beauty would be misplaced. One is almost tempted to say that beauty plays a subordinate role in poetry, or, stated radically and schematically, beauty is not the object of poetry. That which causes the poem to be written, its content, theme, and subject, need not be beautiful. It can equally well be ugly. Where then does beauty come in? At the point of reproducing that theme or content.

What he has seen and experienced the poet is able to reproduce with precision only in a fixed and beautiful form. Why beautiful? Because triviality is false, unclear, and imprecise, and because beauty overcomes triviality which otherwise is the atmosphere in which everything is seen. The world, nature, things are brought close to us in a manner which is revelational in character. The poetic experience is by no means limited to an experience of the world, of nature, and of things in their beauty. It is more than this. It is revelation and nearness; and beauty is so to speak its means in that beauty destroys triviality.

The beauty is indeed the means inasmuch as when we hear or read the poem we are intent upon the reproduction itself. This we cannot be in the case of conversation where under the spell of the speaker we are intent upon that of which he is speaking. In the case of the poem, on the other hand, we take advantage of the poet's absence in order to give attention to the language itself. Nor would the case be altered if the poet were present to read his poem aloud for us since the situation created by the poem itself is and remains different from the ordinary lecture situation.

In conversation both the speaker and the listener are satisfied with the approximate and general meaning of words. Here we need only take note of what the words refer to; we may ignore the words themselves in the interest of what they describe and express. We already have some knowledge regarding the matter at hand, since the purpose of the talk is to orient us further concerning it.

It is different in the case of poetry. Poetry is not satisfied with the approximate and general meaning of words. Its purpose is not to inform but to conjure up a world. This is what has been called the magic of poetry. This conjuring is done by means of a fixed form which brings into play the words' power of expression and their content. Therefore, while in everyday, informative speech it is a matter of indifference whether a particular word or its synonym is used, it is by no means a matter of indifference in the case of poetry. Only one particular word rhymes. In poetry the demand for precision is infinitely greater because poetry brings into play a great deal more of that which the word expresses. The richer the word and the greater its expressive power, the more fatal it is to use a wrong word. But it is self-evident that if the poem is to conjure up a world, the reader must allow himself to be influenced by everything which the fixed form has conjured up. And to this end he must be intent upon the reproduction, upon the language as such.

The antithesis of poetry is triviality. However, triviality is not only an aesthetic category. It is also an ethical category. Triviality is to make oneself self-satisfyingly diffuse. To make oneself comfortable with triviality is to cultivate one another's self-righteousness, possibly so continuously that it is actually reflected in the voice, so that regardless of what is being related —accidents, crimes, illnesses, or deaths—it is recounted in the most self-satisfied tone of voice intended to make the other person comfortable. But this raises the question concerning the relationship between the poetic and the ethical outlook on life.

The Semantic and Expressive Functions of the Word

Ole Wivel takes up this question in his collection of essays on *Poetry and Existence.* He approaches the question from two directions. From one direction he attacks all kinds of separation between poetry and ethics through which poetry becomes cynical aestheticism. And from the other direction, he attacks poetry's acknowledgment of ethics as a concession to the demand of the day for a political-moral mobilization; he insists that the ethical outlook comes from within, from the poetic outlook.

But what are we to understand by the poetic outlook? Wivel speaks of the "presence of life" and says that poetry is not so much a case of personality mastering the world as it is of personality's return to and disappearance in the world.[6]

Let us attempt an explanation. Normally our relation to the world is based primarily on information. Oriented as we are toward things, particularly those things we can see, we determine ourselves. We give names to things, and in the very act of establishing and determining the things we also limit and determine ourselves in terms of the reality thus acknowledged.

All of this is different in the case of poetry. Here we do not determine ourselves; we are determined. The poet does not possess the particular freedom which is normally ours through information. Poetic openness does not disclose information. Moreover, that which it does disclose is far more basic, having about it always a kind of cosmic character. It involves a disclosure not of a certain number of isolated things, but of existence itself. For this reason alone a person cannot restrict or determine his relation to the world on the basis of poetry in the same way that he can on the basis of information.

There is another and perhaps more decisive reason why we cannot determine our relation to the world on the basis of poetry, namely, because we are ourselves drawn into the existence which reveals itself through the poetic openness. The cosmic character of the disclosure is that it is all-inclusive, embracing also the person who is open to it.

Both reasons must be taken into account. A person is in the power of the poetic outlook, and he is identified with the world which reveals itself through the poetic outlook. Thus the poetic outlook gives no opportunity for adopting a stance or attitude, and thereby placing himself in relationship with something tangible and comprehensible.

6. Ole Wivel, *Poesi og Eksistens* (Copenhagen: Gyldendal, 1953), pp. 59–60.

Openness to the world is different from information concerning it, and in this difference, which the poet calls openness, there is an identification with things, with nature, with the outside world. "Identification" means that things are present in a more fundamental sense than they are through some particular interest one may have in them.

In what sense are they more fundamentally present? What is it that reveals itself through the poetic openness? To this question there is no unambiguous answer. The answer can be given only through an interpretation. Whatever lies beyond information is so to speak inexpressible. In order to interpret, the poet must surrender himself to the openness, surrender himself to the inexpressible which is contained in the openness. The inexpressible can come to expression only through rhythm and timbre, through picture and metaphor. It cannot be communicated in the ordinary sense of that term. It can only be disclosed indirectly, by way of suggestion.

Interpretation by way of symbols is not peculiar to poetry. We can neither gain nor communicate information without the use of symbols. What we communicate to one another is that which the symbol, primarily the word, points to.

However, in poetry the symbol functions in a different way. Does this mean that in poetry the symbol is only expressive? The reason for such a question is the philosophical idea that the word has a partly semantic and a partly expressive function. Semantically, the function of words is to describe objects. To understand the word is to be referred to the object which it describes. The intention of the word is not that we relate ourselves to it but to the object it represents. Expressively, the words function as expressions of that which moves a person, for example, his feelings, his attitudes. The words are symptoms of what he is experiencing.[7] It is clear that the poetic word or picture has no semantic function. If that were its function, it would be written only for the purpose of aiding our lively interest in the tangible and comprehensible surrounding

7. Jørgen Jørgensen, *Psykologi på biologisk grundlag* (Copenhagen: Munksgaard, 1941), pp. 455–456.

world. We therefore conclude that the poetic words must have an expressive function. Their intention is to mediate to us the poet's subjective experience, his feelings, his changing moods. The reader is transported by the poem into an emotional situation similar to that of the poet himself. To use an expression borrowed from psychology, the idea is that the reader enters into an emotive person-identification with the poet; it is only the experience which here is of a peculiar character. The symbol is picture and metaphor, rhythmically and colorfully arranged in order to communicate the peculiar experience.

Nevertheless, if we agree with philosophy in its contention that there are only the two possibilities—the semantic and the expressive—then we ignore the poet's own purpose and the reader's experience. Thus viewed, it is probably true that the word has only a semantic and an expressive function, and that there is no third possibility. And still, poetry claims that it is in its way a third possibility. At any rate if we maintain that the poetic word and picture have only expressive significance, then we have not understood what for the poet is the heart of the matter. To him merely having had an experience is not the meaning of the experience. In this sense it is not subjective. The content of the experience includes things, nature, and the world. The purpose of the poetic word and picture is to express, always if possible with unique precision, the presence of things, nature, and the world through a commitment which is pure openness. To the outside observer, from a scientific viewpoint, the poetic symbol is only expressive. Seen from the inside, from the poetic viewpoint, the experience expressed by the symbol is not subjective. On the contrary, it is an experience through which the world is brought as close to one as it can come through an openness in comparison with which all mere information—however great the degree of interest—has the appearance of reservation.

Neither in everyday language nor in philosophical language do we have words adequate to express the intimate character of the objects experienced through poetic openness. It can be expressed only poetically. Neither can a psychological description do justice to it. No poet experiences the presence of things as a reflection of the openness of his own mind. On the contrary, it is of the character of experience that it is itself created by the presence of the objects.

If, however, we are confined in the world rendered unmysterious through our informational knowledge of it, there is no other possibility of understanding the poetic openness than in terms of psychology. This does not necessarily mean that the poetic openness is considered a curiosity. In fact it may very well be regarded as an enrichment we would not want to forego. We are grateful to the poet for his ability to give permanence to the fleeting experience. However, the psychological consideration is not thereby abandoned. "Enrichment" is, so to speak, a psychological concept. As an interpretation of existence, as knowledge, the poem may be an enrichment of our existence without necessarily moving us.

It is different with the poet. He is pressed by the very mysteriousness of existence, and he attacks it head on. In the interest of the interpretation of existence his sole concern is poetic openness, because through it life's mysteriousness is present in a unique manner. Paradoxically, the mysteriousness increases the nearer the mystery is to being solved.

Enrichment and knowledge are the two different horizons between which the poetic experience can be understood. No poetry results exclusively from the desire for enrichment.

Is the claim that the word can only have either a semantic or an expressive function perhaps simply a philosophically crystallized expression of the presuppositions with which the reader usually approaches the reading of a poem? If it is, then there is probably very often a discrepancy between the poet's understanding and the reader's understanding of the nature of the poem. The poet himself wants the poem—and art generally— to be understood as knowledge, a different kind of knowledge than the knowledge which is informative, but a knowledge fully as good. The reader, however—assuming that he accepts the philosophical claim that our words function either semantically or expressively—does not think of the poem as a medium of knowledge but of expressiveness. Martin A. Hansen has accurately characterized this attitude to art when he says: "Even though it (art) were in the future given an honorable discharge as a type of knowledge, it can continue to potter about with that which is expressive in nature." However, Hansen characterizes this attitude only in order to protest against it: "But is it (art) then able to do so? One wonders if it still possesses that ability." And a little later he says it still more plainly. Expressiveness is not its own goal. The poet has left the pictures behind: "He has not made them spurious and hidden himself in them, saying as it were: See, here is a corner in my peculiar soul. By dismissing them they have received perpetual freshness. Poetry must be used for something; it cannot be content only to aestheticize. It must serve some purpose if it is to be itself and remain fresh. I do not believe that art can be content with the task of portraying the expressiveness of things. In that event it would be unable to portray it. If art were at all able to survive, it would turn into narcissism; it would see its own reflection in the objects. It must be involved in the departure, in the dismissal, in the movement, and it must believe that it can be used. But it must not go blindly."[8]

We must not, of course, simply assume that in a debate between the poet and the reader regarding the essence of the poem it is always the poet who is right and the reader who is wrong. But we can at least say one thing: The problem is intensified to the limit by the poet's insistence that were he to recognize the reader's attitude to the poem he would be without any source of inspiration.

Fanaticism and Openness

The decisive question regarding the relationship between the poetic and the ethical outlooks has still to be faced. The openness, the presence in its cosmic character overpowers man who is, so to speak, identified with existence as it reveals itself through the disclosure. What is there to prevent the person

8. Martin A. Hansen, *Leviathan* (Copenhagen: Wivels Forlag, 1950), pp. 47, 49.

who has been poetically overpowered to use this as an occasion for just letting things go in a directionless manner? "The fanatic abandons himself to his moods. He relaxes his restraints in order to drown himself in feelings. He tries to rediscover himself in nature—only this is not an experience, not the fate of an encounter."[9] No wonder that the word "mood" often and perhaps usually carries the connotation of an altogether artificial condition. But what is there to prevent commitment to the point of identification from turning into fanaticism? The fact is that poetic openness involves at one and the same time a disclosure in a cosmic sense and a dissolution of personality. We hear it said that the person disappears in the world. This is necessary. Without the dissolution of personality the commitment is not really commitment.

More precisely, the question concerning what it means that an ethical outlook is implied in a poetic outlook is another way of asking what there is to prevent poetic openness from becoming a personality-dissolving fanaticism in which we, as Lipps puts it, separate ourselves from all ties in order to submerge ourselves in feeling.

Is it possible by a roundabout route to arrive at an answer to this question? We might for just a moment try once again to ignore the poem and give our attention to human fellowship and its conversation. And in this instance we shall not as before consider it in its suspicious but in its trusting form. Everything which is said is given the best construction. No one lies in wait to see whether we expose ourselves. Awkwardness is not taken advantage of for the purpose either of attack or of reservation. However, this does not mean that no demands are placed upon us, for there are demands—fixed and definite albeit unspoken demands. Not everything is allowed to take place. If someone makes use of the friendliness of the situation for self-centered arrogance, for ingratiating himself with flattery, or for angling for support in his hate, he will encounter opposition.

9. Hans Lipps, *Die menschliche Natur* (Frankfurt: Klostermann, 1942), p. 97.

Not only the content of what is said, however, but also its expressiveness is filtered by the fellowship and conversation— in a twofold sense. The filtering takes place through the fact that the emotions, enthusiasm, feelings, and experience are out in the open. Their genuineness is tested in the light in which these phenomena are seen in their expressiveness. If the expression is false, the light exposes it.

Furthermore, the other person or persons by their mere presence function as a touchstone, as authority. Voice, tone, and gesture as such, however spontaneous, are always an unspoken invitation to the other person or persons to adjust and respond to them. Therefore, there is something absurd about uninhibited and unrestrained expressions. As expressions they are invitations to the other person or persons to join in. At the same time, due to their unrestrained character, they ignore the other person's existence. And as concerns the self-indulging and self-pitying expressions, for example, they downgrade the other person's existence through their—unspoken—invitation to his understanding and sympathy.

We may return now to the poem. On the basis of what was said concerning conversation we might say about fanaticism that here a person speaks as though he were not speaking to anyone. There is no concern or consideration either for the daylight or for the other person's authority or his judgment. Through his feelings, emotions, and passions the fanatic arrogantly indulges in bombast, intimacy, and verbosity.

But is this sufficient to establish the difference between the fanatic condition and the poetic openness? Hardly! If we suppose that by applying these reflections to poetry we have said all that is to be said, we err in two respects. In the first place, we would be making a too sharp distinction between experience and a linguistic formulation of it. In the second place, we would not only be letting the linguistic formulation betray whether the experience was genuine or false, but we would be allowing the formulation to determine the nature of the experience. Both would be wrong. The relationship between experience and its linguistic formulation is undoubtedly more intimate than that. (One can hardly imagine that it should be less intimate than the relationship between thought and its formulation in speech.) This in turn means that the difference between poetic openness and fanaticism includes the experience, includes experience plus its formulation.

Experience and Existence

But what then constitutes the difference between the fanatic condition and poetic openness? Is it the contradictions experienced in the act of commitment, both the contradictions peculiar to life itself and the contradictions in which the poet himself and his reader find themselves in relation to that which is experienced? The poetic experience is contradicted by one's own personal existence, inasmuch as no one lives out of the poetic experience. It is precisely only experience, a glimpse retained in the poem but too fleeting to be retained in the world of personal relationships.

Stated differently, the commitment and its identification belong to experience and not to existence. In the act of commitment one becomes aware of the contradiction between experience and existence. And this contradiction is what constitutes the person. Personality is not constituted outside of commitment. It never skirts commitment, but arises in the act of commitment, because commitment would not really be commitment if it did not disclose the contradiction. Does not poetic openness mean the greatest imaginable tension between the dissolution and the constitution of personality? Is not this the difference between fanaticism and the poetic openness?

Identification may mean two different things. Through his mood a person is identical with that which causes his mood. I am as dismal as the rainy day is dismal. What is here called identification depends upon the peculiarity of a person's mood, namely, that it does not represent anything. It does not point to something. I do not through my mood relate myself to anything in the sense that I let my mood symbolize it for me. I do not, via my mood as a symbol, relate myself to something in order thus to encounter it.

Nor is poetic openness itself a symbol. In this respect there
is no difference between it and mood. Neither mood nor poetic
openness has anything whatever to do with the communication
of information. In this respect it is correct to say that they have
no semantic function. The poet himself creates the symbol
through his interpretation of existence. But then what distinguishes the poetic from the emotional? The answer is, perse-
verance in the commitment. Only through commitment does
life's contradiction of experience become a part of the experience, so that it eventually becomes a demand upon our existence—a demand which has received its content from the
experience. It is not a demand from outside of experience,
one that skirts experience; a person knows its content from
the existence with which he becomes identified through the
experience.

The constant temptation of the poetic outlook is therefore
to remain in the act of commitment, abandon itself to feeling,
and let its emotional intoxication become the source of its
productivity. The contradiction does not become a part of the
experience, and the demand becomes poetry's enemy. And since
the contradiction is indeed a fact, the experience becomes
fanaticism if the contradiction is ignored.

To this we must add a comment by Ole Wivel: Usually the
contradiction is unspoken, and this is quite in order. If we
were to demand that it be expressed, we would lapse into the
rhetorical.

But does not experience then become illusory from its
being disputed by existence? This is precisely the claim of
existentialism. In the opinion of existentialism existence is
disclosed only by the demand but never by experience. This is
the crux of the matter. But on what grounds does existentialism make this claim? How does it know that the content of
the demand never coincides with the content of experience?
How can it exclude the possibility that the demand might get
perspective from experience if both had the same content?
The answer is simple. It knows this on the basis of the empti-

ness of the demand. Having emptied the demand of all content, existentialism can with absolute certainty maintain that demand and experience have nothing to do with each other.

This brings us to a consideration of the relationship between demand and experience from the viewpoint of the ethical outlook. Earlier we tried to understand how an ethical outlook is implied by the poetic outlook. Is there a corresponding poetic outlook implicit in the ethical outlook? In an existentialistic age the question is compromising—which does not necessarily mean that there is nothing to it.

Is the demand able to do without the experience? Is the ethical outlook able to do without the poetic outlook? Words have their history, and this is true also of such a word as "experience," as loaded as that word is. But can we do without it in its meaning that an idea must be just as fully present as it is clear?

Philosophy can at best make an idea clear. Poetry can make it a present reality.

The idea of the poetic experience being contradicted by existence must therefore not be pressed to the point where we use the contradiction as an occasion for making existence and poetic experience mutually exclusive. If we were to do this, poetry would become esoteric, and the outlook on life would become existentialistic.

Poetry becomes esoteric or fanatical—which is the same thing—if it remains unaffected by the contradiction and if we ignore the fact that life's contradiction is incorporated into the poetic experience either as an unspoken or as an expressed element in it and as something which contributes to its character.

The outlook on existence becomes existentialistic if we forget that we live by what we contradict. Existence for its part is therefore not unaffected by the poetic experience. That which is present to a person through the poetic openness makes his existence problematical. It helps to disclose his existence in its fragmentariness, not only in its aesthetic but also in its ethical triviality. Poetry brings a message from an existence in which a person already finds himself. It is not something strange from the outside which breaks into his accustomed and familiar world. But the world, the nature, and the things which surround him and in which he is entangled through the information afforded by his senses and his intellect, through calculation and technology—all of these are made present in a new and different manner. The contradiction in our existence, which poetry reveals, is that we are blind and deaf to the world in which we live.

The poetic experience's contradiction of a person's existence belongs to that existence in the same way that life's contradiction of the poetic experience belongs to the poetic experience.

12.

The Impossible Demand
and the Proclamation of Jesus

We took the proclamation of Jesus as the point of departure for our reflection upon the ethical demand. Now that we have tried in a purely human manner to account for the silent, radical, one-sided, and impossible character of the ethical demand, we shall in conclusion return to our point of departure.

It is self-evident that one person cannot speak to another person on behalf of the silent, radical, and one-sided demand and the claim that it can be fulfilled. We are not able to speak to one another on behalf of existence. A person cannot proclaim to another person a demand which purports to be fulfillable when he who proclaims it must, so far as he himself is concerned, acknowledge that it is not fulfillable. It is a generally accepted principle that to demand something of another person, to admonish and urge him to do something which we who do the admonishing and urging have not done and cannot do ourselves is reprehensible. Not even if we accept life's demand through an admission that its impossibility is our own fault do we have a right to proclaim that demand to another person. The only thing we can do is—in a strictly philosophical manner, we might say—to set forth the contradiction and the guilt.

This may also be expressed in another way if we consider the fact from which the demand derives, namely, that we are

219

one another's world, the one being delivered over to the other—if we consider that this fact is at the same time the blessing of our life. Along with this blessing of our life as a life that we have together, existence has given us everything necessary for the fulfillment of its demand. If a person were to proclaim life's demand of another person, he would then himself have to be such a blessing in the life of that person that his own life would be all that the other person needs to fulfill the demand. Furthermore, this would have to include that he care for that person's life in unlimited unselfishness. However, both of these conditions are outrageous. Regardless of how much one person means to another person—and he may mean very much to him—there is always an infinite difference between his meaning much and his meaning everything. To deny this is to pervert the relationship into something religious. And as concerns the idea of unlimited unselfishness, our nature ridicules that, as already mentioned.

According to the proclamation of Jesus as it has been transmitted to us, here was a person who could declare as God's demand—and his own—the demand of existence. Furthermore, he referred quite specifically to its radicality. Again and again he emphatically refused to make any concessions to man's perverse nature. When he was asked how often a person should forgive his brother, he answered: Not seven times but seventy times seven. He rejected every concession to a person's natural right to live and exalt himself and in the name of mutuality to make demands upon others, because such concession would reduce the radicality of the demand. But in spite of the fact that the issue is the radicality of the demand, his words were as far removed from a philosophical analysis as one can imagine. The radicality of the demand does not arise from an analysis of people's life together. It is not cast up as an idea, neither does it come from a sentence or aphorism in a learned discussion about the law. On the contrary, the radicality expresses itself through the most direct demands and appeals to the bystanders, as well as to each individual among them. Though it is not possible to survey the consequences of obedient response, Jesus' demand and appeal are nevertheless addressed to the individual as directly and naturally as when one person orders another to do something whose consequences are perfectly obvious.

The inevitable question, therefore, is: By what authority did Jesus do this, or upon what authority did the Gospel writers have him speak in this manner? The question about who Jesus of Nazareth was, therefore, does not arise because what he said had never been said before. The question would still be with us even if some day it were established that the Pharisees or people on the other side of the globe had entertained equally radical ethical ideas. The issue is not whether these radical words were historically unique; the issue is that they were spoken in his own name and in God's name as a demand addressed directly to the individual. This was the authority with which, according to the Gospels, he spoke—an authority different from that of the Pharisees.

From a philosophical point of view the Sermon on the Mount can be kept; that is, it is possible to set forth its content. In part, this is really what we are trying to do here. As proclamation, however, the Sermon on the Mount cannot be kept; it cannot be proclaimed. Yet this is precisely what Jesus did.

The Source of Jesus' Authority

The question regarding the source of the authority with which Jesus spoke is answered in his own proclamation. It consisted not only in his giving expression to the demand of God and of human existence. He also announced that the love upon which our life depends but which our own self rejects is a divine reality in spite of our rejecting it. This divine reality is ours through forgiveness. But how does his proclamation of God's forgiveness give him his authority?

In order to clarify this question we should first inquire into the meaning of forgiveness between men. If we are to have anything to do with a person, there must be something in him which we can always be sure of meeting. There must be an identity, something constant, something on which we can rely in our relation to him. Succinctly stated, love is distinguished from forbearance in that our expectation of the other person is so absolute that it has the character of a demand. This is why in a certain sense love also involves the possibility of a breach in the relationship. This is not to say that we anticipate such a breach; in our relationships with other people we like we assume that a breach is out of the question. But we regard it out of the question, not on the assumption that our love will bear with everything, but because we rely upon the other person. In that sense the demand is inherent in love, and along with the demand there is the possibility of a breach. And when we exclude the possibility of a breach, it is because we believe an infidelity on the part of the other person is impossible. If it were otherwise, there would be no such thing as forgiveness between people in any real sense.

There are therefore two instances in which it makes no sense to speak about forgiveness. One of these is the case of a person who has only become guilty of what we commonly refer to as "pardonable" wrongs. It is one of the paradoxes of everyday language that it makes no sense to forgive "pardonable" wrongs. Why not? Because in the case of "pardonable" wrongs the relationship between the two parties has not been broken. The "pardonableness" of what was done means that the thing was too insignificant to cause a breach of the relationship. It makes no sense either to speak of forgiveness in instances where a person has fallen short in relation to an impossible demand. In such a case the only reasonable thing is to take into account the discrepancy between the demand and the person's nature and ability to conform to the demand, and admit that what he did could not be avoided.

When then does the word "forgiveness" apply in its full meaning? Two things are required: First, the offense must have been of such gravity as to jeopardize the mutual relationship. In fact the offense must in reality have been so "unforgivable" that the relationship was indeed broken and had to be restored—through forgiveness. This is again the paradox of everyday language that we can speak of forgiveness only when a so-called unpardonable wrong has been committed, inasmuch as only unpardonable wrongs break the relationship —and forgiveness means precisely the restoration of a broken relationship. To be forgiven in the real sense of the word has meaning only when we have to such an extent been untrue to someone's confidence that we have destroyed our relationship with him, and we do not know whether it can be reestablished until we are assured by him that in spite of everything he has decided to continue his relationship with us. Forgiveness is an unforeseen event. It is a historical act through which the offended person restores the relationship with the person who committed the offense. Second, forgiveness in its full meaning implies that the offense could have been avoided. Fulfillment of the demand must have been possible.

The decisive question before us now is whether these two conditions apply in the case of the relationship between God and man.

Let us first consider what it would mean if they did not. It would mean that because the love at issue is the love of God it would *necessarily* have to manifest itself through forgiveness. This would in turn imply a denial of God's claim that his demand can be fulfilled. Forgiveness which is necessary makes the transgression necessitating the forgiveness a necessary transgression. To concede that God must necessarily forgive is therefore to concede that the demand is an impossible demand. But this destroys everything. This turns the demand into pretense, because he who makes the demand withdraws his claim that it can be fulfilled. Forgiveness becomes empty; it becomes only an admission that the demand cannot be fulfilled. The contradiction is solved and completely removed. A person is no longer called upon to decide whether or not to accept the impossibility of the demand as his own fault, because it has been determined in advance that he is not guilty, forgiveness being a concession that the demand is impossible. Constantly to speak of demand, forgiveness, and guilt in spite of their emptiness is to live in a world of unreality.

Jesus' proclamation of God's forgiveness therefore confronts us with a definite decision. To be sure, we may regard him also in this matter as a teacher, a rabbi. We may regard his proclamation as unique in having a more profound insight into God's being than that of other rabbis. Or, we may think that his unique desire for religious consistency and radicality, enables him to know that because of its divine nature the love of God must necessarily manifest itself in forgiveness. In that event his proclamation, if we accept it, leads us into a highly intense effort at pseudopiety. Jesus turns the demand, guilt, and forgiveness of which he speaks into empty concepts through the manner in which he speaks about them. If we accept his proclamation, it therefore becomes our own responsibility to give it content through our own psychic maneuvering. He takes us out of our life's contradiction and abandons us to the processes of our own consciousness.

If, on the other hand, the proclamation of Jesus does not mean the dissolution of everything with which it deals, then this must mean that God accepts the word of Jesus as his own unforeseen word, and the work of Jesus as his own unforeseen work. It means that through the message of Jesus we hear God's own promise to us. Only God can prevent the proclamation of Jesus from becoming a spur to pseudopiety.

The question whether God counts the word and work, the life and death of Jesus as his own is therefore a question determinative of a person's life. If we believe that it is God himself whom we meet in the life of Jesus, then the demand, the guilt, and the forgiveness, which are the central content of his proclamation, become realities. If we reject this, without daring to reject him as a false teacher and demagogue as his contemporaries did, then his proclamation turns our life into a life of unreality.

Our point of departure was the question about what right Jesus had to address the radical demand to the individual in such a uniquely direct way. The answer is that he had to do so and could not do otherwise—if it is true that through his word we hear God's word of forgiveness. God's forgiveness is not an admission that his demand, all things considered, is an impossible demand. God's forgiveness is rather forgiveness in the full sense of an unexpected reestablishment of God's relationship with us. But this means that through his forgiveness God confronts us with his demand and his claim that it can be fulfilled. And if it is true that, for faith, God counts Jesus' word of forgiveness as his own, it is also true that God counts Jesus' demand as his own demand. This is the meaning of Jesus' uniquely direct word to the individual.[1]

His proclamation of the radicality of the demand thereby received a new motive. Its radicality is that it excludes every concession to our perverse nature that might involve a moderation of the demand for love. It rules out any resolution whatsoever of the contradiction between the demand and our self-assertion whereby the demand would be modified as a concession to the self-assertion. The new motive consists in this: that any limitation of love's demand designed to leave reasonable room for one's own demands upon life is equivalent to a refusal of God's forgiveness.

The Mission and Proclamation of Jesus

There is a very definite difference, a purely factual and historical difference, between our attitude to Jesus and that of his contemporaries. To his contemporaries Jesus' life, together with his words and works, could be understood and reacted to in only one of two ways. Either his life, words, and works were God's own life, words, and works, in which event the authority in the demand and the unexpected forgiveness were God's or his life was a life of blasphemy. Both views were held, and people reacted to him according to which of the two views they held.

---

1. Theologically speaking, it is of decisive importance that God's relation to man is spoken of in anthropomorphic terms. This is a main idea in H. Østergaard-Nielsen's study of Luther: *Scriptura sacra et viva vox* (Munich, 1957).

Speaking anthropomorphically, God's relation to man has the character of event. Forgiveness is unexpected. And through Jesus' proclamation of this forgiveness the kingdom of God has come to us.

On the other hand, speaking in speculative terms, the radicality of God's relation to man is transformed into a play of forces, the rules of which we think can be derived from an insight into God's nature. This makes the forgiveness inevitable, which Jesus as the greatest among the Pharisees saw well.

The reason for this difference of opinion and reaction was that in the view of his contemporaries Jesus' mission and the content of his proclamation could not be separated. This accounts for the violence of the dispute concerning his discourse about the law and forgiveness. Upon this issue of law and forgiveness rested his identity, whether he had been sent from God or from Beelzebub. There was no intention of engaging in a calm theological discussion of whether the ideas he proclaimed about God's law and God's mercy were correct—as if such a question had nothing to do with his mission.

Regardless of whether or not Jesus was conscious of his messianic role, he must have regarded his words and works as God's words and works. According to their own content they would otherwise be meaningless. In this respect his enemies were in agreement with him: If his proclamation was true, then it was God himself speaking to them, and then it was the works of God they were witnessing. Therefore, it was a matter of life and death importance. Gogarten expressly calls our attention to the fact that the prophetic zeal lived on in the Pharisees.[2] This was reflected in their inability to separate the question concerning the proclamation of Jesus from the question concerning his mission.

Today, however, our position with respect to Jesus of Nazareth involves two different questions. The one is the question concerning his mission, whether it is God who speaks and works through the words and works of Jesus. Expressed in the traditional language of the church, it is the question whether Jesus is the Son of God, whether he reveals God. The other is the question concerning the content of his proclamation and his works. In contradistinction to the contemporaries of Jesus we have separated these two questions from each other to this extent that we are able in a philosophically objective manner to discuss whether the words and works of Jesus in their ethical-religious sense are true or not, the results

2. See Friedrich Gogarten, *Die Verkündigung Jesu Christi* (Heidelberg: Schneider, 1948), pp. 56–58.

of the discussion implying no necessary decision about who he was. If we conclude that his proclamation does not contain God's truth concerning our existence, we do not on that account necessarily declare him to be a blasphemer; we mean merely that he had not yet attained to sufficient clarity. If on the other hand we conclude that it *is* God's truth concerning our existence, it does not necessarily follow that it is God himself whom we meet through Jesus' words and works; it is God's truth because of Jesus' unique religious insight and his sense of religious consistency and radicality. Regardless of what conclusion we come to, we have not thereby taken a position with respect to Jesus' mission.

The purely historical difference between the position Jesus' contemporaries took toward him and that which we take in our day can also be expressed in this way, that to his contemporaries the offense—or to use a theological expression, the paradoxicality—lay both in the content of his proclamation and in his declared mission. It did not lie in the, so to speak, formal claim that through him they might meet God—apart from what his proclamation may otherwise have meant.

To us, on the other hand, the offense and paradoxicality lie in the claim concerning his mission. This is true to the extent that the question concerning the content of his proclamation is often not raised at all.[3] And if the question is raised, we probably do not find anything offensive or paradoxical about what he either said or did.

How do we explain that it is possible in our day to take for granted that everything which Jesus said and did was an expression of God's truth about our existence without this necessarily implying that it is God himself who addresses us through the words and works of Jesus?

The explanation lies in the fact that in our opinion God's truth is truth about our existence in the sense of knowledge

3. At any rate it is characteristic of our cultural situation that we are able to discuss the question about what the basic ethical phenomenon is without touching upon the proclamation of Jesus.

and guidance concerning it. The truth concerning our existence
is not seen as God's own relation to it through his word and
action.[4]

Trust and Interpretation

Our mutual personal relationships have no definitive manifestations; in these relationships we must simply live in trust
and interpretation. An example will clarify what we mean.
Forgiveness does not consist in our letting the other person
know that we are able to forgive him. This would be the same
as to make him the victim of our superiority or affection. If
this is what forgiveness means, he would probably, if he is not
completely depraved, much prefer to remain the object of our
hate or resentment.

How then do we know that we have been forgiven? This we
know from the other person's conduct toward us. How must
he conduct himself in order that we may know? There is no
general answer to that question, because such conduct may
mean all kinds of things. It all depends upon the circumstances.
For example, there may be forgiveness in a reprimand or in
a condemnation of our failure, provided that in and with that
reprimand or condemnation the other person is in fact reestab-
lishing his relationship with us. But we still ask, how can
we know that there is forgiveness in his reprimand and
condemnation, and that it is not just a plain case of self-
justification on his part?

The answer is that we simply interpret his reprimand and
his condemnation of our failure in this way. It is a matter of
interpretation because, strictly speaking, a verification of his
sincerity is impossible. Our interpretation cannot be tested in

4. When we think of the contemporaries of Jesus and why they regarded his
preaching and conduct as blasphemous, we instinctively ask a question which
divides itself into two parts: Was it because he presumed to speak on God's
behalf and declared that with his life and proclamation the kingdom of God
had come to them? Or was it because his proclamation and conduct conflicted
with their conception of God's law and God's forgiveness? But this division of
the question was probably foreign to them.

a manner which does not involve the interpretation itself. We must interpret, there is no way to avoid it.[5]

We may illustrate the point by referring to the interpretation of a text. The text corresponds to the other person's reprimand and his condemnation of our failure. Our interpretation of his reprimand and condemnation corresponds to the interpretation of the text. If we then look for verification of our interpretation by referring to other words and actions, we are always dependent upon our own interpretation of those other words and actions.

There is admittedly a difference between the interpretation of a text and the interpretation of a person's conduct toward us. There is not the gap between the text—our immediate understanding of it—and its interpretation that there is, for example, between the reprimand or condemnation of our failure on the one hand, and the forgiveness on the other hand.

There is a special reason why we must depend upon an interpretation of our mutual relationships, namely, that it is not possible for men to live together without trust. If the interpretation itself must be involved wherever we test our interpretation of a person's actions, this is because we cannot live without trusting one another. It is trust which bridges the gap between the reprimand or condemnation of our failure and our interpretation of it as forgiveness.

It is only through trust that a person knows himself to be forgiven. To "know" means in this context to trust, to believe that we are forgiven, because forgiveness does not conduct itself in a definite manner. It does not manifest itself in an action or a word on which the forgiven person can rely as on a binding promise. If the forgiven person nevertheless insists on a binding promise, he will, for example, have the word "forgiveness" to rely upon as a direct manifestation of the

5. As Rudolf Bultmann expresses it: Trust and love among people are not "based on any trustworthiness or lovableness in another which could be objectively ascertained, but upon the nature of the other apprehended *in* the love and *in* the trust." Rudolf Bultmann et al., *Kerygma and Myth: A Theological Debate*, ed. Hans Werner Bartsch, trans. Reginald H. Fuller (New York: Harper & Row, 1961), p. 202 (italics by Bultmann).

relationship. But by this insistence upon a false certainty he is asking to become the victim of the other person's arrogance and sentimentality. The cost of wanting to live without trust is a distortion of fundamental human relationships.

In day-to-day living we normally give no thought to the fact that we must live in trust and interpretation. It is only when a crisis occurs in the personal relationship between two people that we become aware of the fact that we cannot avoid trust and interpretation in those relationships which are of personal and fundamental character.

But the same is true also of God's relation to man. It too has no definitive manifestations, not even in the case of Jesus of Nazareth. In his words and works, in his life and death there is nothing divine so far as outward evidence is concerned. It could not be otherwise inasmuch as the relationship is of a personal character. If God's word and action concern a person's relation to God and neighbor, it is self-evident that he must rely upon that word and action; he must trust it, and interpret it in the light of that trust.

Indexes

INDEX OF NAMES

233

INDEX OF SUBJECTS

Body, 11 on 13 and 10 on 11 Garamond
Display, Weiss and Garamond